ACCA

Applied Knowledge
Diploma in Accounting and Business

Financial Accounting (FA/FFA)

EXAM KIT

KAPLAN

PUBLISHING

British Library Cataloguing-in-Publication Data

A catalogue record for this book is available from the British Library.

Published by:

Kaplan Publishing UK
Unit 2 The Business Centre
Molly Millar's Lane
Wokingham
Berkshire
RG41 2QZ

ISBN: 978-1-83996-621-7

Acknowledgements

This product contains copyright material and trademarks of the IFRS Foundation®. All rights reserved. Used under licence from the IFRS Foundation®. Reproduction and use rights are strictly limited. For more information about the IFRS Foundation and rights to use its material please visit www.ifrs.org.

Disclaimer: To the extent permitted by applicable law the Board and the IFRS Foundation expressly disclaims all liability howsoever arising from this publication or any translation thereof whether in contract, tort or otherwise (including, but not limited to, liability for any negligent act or omission) to any person in respect of any claims or losses of any nature including direct, indirect, incidental or consequential loss, punitive damages, penalties or costs.

Information contained in this publication does not constitute advice and should not be substituted for the services of an appropriately qualified professional.

The IFRS Foundation logo, the IASB logo, the ISSB logo, the IFRS for SMEs logo, the 'Hexagon Device', 'IFRS Foundation', 'IAS', 'IASB', 'IFRS for SMEs', 'IASs', 'IFRS', 'IFRSs', 'International Accounting Standards' and 'International Financial Reporting Standards', 'IFRIC', NIIF® and 'SIC' are Trade Marks of the IFRS Foundation.

The Foundation has trade marks registered around the world ('Trade Marks') including 'IAS®', 'IASB®', 'IFRIC®', 'IFRS®', the IFRS® logo, 'IFRS for SMEs®', ISSB ®, IFRS for SMEs® logo, the 'Hexagon Device', 'International Financial Reporting Standards®', NIIF® and 'SIC®'.

Further details of the Foundation's Trade Marks are available from the Licensor on request.

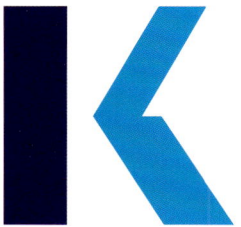

Kaplan Publishing are constantly finding new ways to make a difference to your studies and our exciting online resources really do offer something different to students looking for exam success.

This book comes with free MyKaplan online resources so that you can study anytime, anywhere. **This free online resource is not sold separately and is included in the price of the book.**

Having purchased this book, you have access to the following online study materials:

CONTENT	ACCA (including FBT, FMA, FFA)		FIA (excluding FBT, FMA, FFA)	
	Text	Kit	Text	Kit
Electronic version of the book	✓	✓	✓	✓
Knowledge checks with instant answers	✓		✓	
Material updates	✓	✓	✓	✓
Latest official ACCA exam questions*		✓		
Pocket Notes (digital copy)	✓		✓	
Study Planner	✓			
Progress Test including questions and answers	✓		✓	
Syllabus recap Videos		✓		✓
Revision Planner		✓		✓
Question Debrief and Walkthrough Videos		✓		
Mock Exam including questions and answers		✓		

* Excludes BT, MA, FA, FBT, FMA, FFA; for all other papers includes a selection of questions, as released by ACCA

How to access your online resources

Received this book as part of your Kaplan course?
If you have a MyKaplan account, your full online resources will be added automatically, in line with the information in your course confirmation email. If you've not used MyKaplan before, you'll be sent an activation email once your resources are ready.

Bought your book from Kaplan?
We'll automatically add your online resources to your MyKaplan account. If you've not used MyKaplan before, you'll be sent an activation email.

Bought your book from elsewhere?
Go to **www.mykaplan.co.uk/add-online-resources**
Enter the ISBN number found on the title page and back cover of this book.
Add the unique pass key number contained in the scratch panel below.
You may be required to enter additional information during this process to set up or confirm your account details.

This code can only be used once for the registration of this book online. This registration and your online content will expire when the examinations covered by this book have taken place. Please allow one hour from the time you submit your book details for us to process your request.

Please scratch the film to access your unique code.

Please be aware that this code is case-sensitive and you will need to include the dashes within the passcode, but not when entering the ISBN.

CONTENTS

Section

This document references IFRS® Accounting Standards, which are published by the International Accounting Standards Board (The Board).

Features in this edition

In addition to providing a wide ranging bank of practice questions, we have also included in this edition:

- Details of the examination format.

- Examples of 'objective test' and 'multi-task' questions that will form part of the examination format.

- Exam-specific information and advice on exam technique.

- Our recommended approach to make your revision for this particular subject as effective as possible.

This includes step-by-step guidance on how best to use our Kaplan material (Study Text, Pocket Notes and Exam Kit) at this stage in your studies.

Note that there have been minor changes to the FA/FFA syllabus and study guide for 2025-26. This exam kit reflects the changes to the syllabus and study guide.

You will find a wealth of other resources to help you with your studies on the following sites:

www.MyKaplan.co.uk and www.accaglobal.com/students/

Quality and accuracy are of the utmost importance to us so if you spot an error in any of our products, please send an email to mykaplanreporting@kaplan.com with full details.

Our Quality Co-ordinator will work with our technical team to verify the error and take action to ensure it is corrected in future editions.

INDEX TO QUESTIONS AND ANSWERS

OBJECTIVE TEST QUESTIONS

MULTI-TASK QUESTIONS

EXAM TECHNIQUE

- **Do not skip any of the material** in the syllabus.

- **Read each question** *very* carefully.

- **Double-check your answer** before committing yourself to it.

- Answer **every** question – if you do not know an answer, you don't lose anything by guessing. Think carefully before you **guess**.

- If you are answering a multiple-choice question, **eliminate first those answers that you know are wrong**. Then choose the most appropriate answer from those that are left.

- Remember that **only one answer to a multiple-choice question can be right**. After you have eliminated the ones that you know to be wrong, if you are still unsure, guess. Only guess after you have double-checked that you have only eliminated answers that are *definitely* wrong.

Computer-based exams – tips

- Do not attempt a CBE until you have **completed all study material** relating to it.

- On the ACCA website there is a CBE demonstration. It is **ESSENTIAL** that you attempt this before your real CBE. You will become familiar with how to move around the CBE screens and the way that questions are formatted, increasing your confidence and speed in the actual exam.

- Be sure you understand how to use the **software** before you start the exam. If in doubt, ask the assessment centre staff to explain it to you.

- Questions are **displayed on the screen** and answers are entered using keyboard and mouse. At the end of the exam, you are given a certificate showing the result you have achieved.

- The CBE question types are as follows:

    – Multiple choice – where you are required to choose one answer from a list of options provided by clicking on the appropriate 'radio button'

    – Multiple response – where you are required to select more than one response from the options provided by clicking on the appropriate tick boxes(typically choose two options from the available list

    – Multiple response matching – where you are required to indicate a response to a number of related statements by clicking on the 'radio button' which corresponds to the appropriate response for each statement

    – Number entry – where you are required to key in a response to a question shown on the screen.

- Note that the CBE examination will not require you to input text, although you may be required to choose the correct text from options available.

- You need to be sure you **know how to answer questions** of this type before you sit the exam, through practice.

EXAM-SPECIFIC INFORMATION

THE EXAM

FORMAT OF THE COMPUTER-BASED EXAM

	Number of marks
35 compulsory objective test questions (2 marks each)	70
2 multi-task questions (15 marks each)	30

Total time allowed: 2 hours

- Two mark questions will usually comprise the following answer types:

    (i) Multiple choice with four options (A, B, C or D)

    (ii) Some MCQs may use a multiple response approach (e.g. identify which two of four available statements are correct, with four options to choose from, each option consisting of a combination of two of the available statements). Remember that only one of the four available options will be correct.

- The multi-task questions will test consolidations and preparation of financial statements. The consolidation question could include a small amount of interpretation.

- The examinations contain 100% compulsory questions and students must study across the breadth of the syllabus to prepare effectively for the examination

- The examination will be assessed by a two hour computer-based examination. You should refer to the ACCA web site for information regarding the availability of the computer-based examination.

PASS MARK

The pass mark for all ACCA Qualification examinations is 50%.

DETAILED SYLLABUS, STUDY GUIDE AND CBE SPECIMEN EXAM

The detailed syllabus and study guide written by the ACCA, along with the specimen exam, can be found at:

accaglobal.com/financial-accounting

ACCA SUPPORT

For additional support with your studies please also refer to the ACCA Global website.

KAPLAN'S RECOMMENDED REVISION APPROACH

QUESTION PRACTICE IS THE KEY TO SUCCESS

Success in professional examinations relies upon you acquiring a firm grasp of the required knowledge at the tuition phase. In order to be able to do the questions, knowledge is essential.

However, the difference between success and failure often hinges on your exam technique on the day and making the most of the revision phase of your studies.

The **Kaplan study text** is the starting point, designed to provide the underpinning knowledge to tackle all questions. However, in the revision phase, poring over books is not the answer.

Kaplan online progress tests help you consolidate your knowledge and understanding and are a useful tool to check whether you can remember key topic areas.

Kaplan pocket notes are designed to help you quickly revise a topic area, however you then need to practice questions. There is a need to progress to full exam standard questions as soon as possible, and to tie your exam technique and technical knowledge together.

The importance of question practice cannot be over-emphasised.

The recommended approach below is designed by expert tutors in the field, in conjunction with their knowledge of the examiner.

The approach taken for the Applied Knowledge exams is to revise by topic area.

You need to practice as many questions as possible in the time you have left.

OUR AIM

Our aim is to get you to the stage where you can attempt exam standard questions confidently, to time, in a closed book environment, with no supplementary help (i.e. to simulate the real examination experience).

Practising your exam technique on real past examination questions, in timed conditions, is also vitally important for you to assess your progress and identify areas of weakness that may need more attention in the final run up to the examination.

The approach below shows you which questions you should use to build up to coping with exam standard question practice, and references to the sources of information available should you need to revisit a topic area in more detail.

Remember that in the real examination, all you have to do is:

- attempt all questions required by the exam
- only spend the allotted time on each question, and
- get them at least 50% right!

Try and practice this approach on every question you attempt from now to the real exam.

THE KAPLAN FINANCIAL ACCOUNTING REVISION PLAN

Stage 1: Assess areas of strengths and weaknesses

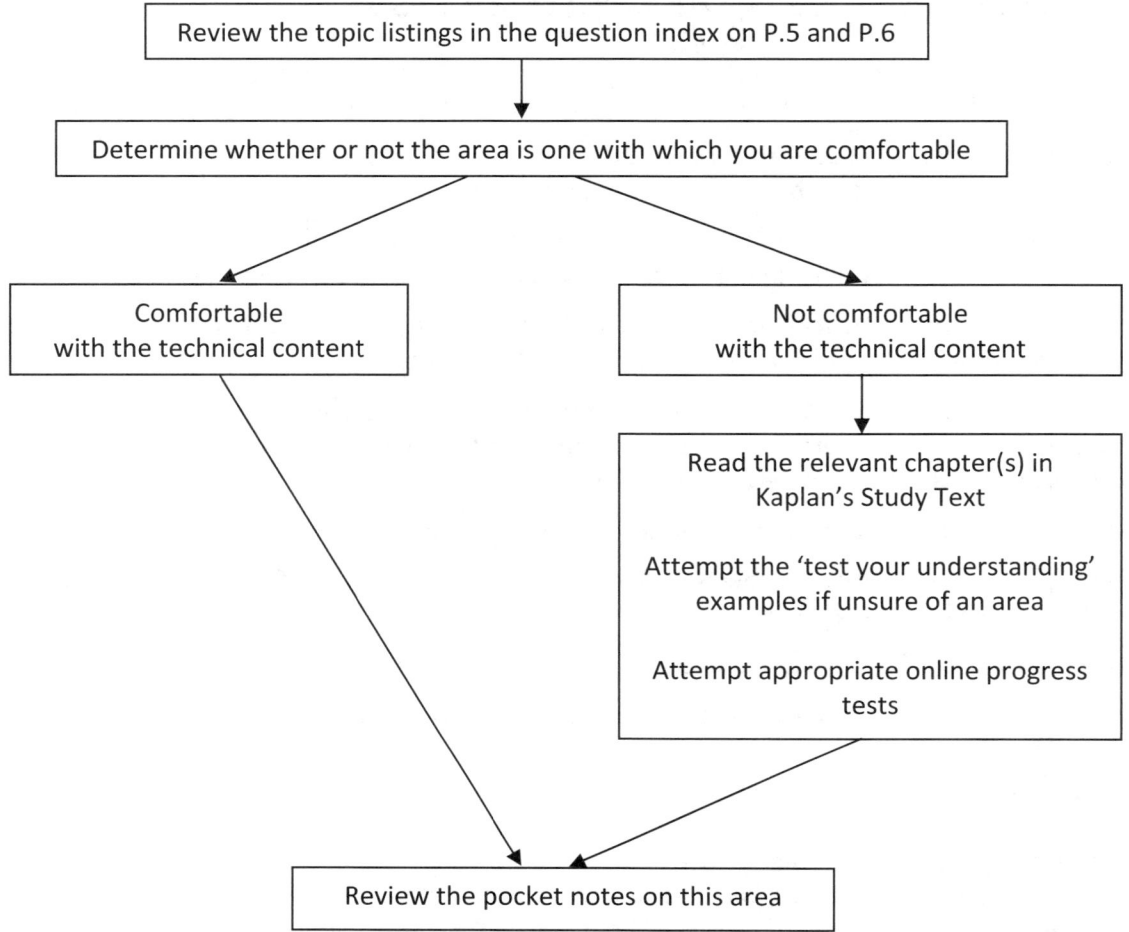

Review the topic listings in the question index on P.5 and P.6

Determine whether or not the area is one with which you are comfortable

Comfortable with the technical content

Not comfortable with the technical content

Read the relevant chapter(s) in Kaplan's Study Text

Attempt the 'test your understanding' examples if unsure of an area

Attempt appropriate online progress tests

Review the pocket notes on this area

Stage 2: Practice questions

Ensure that you revise all syllabus areas as questions could be asked on anything.

Try to avoid referring to text books and notes and the model answer until you have completed your attempt.

Try to answer the question in the allotted time.

Review your attempt with the model answer. If you got the answer wrong, can you see why? Was the problem a lack of knowledge or a failure to understand the question fully?

Fill in the self-assessment box below and decide on your best course of action.

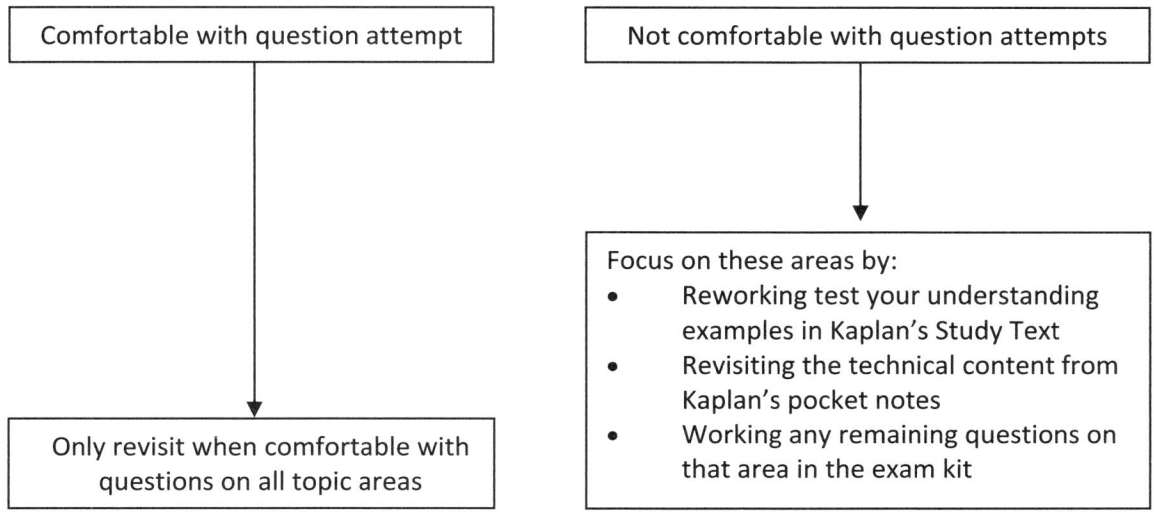

Stage 3: Final pre-exam revision

We recommend that you **attempt at least one two hour mock examination** containing a set of previously unseen exam standard questions.

It is important that you get a feel for the breadth of coverage of a real exam without advanced knowledge of the topic areas covered – just as you will expect to see on the real exam day.

Ideally this mock should be sat in timed, closed book, real exam conditions and could be:

- a mock examination offered by your tuition provider, and/or

- the specimen exam paper in the back of this exam kit.

Section 1

OBJECTIVE TEST QUESTIONS – SECTION A

INTRODUCTION TO FINANCIAL REPORTING

1   **Which of the following statements best defines a statement of financial position?**

    A   It is a summary of income and expenditure for an accounting period

    B   It is a summary of cash receipts and payments made during an accounting period

    C   It is a summary of assets, liabilities and equity at a specified date

    D   It is a summary of assets and expenses at a specified date

2   **Which of the following statements best defines a statement of profit or loss?**

    A   It is a summary of assets and expenses at a specified date

    B   It is a summary of cash receipts and payments made during an accounting period

    C   It is a summary of assets, liabilities and equity at a specified date

    D   It is a summary of income and expenditure for an accounting period

3   **Which of the following user groups is likely to require the most detailed financial information?**

    A   The management of the entity

    B   Investors and potential investors

    C   Government agencies

    D   Employees

4   **Which of the following statements are true?**

    1   Accounting can be described as the recording and summarising of transactions.

    2   Financial accounting describes the production of a statement of financial position and statement of profit or loss for internal use.

    A   1 only

    B   2 only

    C   Both 1 and 2

    D   Neither 1 nor 2

5   What is the main purpose of financial accounting?

A   To record all transactions in the books of account

B   To provide management with detailed analyses of costs

C   To enable preparation of financial statements that provides information about an entity's financial performance and position

D   To calculate profit or loss for an accounting period

6   Which of the following statements does NOT explain the distinction between financial statements and management accounts?

A   Financial statements are primarily for external users and management accounts are primarily for internal users.

B   Financial statements are normally produced annually, whereas management accounts are normally produced more frequently e.g. monthly.

C   Financial statements are more accurate than management accounts.

D   Financial statements are audited by an external auditor and management accounts do not normally have an external audit.

7   Which of the following statements best defines a liability?

A   A liability is an obligation arising from a past transaction or event.

B   A liability is a legally binding amount owed to a third party.

C   A liability is a present obligation of the entity to transfer an economic resource as a result of past events.

D   A liability is anything which results in an outflow of economic benefits from an entity.

8   Which of the following statements best defines an expense?

A   An expense is any outflow of economic benefits in an accounting period.

B   An expense is an outflow of economic benefits resulting from the purchase of resources in an accounting period.

C   An expense is an outflow of economic benefits resulting from a claim by a third party.

D   An expense is decrease in assets, or increase in liabilities, that result in decreases in equity other than those relating to distributions to holders of equity claims.

9   Which of the following statements is true in relation to a partnership?

A   A partnership is a separate legal entity

B   A partnership is jointly owned and managed by the partners

C   A partnership can raise capital by issuing shares to members of the public

D   A partnership is able to own property and other assets in its own name

10   **Which of the following statements is true in relation to a sole trader?**

   A   A sole trader cannot have any employees

   B   A sole trader is able to introduce or withdraw capital from the business at any time

   C   A sole trader has limited liability for the debts of the business

   D   A sole trader can operate a business from only one location

11   **Which of the following statements is true in relation to a limited liability company?**

   A   It can incur liabilities in its own name

   B   It cannot acquire assets in its own name

   C   It cannot incur liabilities in its own name

   D   It can be formed on an informal basis by simple agreement between the first shareholders

12   **Which of the following statements relating to a partnership of twenty persons and a limited liability company with twenty shareholders, each with a five per cent shareholding, is true?**

   A   Both partnerships and limited liability companies are able to own assets in their own name.

   B   The members of a limited liability company have the right to participate in the management of that company, whereas partners do not have the right to participate in the management of their partnership.

   C   The partners have the right to participate in the management of the partnership, whereas members of a limited liability company do not have the right to participate in the management of that company.

   D   Partnerships are subject to the same regulations regarding introduction and withdrawal of capital from the business as a limited liability company.

13   **Which of the following items would NOT be included in a sole trader's capital?**

   A   Equity share capital

   B   Revaluation surplus

   C   Personal drawings

   D   Capital account

14   **Which of the following pairs of items would you expect to see in the financial statements of a partnership?**

   A   Dividends paid and Share premium account

   B   Capital accounts and Profit appropriation account

   C   Profit appropriation account and Dividends paid

   D   Share premium account and Capital accounts

15   Which of the following statements best defines an asset?

A   An asset is a resource owned by the entity with a financial value.

B   An asset is a resource controlled by an entity from which future economic benefits are expected to be generated.

C   An asset is a resource controlled by an entity as a result of past events.

D   An asset is a present economic resource controlled by the entity as a result of past events.

16   Which of the following statements best defines the equity or capital of a business?

A   Equity or capital of a business is represented by the net assets of the business

B   Equity or capital of a business is equivalent to the value of the business

C   Equity or capital of a business is equivalent to the value of the business assets

D   Equity or capital of a business is represented by the total assets of the business

17   Classify each of the following statements as being true or false in relation to the characteristics of a partnership.

	True	False
Each partner has limited liability for the debts of the partnership		
A partner is an employee of the partnership		
Each partner is entitled to participate in the management and running of the business		
There must be a formal partnership agreement signed by all partners which specifies the respective rights, duties and obligations of the partners to each other		

18   Classify each of the following statements as being applicable to either a limited liability company or a partnership.

	Limited liability company	Partnership
Owners or investors may receive a return on their investment in the form of a dividend		
The business cannot own assets and incur liabilities in its own name.		
Annual financial statements are not subject to external audit		
Loans and borrowings for the business may be secured by a floating charge		

19 Which of the following aspects of financial and non-financial performance and position based upon information in the annual financial statements is likely to be of most relevance or interest to a bank that is considering making a long-term loan to a company?

A   Short-term profitability

B   Solvency

C   The total of issued share capital in the statement of financial position

D   Whether the company has made any changes in senior management during the year

20 Which of the following aspects of financial and non-financial performance and position based upon information in the annual financial statements is likely to be of most relevance or interest to a potential investor?

A   The carrying amount of property, plant and equipment in the statement of financial position

B   Solvency

C   Whether the company has developed new products to sell

D   Current and future profitability

21 Which of the following statements explains the concept of consistency in relation to the preparation of the annual financial statements?

A   Consistency relates to the language and terminology used in the annual financial statements from one year to the next

B   Consistency relates to the presentation and classification of information in the statement of profit or loss and the statement of financial position throughout the year and from one year to the next

C   Consistency relates to the presentation and classification of items in the financial statements, including the disclosure notes to the financial statements throughout the year and from one year to the next

D   Consistency relates to the application of IFRS Accounting Standards from one year to the next

22 Which accounting principle is described by the following statement?

'It is an entity-specific aspect of relevance based on the nature or magnitude, or both, of the items to which the information relates in the context of an individual entity's financial report.'

A   Prudence

B   Materiality

C   Going concern

D   Business entity

23 **The principle of consistency is best described by which of the following statements?**

    A   Transactions should be accounted for on a consistent basis within an accounting period only.

    B   Transactions should be accounted for on a consistent basis from one accounting period to another.

    C   Transactions relating to the statement of financial position only should be accounted for on a consistent basis.

    D   Transactions should be accounted for on a consistent basis, both within an accounting period, and from one accounting period to another.

24 **Which accounting principle is described by the following statement?**

'For accounting purposes, a business is separate from its owners.'

    A   Going concern

    B   Materiality

    C   Business entity

    D   Prudence

25 The *Conceptual Framework for Financial Reporting* includes guidance on how assets and liabilities should be classified in the financial statements.

How should each of the following items be classified for inclusion in the financial statements?

	Statement of profit or loss	Statement of financial position
Expenses		
Equity		

26 **Which of the following statements best explains the going concern principle?**

    A   The business is not expected to continue operating for the foreseeable future.

    B   There is a reasonable expectation that the business will continue operating for the foreseeable future.

    C   It is guaranteed that the business will continue operating for the foreseeable future.

    D   The business will terminate its operating activities within the foreseeable future.

27 **Which of the following statements best explains the historical cost principle?**

    A   It is represented by the cost of an asset when it was purchased

    B   It is represented by the cost of replacing an asset

    C   It is represented by the current market value of an asset

    D   It is represented by net realisable value of an asset

28 A business included within its closing inventory valuation some goods that were received before the year end, but invoices were not received until after the year end, but an accrual recognised.

Which accounting concept is this in accordance with?

A   The historical cost concept

B   The accruals concept

C   The consistency concept

D   The materiality concept

29 **Which accounting principle is described by the following statement?**

'Transactions and events are recorded so that assets and income are not overstated whereas and expenses and losses are not understated.'

A   Prudence

B   Materiality

C   Going concern

D   Business entity

30 Every transaction has two effects, which will have an impact upon the elements of the financial statements.

Which accounting concept is this in accordance with?

A   The historical cost concept

B   Materiality

C   Duality

D   The materiality concept

31 Transactions and events should be recorded in the accounting records according to their commercial substance, rather than their strict legal form.

Which accounting concept is this in accordance with?

A   Going concern

B   Offsetting

C   Substance over form

D   Business entity

32 **Which of the following statements concerning the exercise of prudence is correct?**

A   It means that assets and income are not understated.

B   It allows for the overstatement of liabilities or expenses.

C   It requires asymmetry between the recognition of assets and the recognition of liabilities.

D   It requires caution when making judgements under conditions of uncertainty.

33 **Which of the following statements is correct?**

A The going concern concept guarantees that a business will continue in operational existence for at least 12 months after the reporting date.

B To comply with the law, the legal form of a transaction must always be reflected in financial statements.

C If a non-current asset initially recognised at cost is revalued, the surplus must be credited in the statement of cash flows.

D In times of rising prices, the use of historical cost accounting tends to understate assets and overstate profits.

34 **Which of the following statements best explains the principle of faithful representation in relation to the preparation of the annual financial statements?**

A Transactions are presented any way that is considered appropriate.

B Transactions are presented in such a way as to maximise profit for the year.

C Transactions are presented in such a way to maximise asset values in the statement of financial position.

D Transactions are presented to reflect their commercial substance of a transaction rather than their legal form.

35 **Which accounting concept requires non-current assets to be valued at cost less accumulated depreciation, rather than at their enforced saleable value?**

A Prudence

B Relevance

C Comparability

D Going concern

36 **Identify whether each of the following characteristics is a fundamental qualitative characteristic or an enhancing qualitative characteristic of useful financial information according to in the IASB's Conceptual Framework for Financial Reporting.**

	Fundamental qualitative characteristic	Enhancing qualitative characteristic
Comparability		
Timeliness		
Faithful representation		
Understandability		

37 According to the IASB's Conceptual Framework for Financial Reporting, are the following characteristics that enhance the usefulness of financial information or not?

	Yes	No
Relevance		
Comparability		
Faithful representation		
Verifiability		

38 Which of the following pairs of items are the two fundamental qualitative characteristics of useful financial information?

A   Relevance and prudence

B   Relevance and faithful representation

C   Faithful representation and materiality

D   Faithful representation and comparability

39 How should each of the following items be classified according to the *Conceptual Framework for Financial Reporting*?

	Fundamental qualitative characteristic	Enhancing qualitative characteristic
Understandability		
Faithful representation		

40 Which TWO of the following are enhancing qualitative characteristics of financial information according to the *Conceptual Framework for Financial Reporting*?

	Selected answer
Going concern	
Comparability	
Timeliness	
Relevance	

41 Which TWO of the following are fundamental qualitative characteristics of financial information according to the *Conceptual Framework for Financial Reporting*?

	Selected answer
Relevance	
Reliability	
Faithful representation	
Verifiability	

42 **Which of the following are fundamental qualitative characteristics of financial information according to the *Conceptual Framework for Financial Reporting*?**

(i)   Relevance

(ii)   Reliability

A   (i) and (ii)

B   (i) only

C   Neither (i) nor (ii)

D   (ii) only

43 **Which TWO of the following are enhancing qualitative characteristics of financial information according to the *Conceptual Framework for Financial Reporting*?**

	Selected answer
Verifiability	
Materiality	
Historical cost	
Understandability	

44 **Which of the following statements provides a definition of relevance?**

A   Information is relevant if it has the ability to influence the decisions of users

B   Information is relevant if it would have had the ability to influence users had it been available

C   Information is relevant if it is available to be used

D   Information is relevant if it is available immediately

45 **Which of the following statements provides a definition of understandability when considering how financial information should be presented?**

A   It should be presented in a way that is easy to understand by any person

B   It should be presented in a way that is easy to understand by a professionally qualified accountant

C   It should be presented in a way that is easy to understand by a person with a reasonable knowledge of business and economics

D   It should be presented in a way that is easy to understand by business owners

46 **Which of the following statements provides a definition of faithful representation?**

A   Information presented in accordance with its strict legal form

B   Information is presented without bias and in accordance with its commercial substance

C   Information is presented without any errors or omissions

D   Information s presented so that it must be complete and accurate in all respects

THE REGULATORY FRAMEWORK

47 **Which of the following statements is true?**

A The directors of a company are liable for any losses of the company

B A sole trader business is owned by shareholders and operated by the proprietor

C Partners are liable for losses in a partnership in proportion to their profit share ratio

D A company is run by directors on behalf of its members

48 **Which of the following items could be used to encourage executive directors to operate in the best interests of the company?**

A They could be awarded a high salary

B They could receive bonuses based on both individual and company performance

C The could be entitled to large payment on resignation

D The could be asked to attend Annual General Meetings of the company

49 **Which of the following items is the IFRS Advisory Council is responsible for?**

1 To give advice to the IASB or to the trustees.

2 To give advice to the IASB on agenda decisions.

A Both 1 and 2

B 1 only

C 2 only

D Neither 1 nor 2

50 **Are the following statements true or false?**

	True	**False**
IFRS Accounting Standards are effective only if adopted by national regulatory bodies.		
IFRS Accounting Standards provide guidance on accounting for all types of transaction.		

51 **Which of the following is the most obvious means of achieving public oversight of corporate governance?**

A The company establishing a comprehensive web site

B Publication of the Annual Report and Accounts

C Press announcements of all significant developments

D Shareholder access to the Annual General Meeting

52 **Which body is responsible for the issue of IFRS Accounting Standards?**

    A   The IFRS Advisory Council

    B   The International Financial Reporting Interpretations Committee

    C   The International Accounting Standards Board

    D   The European Union

53 **Are the following statements relating to the IASB's Conceptual Framework for Financial Reporting true or false?**

	True	False
It is a financial reporting standard		
It assists in developing IFRS based on consistent concepts		
It assists preparers in developing consistent accounting policies when no Standard applies		
It assists all parties in understanding and interpreting IFRS Accounting Standards		

54 **Who is responsible for the preparation of the annual financial statements of a limited liability company?**

    A   The chair of the board of directors only

    B   The board of directors collectively

    C   The finance director only

    D   The external auditor

55 **Which of the following statements best explains directors' responsibilities in relation to conflicts of interest that may rise between the personal interests of a director and those of the company?**

    A   It is illegal for a conflict of interest to arise between the personal interests of a director and those of the company

    B   A director must resign immediately as soon as they become aware of a conflict between their personal interests and those of the company

    C   A director must disclose a conflict between their personal interests and those of the company as soon as they become aware of it

    D   A director can choose whether or not to disclose a conflict between their personal interests and those of the company

56 Which two of the following statements relating to company directors' responsibilities are true?

	True?
Directors are collectively responsible for the preparation of the annual financial statements	
Directors are always personally responsible for the financial losses incurred as a result of fraud or error in the company accounting records	
All directors are legally required to hold a professional accounting or business qualification	
Directors are collectively responsible for ensuring that the company maintains adequate accounting records	

57 Who is responsible for ensuring that the annual financial statements are issued to shareholders and other stakeholders entitled to receive them?

A   The external auditor

B   The finance director only

C   The chair of the board of directors only

D   The board of directors collectively

58 Which of the following statements defines corporate governance?

A   It is a framework that sets out the objectives and concepts for financial reporting.

B   It is the collective term for all currently valid IFRS Accounting Standards.

C   It is the system by which companies are directed and controlled in the interests of its shareholders and other stakeholders.

D   It is the collective term for the principles and practices used by external auditors when auditing the annual financial statements of a limited liability company.

THE USE OF DOUBLE-ENTRY AND ACCOUNTING SYSTEMS

DOUBLE ENTRY BOOKKEEPING

59 Which of the following statements best describes the purpose of a purchase order?

A   It is issued to a supplier to request supply of goods from them on terms specified within the order.

B   It is issued to a customer to confirm the supply of goods to them on terms specified in the order.

C   It is issued to a supplier as notification of payment.

D   It confirms the price that will be charged by a supplier for goods supplied.

60 **Which of the following statements best describes the purpose of a goods despatched note (delivery note)?**

A   It is issued by a customer returning faulty goods to their supplier.

B   It is issued by a customer to their supplier and specifies the quantity and type of goods they require to be despatched.

C   It is issued by a supplier to their customer and specifies the quantity and type of goods delivered to that customer.

D   It is issued by a supplier to their customer and specifies what goods will be provided to them at a specified future date.

61 **An invoice is best defined by which of the following statements?**

A   An invoice is raised by a business and confirms only the amount due to be paid for goods and services provided.

B   An invoice is raised by business and issued to a supplier as recognition of goods and services received from that supplier.

C   An invoice is raised by a business and issued to a customer to confirm amounts not yet paid.

D   An invoice is raised by a business and issued to a customer to request payment for goods and services provided.

62 **What is the purpose of a credit note?**

A   It acknowledges a purchase on credit

B   It is a reference from an agency detailing the creditworthiness of a new customer

C   It is issued when a deposit is paid on goods

D   It is issued to cancel all or part of a customer (sales) invoice

63 **Which of the following is NOT an internal document for purchases?**

A   Supplier list

B   Delivery note

C   Goods received note

D   Purchase order

64 **What is the purpose of a remittance advice?**

A   To indicate items now paid

B   To identify goods received

C   To advise that a remittance has been received

D   For notification of goods dispatched

65 **What is the purpose of a purchase invoice?**

1   To claim back the sales tax

2   To identify the goods bought

3   To record how much is owed to the supplier

4   To record how much is owed from the customer

A   1, 2 and 3 only

B   1, 2, 3 and 4

C   2 and 3 only

D   1 and 2 only

66 **In the purchasing procedure, which document will usually follow the goods received note?**

A   Delivery note

B   Invoice

C   Statement

D   Advice note

67 Salal received a document from Cullen's Stationery Supplies for eight reams of paper, which they supplied three previously.

How would Salal refer to this document?

A   It is a goods received note

B   It is a receipt

C   It is a purchase invoice

D   It is a credit note

68 **What is the principal document used to record petty cash transactions in the petty cash records?**

A   An invoice

B   A till receipt

C   A petty cash I.O.U.

D   A petty cash voucher

69 **Which of the following is a source document for financial transactions?**

A   Statement of account from a supplier

B   Paying in slip

C   Delivery note

D   Goods received note

70 Nicky runs a sole trader business selling computers. On 12 January 20X7, Nicky employed family member as an administrator for the business and took a computer from the store room for their use in the office.

What is the double entry for this transaction?

A	Dr Drawings	Cr Cost of sales
B	Dr Non-current assets	Cr Cost of sales
C	Dr Cost of sales	Cr Drawings
D	Dr Cost of sales	Cr Non-current assets

71 **Which of the following pairs of items would appear on the same side of the trial balance?**

A   Drawings and accruals

B   Carriage outwards and prepayments

C   Carriage inwards and rental income

D   Opening inventory and purchase returns

72 **The double-entry system of bookkeeping normally results in which of the following balances on the general ledger accounts?**

	Debit balances:	Credit balances:
A	Assets and revenues	Liabilities, capital and expenses
B	Revenues, capital and liabilities	Assets and expenses
C	Assets and expenses	Liabilities, capital and revenues
D	Assets, expenses and capital	Liabilities and revenues

73 **Which of the following entries would be required to account for a reimbursement to the petty cash float of $125 from the bank account?**

A	Dr Petty cash	Cr Bank
B	Dr Bank	Cr Petty cash
C	Dr Drawings	Cr Petty cash
D	Dr Drawings	Cr Bank

74 Sam prepared a draft statement of profit or loss for the business as follows:

	$	$
Revenue		256,800
Cost of sales		
Opening inventory	13,400	
Purchases	145,000	
Closing inventory	(14,200)	
		(144,200)
Gross profit		112,600
Operating expenses		(76,000)
Operating profit		36,600

Sam has not yet recorded the following items:

- Carriage in of $2,300

- Discounts received of $3,900

- Carriage out of $1,950

After these amounts are recorded, what are the revised values for gross and operating profit of Sam's business?

	Gross profit	**Operating profit**
	$	$
A	108,350	36,250
B	108,350	28,450
C	114,200	28,450
D	114,200	36,250

75 Fran started the month with cash at bank of $1,780.

What was the balance carried forward after accounting for the following transactions in June?

1   Fran withdrew $200 per week to cover living expenses.

2   A customer paid for goods with a list price of $600, less trade discount of 5%.

3   An amount of $400 was received from a credit customer.

4   Bankings of $1,200 from canteen vending machines.

$ [   ]

76 After corrections, what should be the balance on the following account?

Bank

	$		$
Overdraft at start of month	1,340	Returns of goods purchased for cash	50
Reimbursement of petty cash float	45	Payments to credit suppliers	990
Receipts from customers	4,400	Rental income	1,300
		Payment of electricity bill	700
		Balance c/f	2,745
	5,785		5,785

$ [   ]

77 Andi started a taxi business by transferring a personally owned car, at a value of $5,000, into the business.

What accounting entries are required to record this transaction?

A Dr Capital $5,000, Cr Car $5,000

B Dr Car $5,000, Cr Drawings $5,000

C Dr Car $5,000, Cr Capital $5,000

D Dr Drawing $5,000 Cr Car $5,000

78 State whether each of the following statements about the journal is true or false.

	True	False
The journal records all bank and cash transactions		
The journal records all accounting transactions		
The journal records correction of errors and year-end adjustments made in the general ledger		
The journal records all credit sales transactions		

79 During the year, Jiva made the following accounting entries to account for the depreciation charge relating to motor vehicles:

Debit Accumulated depreciation – motor vehicles	$5,000
Credit Depreciation expense – motor vehicles	$5,000

What journal entry is required to account correctly for the depreciation charge for motor vehicles for the year?

A   Debit Motor vehicles $5,000, and Credit Accumulated depreciation $5,000

B   Debit Depreciation Expense $10,000, and Credit Accumulated depreciation $10,000

C   Debit Depreciation expense $5,000, and Credit Accumulated depreciation $5,000

D   Debit Accumulated depreciation $10,000, and Credit Depreciation expense $10,000

80 Roshan made the following accounting entries to account for an increase in the allowance for receivables:

Debit Receivables	$4,300
Credit Allowance for receivables	$4,300

What journal entry required to correct the above accounting entries to increase the allowance for receivables for the year?

A   Debit Receivables, and Credit Irrecoverable debts expense

B   Debit Allowance for receivables, and Credit Irrecoverable debts expense

C   Debit Irrecoverable debts expense, and Credit Receivables

D   Debit Irrecoverable debts expense, and Credit Allowance for receivables

81 During the year, Ali made the following accounting entries to account for the cash proceeds received upon disposal of an item of machinery:

Debit Bank	$2,500
Credit Revenue	$2,500

What journal entry is required to account correctly for the disposal proceeds received upon disposal of the item of machinery?

A   Debit Accumulated depreciation $2,500, and Credit Disposal of machinery $2,500

B   Debit Revenue $2,500, and Credit Bank $2,500

C   Debit Disposal of machinery $2,500, and Credit Machinery asset $2,500

D   Debit Revenue $2,500, and Credit Disposal of machinery $2,500

82 **What journal entry is required to correctly account for the depreciation charge for the year of $3,500 relating to buildings?**

A   Debit Depreciation expense $3,500, and Credit Buildings $3,500

B   Debit Buildings $3,500, and Credit Accumulated depreciation $3,500

C   Debit Depreciation expense $3,500 and Credit Accumulated depreciation $3,500

D   Debit Accumulated depreciation $3,500, and Credit Depreciation expense $3,500

83 **What are the accounting entries required to account for settlement discount received of $250 from a credit supplier?**

A   Debit Discount received $250, and Credit Payables $250

B   Debit Payables $250, and Credit Discount received $250

C   Debit Discount received $250, and Credit Payables $250

D   Debit Payables $250, and Credit Revenue $250

84 Perry made the following accounting entries to account for the purchase of goods on credit from a supplier:

Debit Payables	$3,200
Credit Purchases	$3,200

What journal entry is required to account correctly for the purchase of the goods on credit from a supplier?

A   Debit Purchases $3,200, and Credit Receivables $3,200

B   Debit Purchases $3,200, and Credit Payables' $3,200

C   Debit Purchases $3,200, and Credit Suspense $3,200

D   Debit Purchases $6,400, and Credit Payables $6,400

85 Tao used the following balances to prepare the financial statements as at 30 April 20X3.

	$	$
Receivables	6,000	
Bank loan		3,000
Bank overdraft		2,500
Drawings	4,100	
Capital 1 May 20X2		12,500
Purchases and revenue	19,200	22,000
Rent	5,400	
Bank interest	825	
Heat and light	4,475	
	_____	_____
	40,000	40,000
	_____	_____

The business does not hold inventory. No further adjustments were required.

What was Tao's closing capital as at 30 April 20X3?

$ [   ]

86 Which of the following items correctly represents the accounting equation?

    A   Assets = liabilities

    B   Assets = Liabilities – proprietor's capital

    C   Assets = proprietor's capital

    D   Assets = Proprietor's capital + liabilities

87 Which of the following statements best explains the accounting equation?

    A   The accounting equation demonstrates the effect of a transaction upon the assets, liabilities and proprietor's capital of a business.

    B   The accounting equation demonstrates the impact a transaction on the statement of profit or loss for the year.

    C   The accounting equation demonstrates the effect of a transaction upon the assets and income of a business.

    D   The accounting equation demonstrates the effect of a transaction upon the expenses and liabilities of a business.

88 Which of the following transactions would have no impact upon total assets within the accounting equation?

    A   The injection of cash into the business by the owner

    B   A receipt from a credit customer paying the amount due

    C   The settlement of an outstanding payables to a credit supplier

    D   The purchase of a machine on credit

89 State whether each of the following statements about the accounting equation is true or false.

	True	False
Business assets will always equal business liabilities		
Business assets will always exceed business liabilities		
Business assets include proprietor's capital		
Business liabilities include proprietor's capital		

90 Accounting systems consist of inputs, processes and outputs. Which one of the following is an input into the accounting system?

    A   Employee payslips

    B   The trial balance

    C   Financial statements

    D   Purchase invoices

91 **Which one of the following is a source document for financial transactions?**

A   Statement of account from a supplier

B   Paying in slip

C   Delivery note

D   Goods received note

92 **Which one of the following is standing data used when processing the monthly payroll?**

A   Overtime hours worked by an employee

B   Bonus payment awarded to selected employees

C   Standard salary rates of pay

D   A one-off deduction from the salary of an employee to pay for a travel season ticket

93 **Identify the correct sequence of activities in an accounting system.**

A   Processes, followed by outputs, followed by inputs

B   Outputs, followed by inputs, followed by processes

C   Processes, followed by inputs, followed by outputs

D   Inputs, followed by processes, followed by outputs

94 **Which one of the following is not an accounting system process?**

A   Recording sales tax on transactions

B   Calculating account balances

C   Updating general ledger accounts

D   The aged analysis of receivables

95 **Which one of the following is an output of a computerised accounting system?**

A   The trial balance

B   Wages rates

C   Customer account details

D   Summarising expenses incurred

96 **Which one of the following is a definition of cloud accounting?**

A   Cloud accounting is a computerised accounting system

B   Cloud accounting is an accounting system that enables employees to work from home

C   Cloud accounting is an accounting system that enables access to accounting software and data storage hosted on remote servers so that data and information can be accessed at any time by multiple users

D   Cloud accounting is an accounting system which can be used only by persons with a high level of computer-related knowledge

97 State whether each of the following statements is true or false.

	True/False
With a cloud accounting system, an accountant or auditor can be granted remote access to data and information they require	
With a cloud accounting system all employees are granted access to all data and information in the system	

98 Which of the following statements best explains the importance of maintaining financial records?

    A   Financial records should be maintained for the sole purpose of enabling the business owner to make management and control decisions.

    B   Financial records should be maintained for the sole purpose of enabling the business owner to make information available to external interested parties.

    C   Financial records should be maintained for the sole purpose of enabling the business owner to determine any tax liability arising.

    D   Financial records should be maintained to enable a business owner to make decisions regarding the business and to make information available to interested external parties when appropriate to do so.

99 Which of the following statements is NOT true in relation to the importance of a proprietor maintaining financial records for internal use?

    A   Accounting records enable the proprietor to manage and control the business

    B   Accounting records enable the proprietor to reconcile the bank and cash balances

    C   Accounting records enable the proprietor to make investment decisions regarding the business

    D   Accounting records enable the proprietor to provide information that may be of interest to the general public

100 Which of the following statements is NOT true in relation to the importance of a proprietor maintaining financial records for external use?

    A   They enable the proprietor to provide information to lenders and creditors of the business to support credit and loan applications.

    B   They enable the proprietor to make investment decisions relating to the business.

    C   They enable the proprietor to provide information to the tax authorities relevant to the business.

    D   They enable interested parties, such as the general public, to review and evaluate the financial and economic impact that the business has upon the community.

GENERAL LEDGER ACCOUNTS AND JOURNALS

101 State whether each of the following statements is true or false.

	True	False
The general ledger of a computerised accounting system will permit an unequal value of debits and credits to be posted for an individual transaction		
The journal is an integral part of the general ledger		
Equity accounts in a general ledger will normally have credit balances		
The payables general ledger account will include accounting entries for irrecoverable debts written off		

102 The petty cash balance at 30 November 20X9 was $25. The following transactions occurred during November 20X9:

1 Refreshments were purchased at a cost of $7.25.

2 Travel expenses of $12.75 were reimbursed to an employee.

3 The cleaner was paid $15.

What was the petty cash float at 1 November 20X9?

A $25

B $60

C $35

D $50

103 You are given the following figures for revenue and receivables:

	20X7	20X6
	$	$
Receivables at year end	74,963	69,472
Revenue	697,104	
Total cash received from customers	686,912	
Specific allowance for receivables	2,014	1,578
Irrecoverable debts written off	1,697	

What was the value of sales returns during 20X7?

$ _____

104 Which of the following might explain a debit balance on the account of an individual credit supplier?

   A   The business took a settlement discount to which it was not entitled and paid less than the amount due

   B   The business mistakenly paid an invoice twice

   C   The bookkeeper failed to enter a contra with a customer account for the supplier

   D   The bookkeeper failed to post a cheque paid to the account

105 Rahel's payables account in the general ledger has a balance at 1 October 20X8 of $34,500 credit. During October, credit purchases were $78,400, cash purchases were $2,400 and payments made to suppliers, excluding cash purchases, and after deducting settlement discounts of $1,200, were $68,900. Purchase returns during October were $4,700.

   What was the closing balance on Rahel's payables account in the general ledger at 31 October 20X8?

$	

106 The entries in a receivables account in the general ledger for the first accounting period were:

Revenue	$250,000
Bank	$225,000
Returns	$2,500
Irrecoverable debts	$3,000
Returned unpaid cheque	$3,500
Contra with payables	$4,000

   What is the balance on the receivables account in the general ledger at the end of the accounting period?

$	

107 Mehal wrongly paid Nartan $250 twice for goods purchased on credit. Nartan subsequently reimbursed Mehal for the overpayment of $250. How should Mehal account for the reimbursement received from Nartan?

   A   Debit Bank, and   Credit Revenue

   B   Debit Bank, and   Credit Discount received

   C   Debit Bank, and   Credit Receivables

   D   Debit Bank, and   Credit Payables

108 What are the accounting entries required to record sales on credit of $10,000, on which sales tax is applied at the rate of 20%?

    A   Debit Receivables $12,000, Credit Revenue $10,000 and Credit Sales tax $2,000

    B   Debit Receivables $10,000, Credit Revenue $8,000 and Credit Sales tax $2,000

    C   Debit Revenue $10,000, Debit Sales tax $2,000 and Credit Suspense $12,000

    D   Debit Revenue $8,000, Debit Sales tax $2,000 and Credit Suspense $10,000

109 What are the accounting entries required to record the purchase of goods for resale on credit with a gross invoice value of $1,541, which includes sales tax at the rate of 15%? The business is registered to account for sales tax.

    A   Debit Purchases $1,309.85, Debit Sales tax $231.15, and Credit Payables $1,541.00

    B   Debit Purchases $1,340, Debit Sales tax $201, and Credit Payables $1,541

    C   Debit Purchases $1,541.00, Debit Sales tax $231.15, and Credit Payables $1,772.15

    D   Debit Purchases $1,772.15, Credit Sales tax $231.15 and Payables $1,541.00

110 Which of the following best describes the purpose of a purchase invoice?

    A   It is issued by a supplier as a request for payment

    B   It is sent to supplier as a request for a supply

    C   It is issued by supplier listing details of recent transactions

    D   It is sent to the supplier as notification of payment

111 What are the accounting entries required to record the receipt of cash proceeds of $5,400 received following disposal of a non-current asset?

    A   Debit Bank $5,400, and Credit Accumulated depreciation $5,400

    B   Debit Bank $5,400, and Credit Depreciation expense $5,400

    C   Debit Bank $5,400, and Credit Non-current asset disposal $5,400

    D   Debit Bank $5,400, and Credit Non-current asset $5,400

112 What is a ledger account?

    A   A record of all transactions that were initially recorded in the bank ledger account

    B   A record of all transactions that affect the statement of profit or loss

    C   A record of all transactions relating to a specific asset, liability, item of equity, revenue or expense

    D   A record of all transactions that occurred during an accounting period

113 **What is the general ledger?**

    A   It is a record of assets and liabilities of the business

    B   It is a record of all amounts owed to individual suppliers and all amounts owed by individual customers

    C   It contains the statement of profit or loss and the statement of financial position

    D   It contains all of the individual ledger accounts used by a business

114 **What is the purpose of a ledger account?**

    A   To enable a business to classify, record and summarise transactions in an orderly and consistent manner

    B   To enable a business to identify the value of assets and liabilities at any point in time

    C   To enable a business to determine whether it made a profit or a loss during an accounting period

    D   To enable a business to determine the capital account balance of the proprietor at any point in time

115 The following account was extracted from the general ledger of Ali:

Purchases

	$		$
Purchases – Jan	4,700	Journal 25	1,327
Purchases – Feb	3,387		
Purchases – Mar	5,471		
	————		————
	————		————

What is the balance carried down on this ledger account?

$	*Debit/Credit *Delete which does not apply

116 The following account was extracted from the general ledger of Ali:

Revenue account

	$		$
Journal	854	Balance brought forward	18,471
		Sales – Jun	4,200
		Sales – Jul	5,387
		Sales – Aug	7,935

What was the balance brought down on this ledger account?

$	*Debit/Credit *Delete which does not apply

117 What accounting entries are required to record goods returned inwards if the original transaction was made on credit?

A   Debit Revenue, and   Credit Trade payables

B   Debit Returns inwards, and   Credit Trade payables

C   Debit Returns inwards, and   Credit Trade receivables

D   Debit Trade receivables, and Credit Returns inwards

118 What accounting entries are required to record goods returned outwards if the original transaction was made on credit?

A   Debit Payables, and   Credit Returns outwards

B   Debit Returns outwards, and   Credit Payables

C   Debit Returns outwards, and   Credit Receivables

D   Debit Receivables, and   Credit Returns outwards

119 Jo prepared the following journal adjustment:

Debit   Payables $85
Credit   Discount $85

Which of the following is the correct narrative for this journal entry?

A   Settlement discount allowed relating to payables

B   Trade discount received relating to payables

C   Settlement discount received relating to payables

D   Trade discount allowed relating to payables

120 Andi started a taxi business by transferring a car, valued at $5,000, into the business. What accounting entries are required to record the transfer of the car into the business?

A	Debit	Capital	Credit	Motor vehicle
B	Debit	Motor vehicle	Credit	Drawings
C	Debit	Motor vehicle	Credit	Capital
D	Debit	Motor vehicle	Credit	Bank

121 Which of the following is the correct journal entry to write off an irrecoverable debt?

A	Debit	Revenue	Credit	irrecoverable debts
B	Debit	Irrecoverable debts	Credit	Bank
C	Debit	Receivables	Credit	Irrecoverable debts
D	Debit	Irrecoverable debts	Credit	Receivables

RECORDING TRANSACTIONS AND EVENTS

SALES, PURCHASES, SALES TAX AND DISCOUNTS

122 Phoenix is registered to account for sales tax. During May, Phoenix sold goods with a list price of $600, excluding sales tax, to Yan on credit. As Yan was buying a large quantity of goods, Phoenix deducted trade discount of 5% of the normal list price.

If sales tax is charged at 15%, what will be the gross value of the customer (sales) invoice prepared by Phoenix?

$ [   ]

123 At 1 December 20X5, Laurie owed the sales tax authorities $23,778. During the month of December, Laurie recorded the following transactions:

• Sales of $800,000 exclusive of 17.5% sales tax.

• Purchases of $590,790 inclusive of sales tax of 17.5%.

What is the balance on Laurie's sales tax account at 31 December?

$ [   ]

124 If sales (including sales tax) amounted to $27,612.50, and purchases (excluding sales tax) amounted to $18,000, what would be the balance on the sales tax account, assuming all transactions are subject to sales tax at 17.5%?

$ [   ]

125 In the quarter ended 31 March 20X2, Charlie had taxable sales, net of sales tax, of $90,000 and taxable purchases, net of sales tax, of $72,000.

If the rate of sales tax is 10%, how much sales tax is payable to the tax authority by Charlie?

A $1,800 receivable

B $2,000 receivable

C $1,800 payable

D $2,000 payable

126 A summary of the transactions of Ramsgate Co, which is registered to account for sales tax at 17.5% on all transactions, shows the following for the month of August 20X9:

Outputs $60,000 (exclusive of tax)

Inputs $40,286 (inclusive of tax)

At the beginning of the period Ramsgate Co owed $3,400 to the authorities, and during the period Ramsgate Co paid $2,600 to them.

What is the amount due to the tax authorities at the end of the month by Ramsgate Co?

$ [   ]

127 **Which of the following statements best explains the revenue account of a business that is registered to account for sales tax?**

A   It is credited with total revenue, including sales tax

B   It is credited with total revenue, excluding sales tax

C   It is credited with total purchases, including sales tax

D   It is credited with total expenses, excluding sales tax

128 A business sold goods that had a net value of $600 to Lahari.

What entries are required by the seller to record this transaction if sales tax is applied at 17.5%?

A   Dr Receivables $600, Dr Sales tax $105, Cr Sales $705

B   Dr Receivables $705, Cr Sales tax $105, Cr Sales $600

C   Dr Receivables $600, Cr Sales tax $105, Cr Sales $600

D   Dr Sales $600, Dr Sales tax $105, Cr Receivables $705

129 Laker, a customer, returned goods to Streamer that had a net value of $200.

What entries are required by Streamer to record this transaction if transactions are subject to sales tax is payable at 17.5%?

A   Dr Returns inward $200, Dr Sales tax $35, Cr Receivables $235

B   Dr Returns inward $235, Cr Sales tax $35, Cr Receivables $200

C   Dr Purchases $200, Dr Sales tax $35, Cr Receivables $235

D   Dr Receivables $235, Cr Returns inward $200, Cr Sales tax $35

130 Stung Co, which is registered to account for sales tax, purchased furniture on credit at a cost of $8,000, plus sales tax of $1,200.

What are the correct accounting entries to record this transaction?

		$		$
A	Debit Furniture	9,200	Credit Payables	9,200
B	Debit Furniture	8,000	Credit Sales tax	1,200
			Credit Payables	6,800
C	Debit Furniture	8,000	Credit Payables	9,200
	Debit Sales tax	1,200		
D	Debit Furniture	8,000	Credit Payables	8,000

131 **Are the following statements about sales tax true or false?**

	True	False
Sales tax is a form of indirect taxation		
If input tax exceeds output tax the difference is payable to the tax authorities		
Sales tax is included in the reported sales and purchases of a sales tax registered business		
Sales tax cannot be recovered on some purchases		

132 **Based upon the following information, what was the cost of purchases?**

	$
Opening payables	142,600
Cash paid	542,300
Discounts received	13,200
Goods returned	27,500
Closing payables	137,800

$ _____

133 The following information related to Abbey Co's transactions with credit customers:

Receivables at 1 January 20X3	$10,000
Receivables at 31 December 20X3	$9,000
Total receipts during 20X3 (including cash sales of $5,000)	$85,000

What figure should appear for revenue in Abbey Co's statement of profit or loss for the year ended 31 December 20X3?

$ _____

134 Preet is a sole proprietor whose accounting records are incomplete. All the sales are cash sales and during the year $50,000 was banked, including $5,000 from the sale of a business car. Preet paid $12,000 wages in cash from the till and withdrew $2,000 per month as drawings. The cash in the till at the beginning and end of the year was $300 and $400 respectively.

What was the value of Preet's revenue for the year?

A $80,900

B $81,000

C $81,100

D $86,100

135 The following transactions took place during Ashvini's first month of trading:

- Credit sales of $121,000 exclusive of sales tax

- Credit purchases of $157,110 inclusive of sales tax

- Payments to credit suppliers of $82,710 inclusive of sales tax

All transactions are subject to sales tax at 20%.

What was the balance on Ashvini's sales tax account at the end of the first month of trading?

A $1,985 DR

B $1,985 CR

C $15,770 DR

D $15,770 CR

136 Which of the following statements is correct?

A   Carriage inwards and carriage outwards are both accounted for as an expense in the statement of profit or loss.

B   Carriage inwards and carriage outwards are both accounted for as income in the statement of profit or loss.

C   Carriage inwards is treated as an expense and carriage outwards is treated as income in the statement of profit or loss.

D   Carriage inwards is treated as income and carriage outwards is treated as an expense in the statement of profit or loss.

137 Jupiter Co returned unsatisfactory goods to Saturn Co. The goods had been sold on credit by Saturn Co at $100 plus sales tax of $20.

What accounting entries are required by Saturn Co to record the return of goods?

A   Dr Purchases $100, Dr Sales tax $20, Cr Receivables $120

B   Dr Returns outward $100, Dr Sales tax $20, Cr Receivables $120

C   Dr Returns inward $100, Dr Sales tax $20, Cr Receivables $120

D   Dr Receivables $120, Cr Returns outward $100, Cr Sales tax $20

138 Elliott is registered for sales tax. During October, Elliott sold goods with a tax exclusive price of $800 to Kai on credit. As Kai is buying a large quantity of goods, Elliott reduced the price by 8%. Elliott accounts for sales tax on all transactions at 25%.

What was the gross value of the customer (sales) invoice for Kai prepared by Elliott?

$ [   ]

139 ABC Co sold goods with a list price of $1,000 to Smith which was subject to trade discount of 5% and early settlement discount of 4% if the invoice was paid within 7 days. The normal credit period available to credit customers is 30 days from invoice date. At the point of sale, Smith was not expected to take advantage of early settlement terms offered.

If Smith subsequently paid within 7 days and was eligible for the settlement discount, what accounting entries should be made by ABC Co to record settlement of the amount outstanding?

A   Debit Bank $950, Debit Revenue $50 and Credit Receivables $1,000

B   Debit Bank $950, Credit Revenue $38 and Credit Receivables $912

C   Debit Bank $912, Debit Revenue $38 and Credit Receivables $950

D   Debit Bank $912, and Credit Receivables $912

140 ABC Co sold goods with a list price of $2,500 to Jones which was subject to trade discount of 5% and early settlement discount of 4% if the invoice was paid within 7 days. The normal credit period available to credit customers is 30 days from invoice date. At the point of sale, Jones was expected to take advantage of the early settlement terms.

If Jones subsequently paid within 7 days and was eligible for the settlement discount, what accounting entries should be made by ABC Co to record settlement of the amount outstanding?

A   Debit Bank $2,280, Debit Revenue $95 and Credit Receivables $2,375

B   Debit Bank $2,280 and Credit Receivables $2,280

C   Debit Bank $2,375, Debit Revenue $125 and Credit Receivables $2,500

D   Debit Bank $2,500, and Credit Receivables $2,500

141 ABC Co sold goods with a list price of $4,500 to Black which was subject to trade discount of 5% and early settlement discount of 4% if the invoice was paid within 7 days. The normal credit period available to credit customers is 30 days from invoice date. At the point of sale, Black was expected to take advantage of the early settlement terms offered.

If, on this occasion, Black did not pay within 7 days and was not eligible for the settlement discount, what accounting entries should be made by ABC Co to record settlement of the amount outstanding?

A   Debit Bank $4,104, Debit Revenue $396 and Credit Receivables $4,500

B   Debit Bank $4,275, Debit Discount received $171 and Credit Receivables $4,104

C   Debit Bank $4,275 and Credit Receivables $4,275

D   Debit Bank $4,275, Credit Receivables $4,104 and Credit Revenue $171

142 ABC Co sold goods with a list price of $3,700 to White which was subject to trade discount of 5% and early settlement discount of 4% if the invoice was paid within 7 days. The normal credit period available to credit customers is 30 days from invoice date. At the point of sale, White was not expected to pay early and take advantage of the early settlement terms offered.

If, as expected, White did not pay within the settlement discount period, what accounting entries should be made by ABC Co to record settlement of the amount outstanding?

A   Debit Bank $3,515, and Credit Receivables $3,515

B   Debit Bank $3,515, Credit Discount received $140.60 and Credit Receivables $3,374.40

C   Debit Bank $3,374.40 and Credit Receivables $3,374.40

D   Debit Bank $3,515, Debit Revenue $185 and Credit Receivables $3,700

143 ABC Co sold goods with a list price of $1,400 to Green which was subject to trade discount of 4% and early settlement discount of 5% if the invoice was paid within 7 days. The normal credit period available to credit customers is 30 days from invoice date. At the point of sale, Green was expected to take advantage of the early settlement discount terms offered.

If, on this occasion, Green did not pay within the settlement discount period, what accounting entries should be made by ABC Co to record settlement of the amount outstanding?

A   Debit Bank $1,400 Credit Receivables $1,400

B   Debit Bank $1,344, Credit Receivables $1,276.80 and Credit Revenue $67.20

C   Debit Bank $1,344 and Credit Receivables $1,344

D   Debit Bank $1,276.80, and Credit Receivables $1,276.80

CASH

144 **Which of the following explains the imprest system of operating petty cash?**

A   Weekly expenditure cannot exceed a set amount

B   The exact amount of expenditure is reimbursed at intervals to maintain a fixed float

C   All expenditure out of the petty cash must be properly authorised

D   Regular equal amounts of cash are transferred into petty cash at intervals

145 Lei operates the imprest system for petty cash. At 1 July there was a float of $150, but it was decided to increase this to $200 from 31 July onwards. During July, the petty cashier received $25 from staff for using the photocopier and a cheque for $90 was cashed for an employee. In July, cheques were drawn for $500 for petty cash.

How much cash was paid out as cash expenses by the petty cashier in July?

$ [   ]

146 Sarin uses the imprest method of accounting for petty cash. Sarin counted the petty cash and had $66.00 in hand. There were also the following petty cash vouchers:

	$
Sundry purchases	22.00
Loan to sales manager	10.00
Purchase of staff drinks	19.00
Sundry sales receipts	47.00

What is Sarin's imprest amount?

$ [   ]

147 Hanna operates an imprest petty cash system. At the end of each month, it is agreed that the cash float should be $250. During the current month, Hanna had the following petty cash transactions:

	$
Postage	20
Newspapers	5
Window cleaner	10
Cash repaid by employee for personal expense	3

How much cash should be paid into petty cash at the end of the month?

$ [   ]

INVENTORY

148 An item of inventory was purchased for $500. It is expected to be sold for $1,200 although $250 will need to be spent on it in order to achieve the sale. To replace the same item of inventory would cost $650.

At what value should this item of inventory be included in the financial statements?

$ [   ]

149 Closing inventory may be valued using first-in, first-out (FIFO) or average cost (AVCO).

Which of the following statements is true assuming that prices have fallen throughout the year?

A   Closing inventory and profit are higher using FIFO rather than AVCO

B   Closing inventory and profit are lower using FIFO rather than AVCO

C   Closing inventory is higher and profit lower using FIFO rather than AVCO

D   Closing inventory is lower and profit higher using FIFO rather than AVCO

150 Appleby buys and sells inventory during the month of August as follows:

		No. of units	$
Opening inventory		100	2.52/unit
4 August	Sales	20	
8 August	Purchases	140	2.56/unit
10 August	Sales	90	
18 August	Purchases	200	2.78/unit
20 August	Sales	180	

Which of the following statements is true?

A   Closing inventory is $19.50 higher when using the FIFO method instead of the periodic weighted average.

B   Closing inventory is $19.50 lower when using the FIFO method instead of the periodic weighted average.

C   Closing inventory is $17.50 higher when using the FIFO method instead of the periodic weighted average.

D   Closing inventory is $17.50 lower when using the FIFO method instead of the periodic weighted average.

151 Dylan performs an inventory count on 30 December 20X6 ahead of the 31 December year end. Dylan counts 1,200 identical units, each of which cost $50. On 31 December, Dylan sold 20 of the units for $48 each.

What figure should be included in Dylan's statement of financial position for inventory at 31 December 20X6?

$ [   ]

152 **Identify whether each of the following statements relating to the accounting treatment of inventory and work in progress in financial statements is true or false.**

	True	False
Inventory should be valued at the lower of cost, net realisable value and replacement cost.		
When valuing work in progress, materials costs, labour costs and variable and fixed production overheads must be included.		
Inventory items can be valued using either first in, first out (FIFO) or weighted average cost.		
An entity's financial statements must disclose the accounting policies used in measuring inventories.		

153 Ki's interior design business received a delivery of fabric on 29 June 20X6 and was included in the inventory valuation at 30 June 20X6. As at 30 June 20X6, the invoice for the fabric had not been accounted for.

What effect(s) will this have on Ki's profit for the year ended 30 June 20X6 and the inventory valuation at that date?

1   Profit for the year ended 30 June 20X6 will be overstated.

2   Inventory at 30 June 20X6 will be understated.

3   Profit for the year ended 30 June 20X7 will be overstated.

4   Inventory at 30 June 20X6 will be overstated.

A   1 and 2

B   2 and 3

C   1 only

D   1 and 4

154 **What journal entry is required to record goods taken from inventory by the owner of a business for personal use?**

A   Dr Drawings   Cr Purchases

B   Dr Sales   Cr Drawings

C   Dr Drawings   Cr Inventory

D   Dr Inventory   Cr Drawings

155 A business had opening inventory of $180,000 and closing inventory of $220,000 in its financial statements for the year ended 31 December 20X5.

Which of the following accounting entries are required to account for opening and closing inventory when preparing the financial statements of the business?

		Debit	Credit
		$	$
A	Inventory account	180,000	
	Statement of P/L		180,000
	Statement P/L	220,000	
	Inventory account		220,000
B	Statement of P/L	180,000	
	Inventory account		180,000
	Inventory account	220,000	
	Statement of P/L		220,000
C	Inventory account	40,000	
	Purchases account		40,000
D	Purchases account	40,000	
	Inventory account		40,000

156 Jay's annual inventory count took place on 7 July 20X6. The inventory value on this date was $38,950. During the period from 30 June 20X6 to 7 July 20X6, the following took place:

Sales $6,500

Purchases $4,250

The mark up is 25% on cost.

What is Jay's inventory valuation at 30 June 20X6?

$ [   ]

157 Inventory movements for product X during the last quarter were as follows:

Opening inventory at 1 January was 6 items valued at $15 each.

January	Purchases	10 items at $19.80 each
February	Sales	10 items at $30 each
March	Purchases	20 items at $24.50
	Sales	5 items at $30 each

What was gross profit for the quarter, if inventory is valued using the continuous weighted average cost method?

$ [   ]

158 A business values inventory using the periodic weighted average cost method. At 1 October 20X8, there were 60 units in inventory valued at $12 each. On 8 October, 40 units were purchased for $15 each, and a further 50 units were purchased for $18 each on 14 October. On 21 October, 75 units were sold for $1,200.

What was the value of closing inventory at 31 October 20X8?

$ [   ]

159 Wei is a book wholesaler. On each sale, commission of 4% is payable to the selling agent. The following information is available in respect of total inventories of three of the most popular titles at Wei's financial year-end:

	Cost $	Selling price $
Henry VII – Shakespeare	2,280	2,900
Dissuasion – Jane Armstrong-Siddeley	4,080	4,000
Pilgrim's Painful Progress – John Bunion	1,280	1,300

What is the value of these inventories in Wei's statement of financial position?

A $7,368

B $7,400

C $7,560

D $7,640

160 A business had inventory at 1 July comprising 15 units at a cost of $3.00 each. The following inventory movements occurred in July:

3 July 20X4   5 units sold at $3.30 each

8 July 20X4   10 units bought at $3.50 each

12 July 20X4   8 units sold at $4.00 each

What was the value of closing inventory at 31 July, if the FIFO method of inventory valuation is used?

A $31.50

B $36.00

C $39.00

D $41.00

161 **What would be the effect on an entity's profit for the year of discovering that inventory with cost of $1,250 and a net realisable value of $1,000 had been omitted from the original inventory valuation?**

A   An increase of $1,250

B   An increase of $1,000

C   A decrease of $250

D   No effect

162 S Co sells three products – Basic, Super and Luxury. The following information was available at the year-end:

	Basic	Super	Luxury
	$ per unit	$ per unit	$ per unit
Original cost	6	9	18
Estimated selling price	9	12	15
Selling expenses	1	4	5
	units	units	units
Units in inventory	200	250	150

What was the value of inventory at the year-end?

$ [   ]

163 **In times of rising prices, the valuation of inventory using the first in, first out method, as opposed to the weighted average cost method, will result in which of the following combinations?**

	Cost of sales	Profit	Closing inventory
A	Lower	Higher	Higher
B	Lower	Higher	Lower
C	Higher	Lower	Higher
D	Higher	Higher	Lower

164 If an entity uses the periodic weighted average cost method to value closing inventory, which of the following statements is true?

    A   Unit average cost is recalculated each time there is a purchase of inventory

    B   Unit average cost is recalculated each time there is a sale of goods

    C   Unit average cost is calculated once only at the end of an accounting period

    D   Unit average cost is recalculated each time there is a purchase or a sale

165 If an entity uses the continuous weighted average cost method to value closing inventory, which of the following statements is true?

    A   Unit average cost is recalculated each time there is a purchase of inventory

    B   Unit average cost is calculated once only at the end of an accounting period

    C   Unit average cost is recalculated each time there is a sale of goods

    D   Unit average cost is recalculated each time there is a purchase or a sale

166 If an entity uses the continuous weighted average cost method to value closing inventory, what is the value of closing inventory based upon the following information?

    2 Feb   Purchased 10 units at a cost of $5.00 per unit

    5 Feb   Sold 6 units at a price of $8 per unit

    7 Feb   Purchased 10 units at a cost of $6.50 per unit

    $ _____

167 If an entity uses the periodic weighted average cost method to value closing inventory, what is the value of closing inventory based upon the following information?

    12 Apr   Purchased 10 units at a cost of $5.00 per unit

    15 Apr   Sold 6 units at a price of $8 per unit

    17 Apr   Purchased 10 units at a cost of $6.50 per unit

    $ _____

168 Using the periodic weighted average cost method to value closing inventory, what is the value of cost of sales for April based upon the following information?

    1 Apr   Opening inventory 4 units at a cost of $4.00 per unit

    12 Apr   Purchased 10 units at a cost of $5.00 per unit

    15 Apr   Sold 6 units at a price of $8 per unit

    17 Apr   Purchased 10 units at a cost of $6.00 per unit

    25 Apr   Sold 8 units at a price of $8.50 per unit

    $ _____

169 Using the continuous weighted average cost method to value closing inventory, what is the value of cost of sales for April based upon the following information?

1 Apr   Opening inventory 4 units at a cost of $4.00 per unit

12 Apr   Purchased 10 units at a cost of $5.00 per unit

15 Apr   Sold 6 units at a price of $8 per unit

17 Apr   Purchased 10 units at a cost of $6.00 per unit

25 Apr   Sold 8 units at a price of $8.50 per unit

$ [   ]

170 From a financial reporting perspective, why should an entity maintain continuous and period end inventory records?

A   They help to determine the average cost of a unit of inventory

B   They help to identify variances between the expected usage and actual usage of inventory in an accounting period

C   They help to determine the quantity and cost of inventory for inclusion in the financial statements

D   They help management to make decisions regarding the selling price of products

TANGIBLE NON-CURRENT ASSETS

171 The non-current asset register shows a carrying amount for non-current assets of $85,600; the general ledger accounts include a cost balance of $185,000 and an accumulated depreciation balance of $55,000.

Which of the following statements may explain the discrepancy?

A   The omission of an addition of land costing $30,000 from the ledger account and the omission of the disposal of an asset from the register (cost $25,600 and accumulated depreciation at disposal $11,200).

B   The omission of the revaluation of an asset upwards by $16,600 and the depreciation charge of $20,000 from the ledger account and the omission of the disposal of an asset with a carrying amount of $41,000 from the register.

C   The omission of the disposal of an asset from the ledger accounts (cost $25,600 and accumulated depreciation at disposal $11,200) and the omission of an addition of land costing $30,000 from the register.

D   The omission of an upwards revaluation by $16,400 from the register and the accidental debiting of the depreciation charge of $28,000 to the accumulated depreciation ledger account.

172 Laurie bought an asset on the 1st January 20X4 for $235,000 and depreciated it at 30% using the reducing balance method. On 1st January 20X7, Laurie revalued the asset to $300,000.

What accounting entries should Laurie post to record the revaluation?

		$		$
A	Dr Non-current asset	65,000	Cr Revaluation surplus	219,395
	Dr Accumulated depreciation	154,395		
B	Dr Non-current asset	65,000	Cr Revaluation surplus	276,500
	Dr Accumulated depreciation	211,500		
C	Dr Revaluation surplus	219,395	Cr Non-current asset	65,000
			Cr Accumulated depreciation	154,395
D	Dr Revaluation surplus	276,500	Cr Non-current asset	65,000
			Cr Accumulated depreciation	211,500

173 **Which of the following statements is true in relation to the non-current asset register?**

A It is an alternative name for the non-current asset ledger account.

B It is a list of the physical non-current assets rather than their financial cost.

C It is a schedule of planned maintenance of non-current assets for use by the plant engineer.

D It is a schedule of the cost and other information about each individual non-current asset.

174 The plant and equipment cost account in the records of C Co for the year ended 31 December 20X6 is as follows:

Plant and equipment – cost

	$		$
Balance b/f	960,000		
1 July Cash	48,000	30 Sept Disposals	84,000
		Balance c/f	924,000
	———		———
	1,008,000		1,008,000
	———		———

C Co's policy is to charge straight line depreciation at 20% per year on a pro rata basis.

What should be the charge for depreciation in C Co's statement of profit or loss for the year ended 31 December 20X6?

$ [_____]

175 On 1 January 20X7, Z Co purchased an item of plant. The invoice showed:

	$
Cost of plant	48,000
Delivery to factory	400
One year warranty covering breakdown	800
	———
	49,200
	———

Modifications to the factory building costing $2,200 were necessary to enable the plant to be installed.

What amount should be capitalised for the plant in Z Co's accounting records?

$ [   ]

176 A non-current asset was purchased at the beginning of Year 1 for $2,400 and depreciated at 20% per annum using the reducing balance method. At the beginning of Year 4 it was sold for $1,200.

What was the profit or loss on disposal?

A $240.00 loss

B $28.80 loss

C $28.80 profit

D $240.00 profit

177 A business' non-current assets had a carrying amount of $125,000. An asset which had cost $12,000 was sold for $9,000, at a profit of $2,000.

What is the revised carrying amount of non-current assets?

A $113,000

B $118,000

C $125,000

D $127,000

178 W Co bought a new printing machine from abroad. The cost of the machine was $80,000. The installation costs were $5,000 and the employees received training on how to use the machine, at a cost of $2,000. Before using the machine to print customers' orders, pre-production safety testing was undertaken at a cost of $1,000.

What should be the cost of the machine in W Co's statement of financial position?

$ [   ]

179 A non-current asset was disposed of for $2,200 during the last accounting year. It had been purchased exactly three years earlier for $5,000, with a residual value of $500, and had been depreciated on the reducing balance basis, at 20% per annum.

What was the profit or loss on disposal?

A $360 loss

B $150 loss

C $104 loss

D $200 profit

180 At the end of its financial year, Tanner Co had the following non-current assets:

Land and buildings at cost	$10.4 million
Land and buildings: accumulated depreciation	$0.12 million

Tanner Co decided to revalue its land and buildings at the year-end to $15 million.

What will be the value of the revaluation surplus if the revaluation is accounted for?

$ _____

181 **Which of the following items should be accounted for as asset expenditure?**

A The cost of painting a building

B The replacement of broken windows in a building

C The purchase of a car by a car dealer for re-sale

D Legal fees incurred on the purchase of a building

182 F Co purchased a car for $12,000 on 1 April 20X1 which has been depreciated at 20% each year straight line, assuming no residual value. F Co's policy is to charge a full year's depreciation in the year of purchase and no depreciation in the year of sale. The car was traded in for a replacement vehicle on 1 August 20X4 for an agreed figure of $5,000.

What was the profit or loss on the disposal of the vehicle for the year ended 31 December 20X4?

A Loss $2,200

B Loss $1,400

C Loss $200

D Profit $200

183 At 30 September 20X2, the following balances existed in the records of Lambda Co:

Plant and equipment:

Cost $860,000

Accumulated depreciation $397,000

During the year ended 30 September 20X3, plant with a written down value of $37,000 was sold for $49,000. The plant had originally cost $80,000. Plant purchased during the year cost $180,000. It is Lambda Co's policy to charge a full year's depreciation in the year of acquisition of an asset and none in the year of sale, using a rate of 10% on the straight line basis.

What was the carrying amount that should appear in Lambda Co's statement of financial position at 30 September 20X3 for plant and equipment?

$ _____

184 **Which of the following statements best describes depreciation?**

A   It is a means of spreading the payment for non-current assets over a period of years.

B   It is a decline in the market value of the assets.

C   It is a means of spreading the cost of non-current assets over their estimated useful life.

D   It is a means of estimating the amount of money needed to replace the assets.

185 On 1 January 20X8, Wootton Co had a building in its books which cost $500,000 with a carrying amount of $405,000. On 1 July 20X8, the asset was valued at $600,000 and Wootton Co wishes to include that valuation in its books. Wootton Co's accounting policy is to depreciate buildings at the rate of 2% on a straight-line basis.

What was depreciation charge included in the statement of profit or loss for the year ended 31 December 20X8?

$ _____

186 **The reducing balance method of depreciating non-current assets is more appropriate than the straight-line method in which of the following situations?**

A   There is no residual value for the asset

B   The useful life of the asset is not capable of being estimated

C   The asset is expected to be replaced in a short period of time

D   The asset decreases in value less in later years than in the early years of use

187 SSG Co bought a machine at a cost of $40,000 on 1 January 20X1. The machine had a useful life of six years and a residual value of $10,000. The machine was depreciated using the straight-line basis on a monthly basis. At 31 December 20X4, the machine was sold for $15,000.

What was the profit or loss on disposal for inclusion in SSG's financial statements for the year ended 31 December 20X4?

$ _____   Profit / loss*   * Delete which does not apply

188 A car was purchased by a newsagent business in May 20X1 as follows:

	$
Cost	10,000
Vehicle tax – 1 year	150
Total	10,150

The business adopted a date of 31 December as its accounting year-end.

The car was traded in for a replacement vehicle in August 20X5 at an agreed value of $5,000. It was depreciated at 25% per annum using the reducing-balance method, charging a full year's depreciation in the year of purchase and none in the year of sale.

What was the profit or loss on disposal of the vehicle during the year ended December 20X5?

A   Profit: $718

B   Profit: $781

C   Profit: $1,788

D   Profit: $1,836

189 Li runs a picture framing business and bought a guillotine for $20,000 on 1 July 20X7. Li expected the guillotine to have a useful life of ten years and a residual value of $500. On 1 July 20X8, Li revised these estimates and now believes the guillotine to have a remaining useful life of 5 years and no residual value.

What was the depreciation charge for the year ended 30 June 20X9?

$ [   ]

190 A business has an accounting year end of 31 March. It purchased a truck on 1 April 20X3 at a total cost of $21,000, including $1,000 for one year of insurance cover.

At the date of purchase, the truck had an estimated useful life to the business of eight years and had an estimated residual value of $3,000. The truck was traded in for a replacement vehicle on 31 March 20X8 at an agreed valuation of $10,000. The truck was depreciated on a straight-line basis, with a pro-rated charge in the year of acquisition and disposal.

Calculate the profit or loss on disposal of the truck.

$ [   ]   Profit / loss*   * Delete which does not apply

191 The following information of P Co is available for the year ended 31 October 20X2:

Property	$
Cost as at 1 November 20X1	102,000
Accumulated depreciation as at 1 November 20X1	(20,400)
	81,600

On 1 November 20X1, P Co revalued the property to $150,000.

P Co's accounting policy is to charge depreciation on a straight-line basis over 50 years. On revaluation there was no change to the overall useful life. It has also chosen not to make an annual transfer of the excess depreciation on revaluation between the revaluation surplus and retained earnings.

What should be the balance on the revaluation surplus and the depreciation charge as shown in P Co's financial statements for the year ended 31 October 20X2?

	Depreciation charge	Revaluation surplus
	$	$
A	3,750	68,400
B	3,750	48,000
C	3,000	68,400
D	3,000	48,000

192 **Complete the following statement by making one choice from each option available.**

When an entity has revalued a non-current asset, it is (Option 1)..............to account for excess depreciation arising on the revaluation. When excess depreciation is accounted for, the accounting adjustment is reflected in (Option 2).........................

Option 1   compulsory/optional

Option 2   profit or loss/other comprehensive income/the statement of changes in equity

193 On 1 January 20X8, Barnstorm Co owned a building which cost $480,000 with a carrying amount of $384,000. On that date the building was valued at $600,000 and Barnstorm Co wishes to include that valuation in its financial statements. Barnstorm Co's accounting policy is to depreciate buildings at the rate of 2% on a straight-line basis and to make the annual transfer of 'excess depreciation'.

What is the amount of the annual transfer of 'excess depreciation' that Barnstorm Co will make as a result of the revaluation?

$	

194 Draper Co uses the revaluation model when accounting for land and buildings and makes the annual transfer of 'excess depreciation'. Following the most recent revaluation, Draper Co calculated that the annual amount of the excess depreciation was $8,000.

What accounting entries should Draper Co post to make the annual transfer of 'excess depreciation'?

		$		$
A	Dr Non-current assets	8,000	Cr Profit or loss	8,000
B	Dr Non-current assets	8,000	Cr Revaluation surplus	8,000
C	Dr Revaluation surplus	8,000	Cr Retained earnings	8,000
D	Dr Retained earnings	8,000	Dr Revaluation surplus	8,000

195 **Which of the following statements is correct?**

Statement 1 If the revaluation model is used for property, plant and equipment, revaluations must subsequently be made with sufficient regularity to ensure that the carrying amount does not differ materially from the fair value at each reporting date.

Statement 2 When an item of property, plant and equipment is revalued, there is no requirement that the entire class of assets to which the item belongs must be revalued.

	Statement 1	Statement 2
True		
False		

196 The following information of Premium Co is available for the year ended 31 October 20X2:

Property	$
Cost as at 1 November 20X1	102,000
Accumulated depreciation as at 1 November 20X1	(20,400)
	———
	81,600

On 1 November 20X1, P Co revalued the property to $120,000.

Premium Co's accounting policy is to charge depreciation on a straight-line basis over 50 years. On revaluation there was no change to the overall useful life. It has also chosen to make the annual transfer of excess depreciation on revaluation in equity.

What should be the balance on the revaluation surplus and the depreciation charge as shown in Premium Co's financial statements for the year ended 31 October 20X2?

	Depreciation charge	Revaluation surplus
	$	$
A	3,000	37,440
B	3,000	38,400
C	2,400	39,360
D	2,400	18,000

197 State whether each of the following statements is true or false.

Statement 1 If the revaluation model is used for property, plant and equipment, all items of property, plant and equipment must be subject to revaluation.

Statement 2 When an item of property, plant and equipment is revalued, it is compulsory to make the annual transfer of excess depreciation within equity.

	Statement 1	**Statement 2**
True		
False		

198 On 31 January 20X8, Westvale Co disposed of a building for $450,000. The building was accounted for using the revaluation model. At the date of disposal, after deduction of accumulated depreciation of $90,000, the building had a carrying amount of $310,000. It also had a revaluation surplus in equity of $30,000.

What was Westvale Co's profit on disposal of the building for inclusion in the statement of profit or loss for the year ended 31 December 20X8?

$ ☐

199 When a revalued building is disposed of, how is the revaluation surplus relating to that asset at the date of disposal accounted for?

A It is transferred from revaluation surplus to accumulated depreciation

B It is transferred from revaluation surplus to property, plant and equipment

C It is transferred from revaluation surplus to the statement of profit or loss

D It is transferred from revaluation surplus to retained earnings within equity

200 A business has an accounting year end of 30 June. It purchased an item of plant on 1 April 20X5 as follows:

	$
Cost	15,000
3-year maintenance agreement	450
Total	15,450

At the date of purchase, the item of plant and equipment had an estimated useful life to the business of five years and an estimated residual value of $2,000. This item of plant was traded in for a replacement item on 30 September 20X8 at an agreed valuation of $5,000.

It has been depreciated at 20% per annum on a straight-line basis, with a pro-rated charge in the year of acquisition and disposal.

Calculate the profit or loss on disposal of the item of plant.

$ ☐ Profit / loss* * Delete which does not apply

201 On 1 January 20X8, a new property was acquired at a cost of $750,000. Also, on 1 January 20X8 additional associated costs incurred were as follows:

	$
Legal costs of purchase	7,500
Architect's fees	9,200
Annual maintenance contract	6,000
Alterations to property	25,000

The property is to be depreciated over its useful life of 20 years. The company prepares financial statements at 31 December each year.

What is the carrying amount of the property in the statement of financial position as at 31 December 20X8?

$ [   ]

202 Motor expenses of $320 have been debited to the motor vehicles at cost account and correctly recorded in the cash book. Depreciation had been charged on the motor vehicles at 25% straight-line, with a full year's charge in the year of acquisition.

Which of the following journal entries will correct this error?

1	Dr Motor expenses $320	Cr Motor vehicles at cost $320
2	Dr Motor vehicles at cost $320	Cr Motor expenses $320
3	Dr Depreciation expense $80	Cr Accumulated depreciation $80
4	Dr Accumulated depreciation $80	Cr Depreciation expense $80

A   1 and 4

B   2 and 4

C   1 and 3

D   2 and 3

203 Fawad purchased machinery costing $30,000 on 1 July 20X2 with a useful life of ten years and which is depreciated on a straight-line basis. On 1 July 20X5 Fawad reassessed the original useful life to 15 years.

What is the depreciation charge for the machinery in the year ended 30 June 20X6?

A $1,400

B $1,750

C $2,000

D $2,500

204 A business buys a machine on 31 August 20X5:

Cost	$50,000
Expected useful life	Seven years
Estimated residual value	$1,000

On 1 January 20X8, the machine is revalued to $41,000 with no change in residual value or useful life.

The accounting policy for depreciating machinery is straight line, with a full year's charge in both the years of acquisition and disposal.

What should the depreciation charge be in the statement of profit or loss for the year ended 31 December 20X8?

$ [   ]

INTANGIBLE ASSETS

205 **Which of the following statements is correct?**

A   If all the conditions specified in IAS 38 *Intangible Assets* are met, the directors can choose whether to capitalise the development expenditure or not.

B   Amortisation of capitalised development expenditure will appear as an item in an entity's statement of changes in equity.

C   Capitalised development costs are shown in the statement of financial position as non-current assets.

D   Capitalised development expenditure must be amortised over a period not exceeding five years.

206 **Complete the following statement by selecting the appropriate wording from the choice available.**

When accounting for intangible assets using the revaluation model, movements in the carrying amount are..

A   accounted for in other comprehensive income and other components of equity

B   accounted for in the statement of profit or loss only

C   accounted for in other comprehensive income only

D   accounted for on other components of equity only

207 **What is the correct accounting treatment for an intangible asset with an indefinite useful life?**

A   It is recognised at cost for as long as the entity has the intangible asset.

B   It is recognised at cost and is subject to an annual impairment review.

C   It is recognised at cost and the entity must make an estimate of estimated useful life so that it can be amortised.

D   It cannot be recognised as an intangible asset as it would not be possible to calculate an annual amortisation charge.

208 Identify whether or not each of the following items should be capitalised as intangible assets from the following list.

	Capitalised	Not capitalised
Employment costs of staff conducting research activities		
Cost of constructing a working model of a new product		
Materials and consumables costs associated with conducting scientific experiments		
Licence purchased to permit production and sale of a product for ten years		

209 Complete the following statement by selecting the appropriate wording from the choice available.

When accounting for intangible assets using the cost model, annual impairment charges are:

A   accounted for in other comprehensive income and other components of equity

B   accounted for in the statement of profit or loss only

C   accounted for in other comprehensive income only

D   accounted for in other components of equity only

210 Classify each of the following costs as either a research expense or as an intangible asset.

	Research expense	Intangible asset
Market research costs		
Patented product design costs		
Product advertising		
Employee training costs		

211 Which of the following statements best defines an intangible asset?

A   An intangible asset is an asset with no physical substance

B   An intangible asset is always generated internally by a business

C   An intangible asset is an asset which cannot be sold

D   An intangible asset is a purchased asset which has no physical substance

212 Geranium is engaged in the following research and development projects:

Identify how the costs of each project should be accounted for in the financial statements.

	Written off as an expense	Capitalised as an asset
Project 1 is applying a new technology to the production of heat resistant fabric. On completion, the fabric will be used in the production of uniforms for the emergency services. Geranium has sufficient resources and the intention to complete the project.		
Project 2 is testing whether a particular substance can be used as an appetite suppressant. If this is the case, it is expected be sold worldwide in chemists and pharmacies.		
Project 3 is developing a material for use in kitchens which is self-cleaning and germ resistant. A competitor is currently developing a similar material and, for this reason, Geranium is unsure whether its project will be completed.		

213 Merlot Co is engaged in a number of research and development projects during the year ended 31 December 20X5:

Project A – A project to investigate the properties of a chemical compound. Costs incurred on this project during the year ended 31 December 20X5 were $34,000.

What amount should be expensed to the statement of profit or loss and other comprehensive income of Merlot Co in respect of Project A in the year ended 31 December 20X5?

$

214 The following information relates to the accounting year ended 30 April 20X6 of Arnold Co:

Brand – carrying amount 1 May 20X5 $44,880

Arnold Co amortises the brand on a straight-line basis. It had an estimated useful life of eight years from the date of purchase, with no residual value at the end of that period. At the end of the previous accounting period, there was accumulated amortisation of $20,400 relating to the brand.

What should be the amortisation charge for the year ended 30 April 20X6, along with the balance on the accumulated amortisation account at 30 April 20X6?

	Amortisation charge	Accumulated amortisation
	$	$
A	5,610	26,010
B	8,160	36,720
C	8,160	28,560
D	5,610	39,720

215 Campbell Co purchased a licence at a cost of $3,600,000 to sell a product for a five-year term commencing 1 July 20X3, after which the licence will expire and cannot be renewed. It is Campbell Co's policy to write off the cost of the licence over the five-year term commencing from the date of purchase.

What was the amortisation charge for the year ended 31 March 20X4?

$ [   ]

216 The following information relates to the accounting year ended 31 December 20X6 of Barnaby Co:

	$
Licence – carrying amount 1 January 20X6	17,500

Barnaby Co amortises the licence on a straight-line basis. It had an estimated useful life of six years from the date of purchase, with no residual value at the end of that period. At the end of the previous accounting period, there was accumulated amortisation of $12,500 relating to the licence.

What should be the amortisation charge for the year ended 31 December 20X6, along with the balance on the accumulated amortisation account at that date?

	Amortisation charge	Accumulated amortisation
	$	$
A	5,000	12,500
B	6,000	18,500
C	6,000	11,500
D	5,000	17,500

217 **Identify which THREE of the following statements are true in relation to application of IAS 38 *Intangible Assets*.**

	True
Research costs should be expensed to the statement of profit or loss.	
All types of goodwill can be capitalised.	
Capitalised development costs that no longer meet the criteria specified by IAS 38 must be written off to the statement of profit or loss.	
Capitalised development costs are amortised from the date the assets is available to use or sell.	
Research costs written off can be re-capitalised when the developed asset is feasible.	
Only purchased intangibles can be capitalised.	

218 Merlot Co is engaged in a number of research and development projects during the year ended 31 December 20X5:

Project B – A project to develop a new process which will save production time in the manufacture of widgets. This project commenced on 1 January 20X5 and met the capitalisation criteria on 31 August 20X5. The cost incurred during 20X5 was $78,870 to 31 August and $27,800 from 1 September.

What amount should be expensed to the statement of profit or loss and other comprehensive income of Merlot Co in respect of Project B in the year ended 31 December 20X5?

$ [   ]

219 Merlot Co is engaged in several research and development projects during the year ended 31 December 20X5:

Project C – A development project which was completed on 30 June 20X5. Development costs incurred up to 31 December 20X4 were $290,000, with a further $19,800 incurred between January and June 20X5. Production and sales of the new product commenced on 1 September and are expected to last 36 months.

What amount should be expensed to the statement of profit or loss and other comprehensive income of Merlot Co in respect of Project C in the year ended 31 December 20X5?

$ [   ]

220 **Which of the following statements best describes amortisation?**

A   It is a means of spreading the payment for an intangible asset over a period of years

B   It is a means of spreading the cost of an intangible asset over its estimated useful life

C   It is a means of estimating the amount of money needed to replace the intangible asset

D   It is a measure of the decline in the market value of an intangible asset

221 Identify whether the following costs incurred by Companies Co should be capitalised as INTANGIBLE assets in the year ended 30 November 20X1.

		Capitalised as intangible asset	Not capitalised as intangible asset
1	$48,000 on staff costs relating to the development of a new product that is expected to generate future economic benefits		
2	$35,000 on advertising a new product which was successfully developed during the year. It is expected that the advertising campaign will generate additional economic benefits for Companies Co		
3	$180,000 on laboratory equipment which will be used to build new product prototypes		
4	$22,000 on the cost of testing whether a separately acquired intangible asset is functioning properly		

ACCRUALS AND PREPAYMENTS

222 Leisure Co owns two properties which it rents to tenants. In the year ended 31 December 20X6, it received $280,000 in respect of property 1 and $160,000 in respect of property 2. Balances on the prepaid and accrued income accounts were as follows:

	31 December 20X6	31 December 20X5
Property 1	13,400 Dr	12,300 Cr
Property 2	6,700 Cr	5,400 Dr

What amount should be credited to the statement of profit or loss for the year ended 31 December 20X6 in respect of rental income?

$ [   ]

223 Troy Co has a property rental business and received cash totalling $838,600 from tenants during the year ended 31 December 20X6.

Figures for rent in advance and in arrears at the beginning and end of the year were:

	31 December 20X5	31 December 20X6
	$	$
Rent received in advance	102,600	88,700
Rent in arrears (all subsequently received)	42,300	48,400

What amount should appear in Troy Co's statement of profit or loss for the year ended 31 December 20X6 for rental income?

$ [   ]

224 Details of B Co's insurance policy are as follows:

Premium for year ended 31 March 20X6 paid April 20X5	$10,800
Premium for year ending 31 March 20X7 paid April 20X6	$12,000

What figures should be included in the B Co's financial statements for the year ended 30 June 20X6?

	Statement of profit or loss	Statement of financial position
	$	$
A	11,100	9,000 prepayment
B	11,700	9,000 prepayment
C	11,100	9,000 accrual
D	11,700	9,000 accrual

225 Vine Co sublets part of its office accommodation to earn rental income. The rent is received quarterly in advance on 1 January, 1 April, 1 July and 1 October. The annual rent has been $24,000 for some years, but it was increased to $30,000 from 1 July 20X5.

What amounts for rent should appear in Vine Co's financial statements for the year ended 31 January 20X6?

	Profit or loss	Statement of financial position
A	$27,500	$5,000 in accrued income
B	$27,000	$2,500 in accrued income
C	$27,000	$2,500 in prepaid income
D	$27,500	$5,000 in prepaid income

226 On 1 May 20X0, Bao commenced business and paid an annual rent charge of $1,800 for the period to 30 April 20X1.

What is the charge to Bao's statement of profit or loss and the entry in the statement of financial position for the accounting period ended 30 November 20X0?

A $1,050 charge to statement of profit or loss and prepayment of $750 in the statement of financial position.

B $1,050 charge to statement of profit or loss and accrual of $750 in the statement of financial position.

C $1,800 charge to statement of profit or loss and no entry in the statement of financial position.

D $750 charge to statement of profit or loss and prepayment of $1,050 in the statement of financial position.

227 At 1 September, the motor expenses account showed 4 months' insurance prepaid of $80 and fuel costs accrued of $95. During September, the outstanding fuel bill was paid, plus further bills of $245. At 30 September there was a further outstanding fuel bill of $120.

What was the expense included in the statement of profit or loss for motor expenses for September?

$ [   ]

228 The electricity account of a business for the year ended 30 June 20X3 was as follows:

	$
Opening balance for electricity accrued at 1 July 20X2	300
Payments made during the year:	
1 August 20X2 for three months to 31 July 20X2	600
1 November 20X2 for three months to 31 October 20X2	720
1 February 20X3 for three months to 31 January 20X3	900
30 June 20X3 for three months to 30 April 20X3	840

What was the expense charged to the statement of profit or loss for the year ended 30 June 20X3 and the accrual at 30 June 20X3?

Accrued at June 20X3

$ [   ]

Expense in profit or loss

$ [   ]

229 The annual insurance premium for Shan for the period 1 July 20X3 to 30 June 20X4 was $13,200, which is 10% more than the previous year. Insurance premiums are paid on 1 July.

What is the statement of profit or loss charge for insurance for the year ended 31 December 20X3?

$ [   ]

230 Farthing Co's year-end is 30 September. On 1 January 20X6 Farthing Co took out a loan of $100,000 with annual interest of 12%. The interest is payable in equal instalments on the first day of April, July, October and January in arrears.

How much should be charged to the statement of profit or loss account for the year ended 30 September 20X6, and how much should be accrued on the statement of financial position?

	Statement of profit or loss	Statement of financial position
A	$12,000	$3,000
B	$9,000	$3,000
C	$9,000	$0
D	$6,000	$3,000

231 On 1 January 20X3, a business had prepaid insurance of $10,000. On 1 August 20X3, it paid, in full, the annual insurance invoice of $36,000, to cover the 12 months to 31 July 20X4.

What was the amount charged in the statement of profit or loss and the amount shown in the statement of financial position for the year ended 31 December 20X3?

	Statement of profit or loss	Statement of financial position
	$	$
A	5,000	24,000
B	22,000	23,000
C	25,000	21,000
D	36,000	15,000

232 **Which of the following statements is false?**

A   Accruals decrease profit

B   Accrued income decreases profit

C   A prepayment is an asset

D   An accrual is a liability

233 On 9 October, Ping paid the heat and power bill for the three months ended 30 September 20X4. The bill included a meter rental charge of $60 for the three months ending 31 December 20X4 and a usage charge of $135 for the three-month period to 30 September 20X4. Ping has an accounting year end date of 31 October 20X4.

Which of the following pairs of adjustments is required in relation to the heat and power expense as at 31 October 20X4?

A	Rental accrual of $40	Usage prepayment of $45
B	Rental accrual of $45	Usage prepayment of $40
C	Rental prepayment of $40	Usage accrual of $45
D	Rental prepayment of $45	Usage accrual of $45

RECEIVABLES

234 In the statement of financial position at 31 December 20X5, Yanlin had net receivables of $12,000. During 20X6 Yanlin made sales on credit of $125,000 and received cash from credit customers amounting to $115,500. At 31 December 20X6, Yanlin decided to write off debts of $7,100 and increase the specific allowance for receivables by $950 to $2,100.

What was the net receivables figure reported in Yanlin's statement of financial position at 31 December 20X6?

A $12,300

B $13,450

C $14,400

D $15,550

235 The following balances relate to Putney Co:

	$
Receivables at 1 January 20X8	34,500
Cash received from credit customers	247,790
Contra with payables	1,200
Cash sales	24,000
Irrecoverable debts	18,600
Increase in allowance for receivables	12,500
Discounts received	15,670
Receivables at 31 December 20X8	45,000

What is the revenue figure reported by Putney Co in the year ended 31 December 20X8?

A $275,690

B $278,090

C $320,690

D $302,090

236 The following account has been extracted from the general ledger of Purdey Co:

Receivables

	$		$
Balance b/f	84,700	Irrecoverable debts	4,300
Contra with payables	5,000	Increase in allowance for receivables	6,555
Discounts received	21,100	Cash received from credit customers	625,780
Credit sales	644,000		
Cash sales	13,500	Balance c/f	131,665
	768,300		768,300

After amendment, what is the correct receivables' balance carried forward?

A $100,175

B $93,620

C $89,320

D $97,920

237 Newell Co's receivables account shows a balance at the end of the year of $58,200 before making the following adjustments:

(i) Newell Co decides to write off debts amounting to $8,900 as it believes they are irrecoverable.

(ii) Newell Co also decides to make specific allowance for Carroll's debt of $1,350, Jay's debt of $750 and Mai's debt of $1,416.

Newell Co's allowance for receivables at the previous year end was $5,650.

What is the charge to the statement of profit or loss in respect of the above information?

A $6,766

B $11,034

C $6,829

D $10,971

238 At 1 July 20X5, V Co's allowance for receivables was $48,000. At 30 June 20X6, trade receivables amounted to $838,000. It was decided to write off $72,000 of these debts and adjust the specific allowance for receivables to $60,000.

What are the final amounts for inclusion in V Co's statement of financial position at 30 June 20X6?

	Trade receivables	Allowance for receivables	Net balance
	$	$	$
A	838,000	60,000	778,000
B	766,000	60,000	706,000
C	766,000	108,000	658,000
D	838,000	108,000	730,000

239 In the year ended 30 September 20X8, Gulzar had sales of $7,000,000. The year-end receivables amounted to 5% of annual sales. At the year end, Gulzar's specific allowance for receivables equated to 4% of receivables. Gulzar also identified that this amount was 20% higher than at the previous year end.

During the year irrecoverable debts amounting to $3,200 were written off and debts amounting to $450 and previously written off were recovered.

What was Gulzar's irrecoverable debt expense for the year?

A $5,083

B $5,550

C $5,583

D $16,750

240 On 1 January 20X3 Tipton Co's trade receivables were $10,000. The following relates to the year ended 31 December 20X3:

	$
Credit sales	100,000
Cash receipts	90,000
Contra with payables	800
Discounts received	700

Cash receipts include $1,000 in respect of a receivable previously written off.

What was the value of Tipton Co's receivables at 31 December 20X3?

A $19,300

B $20,200

C $20,800

D $20,700

241 G Co has been notified that a customer has been declared bankrupt. G Co had previously made allowance for this receivable.

Which of the following is the correct double entry?

	Debit	**Credit**
A	Allowance for receivables	Receivables
B	Receivables	Irrecoverable debts account
C	Irrecoverable debts account	Receivables
D	Receivables	Allowance for receivables

242 Headington Co is owed $37,500 by its customers at the start, and $39,000 at the end, of its year ended 31 December 20X8.

During the period, cash sales of $263,500 and credit sales of $357,500 were made, contras against the payables account amounted to $15,750 and discounts received totalled $21,400. Irrecoverable debts of $10,500 were written off. Headington Co also identified that the increase in the specific allowance for receivables required at 31 December 20X8 was $8,750.

How much cash was received from credit customers during the year ended 31 December 20X8?

A $329,750

B $593,175

C $593,250

D $614,650

243 The revenue of J Co was $2 million and its receivables were 5% of sales. J Co wishes to have a specific allowance for receivables of $4,000, which would make the allowance one-third higher than the current allowance.

How will the profit for the period be affected by the change in allowance?

A   Profit will be reduced by $1,000

B   Profit will be increased by $1,000

C   Profit will be reduced by $1,333

D   Profit will be increased by $1,333

244 Abacus Co started the year with total receivables of $87,000 and an allowance for receivables of $2,500.

During the year, two specific debts were written off, one for $800 and the other for $550. A debt of $350 that had been written off as irrecoverable in the previous year was paid during the year. At the year-end, total receivables were $90,000 and the allowance for receivables was $2,300.

What is the charge to the statement of profit or loss for the year in respect of irrecoverable debts and allowance for receivables?

A $800

B $1,000

C $1,150

D $1,550

245 **An increase in the allowance for receivables results in which of the following?**

A   An increase in net current assets

B   A decrease in net current assets

C   An increase in sales

D   A decrease in drawings

246 At the end of 20X7, Charu's receivables' balance was $230,000 and the allowance for receivables was $11,700. Irrecoverable debts of $11,429 should be written off. At the end of the year, Charu wishes to make specific allowance only for Emily's debt of $450 and Lulu's debt of $980.

What amount should be charged or credited to Charu's statement of profit or loss in respect of irrecoverable debts and the allowance for receivables?

A $1,159 Dr

B $1,230 Dr

C $200 Cr

D $12,930 Dr

247 **Which of the following is not a benefit of providing credit to customers?**

A   It may result in increased sales

B   It may encourage customer loyalty

C   It may attract new customers

D   It may improve the cash flow of the business

248 **Which of the following best explains the purpose of an aged receivables' analysis?**

A   To ensure that credit is not extended to unapproved customers

B   To ensure that credit customers regularly purchase goods from the business

C   To keep track of outstanding debts and identify overdue amounts to follow up

D   To keep track of customer addresses

249 On 31 March 20X4, the balance on the receivables of P Co was $425,700. The following adjustments to receivables are required:

Irrecoverable debt recovered $2,000
Specific allowance required $2,400

It was decided that amounts totalling $8,466 should be written off as irrecoverable. The allowance for receivables on 1 April 20X3 was $1,900.

What was the expense for irrecoverable debts and allowance for receivables for the year ended 31 March 20X4?

$ _____

250 **What is the purpose of customer credit limits?**

A   To enable the entity to make a decision regarding whether trade or early settlement discounts should be offered to individual customers

B   To manage the risk of cash customers not being able to pay for goods sold

C   To manage the risk of loss to the business arising from credit customers not being able to pay for goods sold

D   To manage the risk of having inventory shortages

251 **How should an irrecoverable debt recovered be recording in the accounting records?**

A   Debit Bank   Credit Revenue

B   Debit Bank   Credit Receivables

C   Debit Bank   Credit Allowance for receivables

D   Debit Bank   Credit Irrecoverable debts expense

252 Following a mid-year review of its aged receivables' listing, Pluto Co identified three irrecoverable debts totalling $630 which should be written off. One of the debts, for $150, was already included in the allowance for receivables.

What accounting entries should Pluto Co make to write off the irrecoverable debts?

	Debit	Credit
A	Irrecoverable debts $480	Trade receivables $480
B	Irrecoverable debts $630	Trade receivables $630
C	Irrecoverable debts $480 Allowance for receivables $150	Trade receivables $630
D	Irrecoverable debts $630	Trade receivables $480 Allowance for receivables $150

253 At its accounting year end of 30 November 20X6, Venus Co decided to write off irrecoverable debts of $425 and also to increase the allowance for receivables by $160.

What accounting entries should Venus Co make to update the general ledger to reflect these circumstances?

	Debit	Credit
A	Trade receivables $585	Irrecoverable debts $425 Allowance for receivables $160
B	Irrecoverable debts $425 Allowance for receivables $160	Trade receivables $585
C	Irrecoverable debts $585	Trade receivables $425 Allowance for receivables $160
D	Irrecoverable debts $585	Allowance for receivables $585

254 At its accounting year end of 31 October 20X3, Neptune Co decided to write off irrecoverable debts of $673 and also to reduce the allowance for receivables by $184.

What accounting entries should Neptune Co make to update the general ledger to reflect these circumstances?

	Debit	Credit
A	Trade receivables $673	Irrecoverable debts $489 Allowance for receivables $184
B	Irrecoverable debts $184 Allowance for receivables $489	Trade receivables $673
C	Irrecoverable debts $857	Trade receivables $673 Allowance for receivables $160
D	Irrecoverable debts $489 Allowance for receivables $184	Receivables $673

255 During its accounting year end to 31 May 20X7, Jupiter Co unexpectedly received a receipt of $382 in relation to a debt which had been written off earlier during the year.

What accounting entries should Jupiter Co make to update the general ledger to reflect this situation?

	Debit	**Credit**
A	Bank $382	Sundry income $382
B	Bank $382	Receivables $382
C	Bank $382	Allowance for receivables $382
D	Bank $382	Irrecoverable debts $382

256 Magasin Co is a small business which is preparing its financial statements for the year ended 31 December 20X6. The personal account of its only credit customer, Shaun, contains the following information for the year:

	$	
Opening balance as at 1 January 20X6	24,500	(Dr)
Cash received	102,300	
Discounts allowed	3,100	
(not expected to be taken when invoice first issued)		
Interest on overdue payments	1,600	
Contra agreement	8,200	
Credit sales	133,700	
Returns inwards	5,000	

Shaun is disputing $6,700 of items and is arguing that the items were damaged on delivery. Magasin Co decides to write this disputed amount off as an irrecoverable debt.

What amount would Magasin Co show as being owed by Shaun at the year end?

$ ☐

PAYABLES, PROVISIONS AND CONTINGENCIES

257 During its accounting year end to 30 April 20X1, Earth Co agreed with Trader Co, who it both purchased goods from, and sold goods to, on credit terms, to contra an amount of $1,500 off the balances due to each other.

What accounting entries should Earth Co make in its general ledger to record this situation?

	Debit	**Credit**
A	Trade receivables $1,500	Trade payables $1,500
B	Trade payables $1,500	Trade receivables $1,500
C	Sales $1,500	Purchases $1,500
D	Purchases $1,500	Sales $1,500

258 During its accounting year end to 29 February 20X6, Saturn Co agreed with Acme Co, who it both purchased goods from, and sold goods to, on credit terms, to contra the maximum possible amount of the balances due to each other. At the date of this agreement, Saturn Co had a customer account balance for Acme Co of $685 and a supplier account balance of $565.

What accounting entries should Saturn Co make in its general ledger to record this situation?

	Debit	**Credit**
A	Trade payables $685	Trade receivables $685
B	Trade payables $565	Trade receivables $565
C	Trade receivables $565	Trade payables $565
D	Trade receivables $685	Trade payables $685

259 During its accounting year end to 29 February 20X5, Neptune Co agreed with Sun Co, who it both purchased goods from, and sold goods to, on credit terms, to contra an amount that left a balance outstanding from Sun Co due to Neptune Co of $750. At the date of this this agreement, Neptune Co had a customer account balance for Sun Co of $2,685 and a supplier account balance of $2,565.

What accounting entries should Neptune Co make in its general ledger to record this situation?

	Debit	**Credit**
A	Trade payables $1,935	Trade receivables $1,935
B	Trade receivables $1,815	Trade payables $1,815
C	Trade receivables $1,935	Trade payables $1,935
D	Trade payables $1,815	Trade receivables $1,815

260 G Co is both a customer of, and supplier to Zed Co. As at 31 May, 20X4, G Co's accounting records identified the following account balances with Zed Co: a customer account balance of $2,500 and a supplier account balance of $850. G Co and Zed Co agree to contra the maximum possible amount in their respective accounting records.

What accounting entries should G Co make in its general ledger to account for the maximum possible contra with Zed Co?

	Debit	**Credit**
A	Receivables $850	Payables $850
B	Payables $2,500	Receivables $2,500
C	Payables $850	Receivables $850
D	Receivables $2,500	Payables $2,500

261 Which TWO items may be accounted for in a payables account in a general ledger?

	Selection
Discount allowed	
Returns inwards	
Discount received	
Irrecoverable debts	
Returns outwards	

262 What is the purpose of supplier statements?

A   The supplier statement is a demand from the supplier to reconcile that statement with its own records and to inform the supplier of any discrepancies.

B   The supplier statement acts as an immediate demand for full payment from the supplier to a customer

C   It is a record of transactions recorded by a purchaser and issued to a supplier as a request to settle amounts due

D   It is a record of transactions recorded by seller and issued to the customer as a request to settle amount due

263 Manvi is a sole trader who has provided the following information relating to transactions with credit customers and suppliers for the year ended 30 April 20X5:

	$
Trade receivables 1 May 20X4	200,000
Trade payables 1 May 20X4	130,000
Cash received from customers	576,800
Cash paid to suppliers	340,000
Discount received	3,500
Contra between payables and receivables	3,800
Trade receivables 30 April 20X5	240,000
Trade payables 30 April 20X5	150,000

What was the cost of Manvi's purchases for the year ended 30 April 20X5?

$ [   ]

264 For which of the following items is a provision required in accordance with IAS 37 *Provisions, Contingent Liabilities and Contingent Assets*?

	Provision required	Provision not required
A retail outlet has a policy of providing refunds over and above the statutory requirement to do so. This policy is well publicised and customers have made use of this facility in the past.		
A customer has made a legal claim against an entity, claiming that faulty goods sold to them caused damage to their property. The entity's lawyers have advised that the claim will possibly succeed and, if it does, compensation of $10,000 will be payable.		

265 Which of the following statements about the requirements relating to IAS 37 *Provisions, Contingent Liabilities and Contingent Assets* are correct?

1 A contingent asset should be disclosed in the notes if an inflow of economic benefits is probable.

2 No disclosure of a contingent liability is required if the possibility of a transfer of economic benefits arising is remote.

3 Contingent assets must not be presented in the financial statements unless an inflow of economic benefits is virtually certain to arise.

A 1, 2 and 3

B 1 and 2 only

C 1 and 3 only

D 2 and 3 only

266 The following items need to be considered in finalising the financial statements of Q Co:

1 Q Co gives warranties on its products. Q Co's statistics show that about 5% of sales give rise to a warranty claim.

2 Q Co has guaranteed the overdraft of another entity. The likelihood of a liability arising under the guarantee is assessed as possible.

What is the correct action to be taken in the financial statements of Q Co for these items?

	Recognise a provision	Disclose in the notes only	No action
A	1	2	
B		1	2
C	1 and 2		
D		1 and 2	

267 **Which one of the following statements relating to the requirements of IAS 37** *Provisions, Contingent Liabilities and Contingent Assets* **is correct?**

A   A contingent asset must always be recognised and accounted for in the financial statements.

B   A contingent asset must always be disclosed in the notes to the financial statements.

C   A contingent liability must always be disclosed in the notes to the financial statements if it is regarded as possible.

D   A contingent liability must always be disclosed in the notes to the financial statements if it is regarded as probable.

268 **Which one of the following statements relating to the requirements of IAS 37** *Provisions, Contingent Liabilities and Contingent Assets* **is correct?**

A   A contingent asset must be recognised and accounted for in the financial statements if it is regarded as probable.

B   A contingent asset must never be recognised in the financial statements.

C   A contingent liability must either be recognised and accounted for in the financial statements or disclosed in the notes to the financial statements.

D   A contingent liability may not be required to be accounted for or disclosed in the notes to the financial statements under certain circumstances.

269 Consider each of the following statements.

1   A provision will always be classified as falling due for payment within 12 months of the reporting date, whereas a liability may be classified as either current or non-current.

2   A provision requires judgement and estimation to quantify the amount and/or the date of payment, whereas a liability is normally capable of precise calculation and the date of payment can be determined.

3   A provision meets the definition of a liability but is subject to uncertainty regarding the exact amount or date of the future outflow of economic benefits.

Which statements are correct in relation to provisions and liabilities?

A   1 and 2

B   2 and 3

C   1 and 3

D   1, 2 and 3

270 Driller Co undertakes oil and gas exploration activities. One of the conditions of the operating licence is that Driller must make good any damage caused to the local environment as a result of its exploration activities. As at the year-end date of 31 August 20X4, Driller Co estimated that the cost of rectifying damage already caused at current exploration sites at $5 million. At that date Driller Co estimated that that the cost of rectifying expected future damage at current exploration sites at an additional $20 million. Driller Co also estimated that all current exploration sites will operate until 20X7 or beyond that date.

How should this information be reported in the financial statements of Driller Co for the year ended 31 August 20X4?

A   As a provision classified as a current liability for $5 million

B   As a provision classified as a current liability for $25 million

C   As a provision classified as a non-current liability for $5 million

D   As a provision classified as a non-current liability for $25 million

271 Recently, users of a new perfume have suffered blistering of the skin along with considerable pain and discomfort. Following investigation by the manufacturer, Fleur Co, it appears that product contamination occurred during the bottling process which was performed by Bottler. Fleur Co's legal representatives have advised it that it is probable that customers will make valid compensation claims totalling $3 million and that it is probable Fleur Co will be able to successfully counter-claim against Bottler for the same amount.

How should this information be reported in the financial statements of Fleur Co for the year ended 31 August 20X4?

A   There should be a provision for $3 million only recognised in the statement of financial position.

B   There should be a provision and an asset, each for $3 million, recognised in the statement of financial position.

C   No provision or asset should be recognised in the statement of financial position as the two amounts cancel each other.

D   There should be a provision for $3 million in the statement of financial position and a disclosure note only to deal with the contingent asset of the amount which may be recovered from Bottler.

272 Electrode Co manufactures vacuum cleaners and allows customers three months from the date of purchase to return cleaners if they are dissatisfied with the product for any reason. At 31 May 20X8, Electrode Co included a provision of $10,000 in the financial statements relating to the expected return of cleaners which had been sold before the year-end date. At 31 May 20X9, Electrode Co estimated that the amount of the provision should be changed to $13,000.

How should this information be accounted for in Electrode Co's financial statements for the year ended 31 May 20X9?

	Dr	Cr
A	Other comprehensive income $3,000	Provision $3,000
B	Provision $3,000	Other comprehensive income $3,000
C	Profit or loss $3,000	Provision $3,000
D	Provision $3,000	Profit or loss $3,000

273 During the year ended 30 April 20X7 Doolittle Co experienced a number of difficulties with employees. On 1 April 20X7 Doolittle Co dismissed an employee and subsequently received notice of a claim for unfair dismissal amounting to $50,000. Another employee suffered personal injury on 30 March 20X7 whilst operating machinery at work. On 30 May Doolittle Co received notice of a claim from that employee for compensation of $100,000. Doolittle Co's legal representatives have advised that the claim for unfair dismissal will probably be successful and result in a compensation award of $50,000 to the employee. The lawyer also advised that the compensation claim for injury suffered is regarded as possible, but not probable, that compensation will be payable. In the event that compensation was payable for personal injury suffered, an amount of $100,000 is a reliable estimate.

How should this information be accounted for in the financial statements of Doolittle Co for the year ended 30 April 20X7?

A   A provision should be recognised in the financial statement for $50,000 only.

B   A provision should be recognised in the financial statements for $50,000 plus a disclosure note included of the possible compensation payment relating to the personal injury claim.

C   A provision should be recognised in the financial statements for $150,000 only.

D   A provision should be recognised in the financial statements for $150,000 and a disclosure note included of the possible compensation payment relating to the personal injury claim.

274 According to IAS 37 *Provisions, Contingent Liabilities and Contingent Assets*, should the following situations result in the recognition of a provision in the statement of financial position?

	Yes	No
A manufacturer gives warranties to its customers. The terms of the warranty require the company to repair any defects in its products that arise within two years of the date of sale. The company expects that around 2% of sales each year will result in claims under the warranty.		
A coal-mining company operates in a country where there is no legislation requiring the company to repair environmental damage. The company causes environmental damage but has a widely publicised policy of repairing this damage.		

CAPITAL STRUCTURE AND FINANCE COSTS

275 State whether each of the following statements about a rights issue of shares true or false.

	True	False
A rights issue capitalises retained earnings or other components of equity, which can be a disadvantage, as this can reduce the amount available for future dividends.		
A rights issue is offered to the company's existing shareholders and is usually at a discounted price compared to the nominal value of a share.		

276 Which TWO items within the statement of financial position would change immediately following the issue of redeemable preference shares?

	Selection
Bank	
Retained earnings	
Interest expense	
Equity	
Long-term debt	

277 The statement of financial position of Cartwright Co shows closing retained earnings of $320,568. The statement of profit or loss showed profit of $79,285. Cartwright Co paid last year's dividend of $12,200 during the year and proposed a dividend of $13,500 at the year end. This had not been approved by the shareholders at the end of the year.

What is the opening retained earnings balance?

A $241,283

B $387,653

C $254,783

D $253,483

278 Gearing Co had profit before income taxes of $68,000 and an income tax expense of $32,000, resulting in a profit for the year of $36,000 for the year ended 30 April 20X5.

In addition to the profit above:

1   Gearing Co paid a dividend of $21,000 during the year.

2   A gain on revaluation of land resulted in a revaluation surplus of $18,000.

What total amount will be added to retained earnings at the end of the financial year?

$ [   ]

279 Which of the following items would NOT be included in the statement of changes in equity?

A   Equity share capital

B   Bank loans

C   Revaluation surplus

D   Dividends paid

280 Which of the following statements about preference shares is true?

A   All preference shares are classified as a liability in the statement of financial position

B   Irredeemable preference shares are classified as a liability and redeemable preference shares as an equity in the statement of financial position

C   All preference shares are classified as equity in the statement of financial position

D   Irredeemable preference shares are classified as equity and redeemable preference shares as a liability in the statement of financial position

281 Which of the following statements is true in relation to a rights issue of shares by an entity?

A   No cash is received by the entity as a result of making the rights issue

B   The entity issues shares for cash at market price of the shares

C   The entity issues shares for cash at a price less than the market price of the shares

D   A rights issue is not presented in a statement of cash flows

282 Which of the following statements is true in relation to a bonus issue of shares by an entity?

A   The entity issues shares for cash at a price less than the market price of the shares

B   The entity issues shares for cash at market price of the shares

C   No cash is received by the entity as a result of making the bonus issue

D   A bonus issue will be presented in a statement of cash flows

283 State whether each of the following statements about dividends true or false.

	True	False
Dividends paid by an entity are excluded from the statement of changes in equity		
Dividends received by an entity are included in the statement of changes in equity.		
Dividends received by an entity are excluded from the statement of changes in equity.		
Dividends paid by an entity are included in the statement of changes in equity.		

284 When an entity pays a dividend, what accounting entries are required to account for the transaction?

	Debit	Credit
A	Share capital	Bank
B	Share premium	Bank
C	Retained earnings	Bank
D	Profit or loss	Bank

285 An entity made an issue of 20,000 $1 equity shares at a price of $1.75. What accounting entries are required to record the issue of shares?

A   Debit Bank $35,000, and Credit Share capital $35,000

B   Debit Share capital $20,000, Debit Share premium $15,000 and Credit Bank $35,000

C   Debit Bank $35,000, Credit Share premium $20,000 and Credit Share capital $15,000

D   Debit Bank $35,000, Credit Share capital $20,000 and Credit Share premium $15,000

286 An entity, Taylor Co, issued 250,000 equity shares with a nominal value of $0.50 each and a share premium account balance of $100,000.

What accounting entries are required if Taylor Co was to make a bonus issue of one share for four held?

	Debit		Credit	
A	Share capital	$62,500	Share premium	$62,500
B	Share premium	$31,250	Share capital	$31,250
C	Share capital	$31,250	Share premium	$31,250
D	Share capital	$62,500	Share premium	$62,500

287 **Which of the following statements are correct?**

1   A limited company will always have both an equity share capital account and a share premium account.

2   A limited company will always have an equity share capital account, and may also have a share premium account.

3   A limited company will always have either a share premium account or a revaluation surplus account.

A   1 only

B   2 only

C   1 and 3

D   2 and 3

288 **Which of the following would NOT be included in a statement of changes in equity?**

A   Share premium

B   Revaluation surplus

C   Irredeemable preference shares

D   Redeemable preference shares

289 The following information relates to the latest financial year for Garden Co:

1   The company made a loss of $87,445

2   Assets were revalued resulting in an increase in the revaluation surplus of $145,000

3   Interim dividends of $30,000 were paid during the year

4   The final dividend of $25,000 for the prior year was paid at the beginning of the year

What is the total comprehensive income for the year to be reported in the statement of profit or loss and other comprehensive income?

A $145,000 Cr

B $27,555 Cr

C $57,555 Cr

D $2,555 Dr

290 **Which of the following would be included in a statement of changes in equity?**

A   A bank loan, repayable in 10 years' time

B   Dividend paid in the year

C   Dividend received in the year

D   Redeemable preference shares

Total comprehensive income for the period is the profit or loss plus other comprehensive income (OCI) = -$87,455 (loss) + $145,000 (increase in revaluation surplus) = $57,555.

Dividends are not deducted from profit (nor OCI) as they are distributions of profit to the owners of the business (shareholders). Dividends are deducted from retained earnings and disclosed in the statement of changes in equity.

291   At 1 April 20X8, Companies Co had a $300,000 6% loan note in issue. On 1 June 20X8, Companies Co issued a $500,000 9% loan note. On 1 January 20X9, Companies Co repaid the $300,000 6% loan note in full.

What figure should appear in the statement of profit or loss for interest expense for the year ended 31 March 20X9?

A $51,000

B $55,500

C $58,500

D $63,000

292   Companies Co's retained earnings were $119,460 at 31 March 20X5 and $145,710 at 31 March 20X6. During the year ended 31 March 20X6, Companies Co undertook the following transactions:

1   Paid a dividend of $0.45 per share on each of its 100,000 redeemable preference shares

2   Paid a dividend of $0.25 per share on each of its 200,000 ordinary shares

3   Made a rights issue of 50,000 shares at a price of $1.10 per share

4   Made an issue of bonus shares of $25,000 out of retained earnings

What is Companies Co's profit for the year ended 31 March 20X6?

A $26,250

B $101,250

C $146,250

D   201,250

RECONCILIATIONS

BANK RECONCILIATIONS

293 The bank ledger account of Worcester shows a credit balance of $1,350. Cheques totalling $56 have been written to suppliers but not yet cleared the bank; uncleared lodgements amount to $128. The bank has accidentally credited Worcester's account with interest of $15 due to another customer. A standing order of $300 has not been accounted for in the general ledger.

What is the balance on the bank statement?

A $993 Cr

B $993 Dr

C $1,707 Cr

D $1,707 Dr

294 Reema's bank ledger account shows a balance of $190 credit. Reema's bank statement reports a balance of $250 credit.

Which of the following will explain the difference in full?

A   Unpresented cheques of $100 and an uncleared lodgement of $30

B   Unpresented cheques of $150, the misposting of a cash receipt of $130 to the wrong side of the bank ledger account and unrecorded bank interest received of $30

C   An unrecorded direct debit of $30, a dishonoured cheque of $70 and an uncleared lodgement of $40

D   An unrecorded standing order of $60, an unpresented cheque of $110 and a bank error whereby Reema's account was accidentally credited with $110

295 State whether each of the following statements true or false.

	True	False
When preparing a bank reconciliation, unpresented cheques must be deducted from a balance of cash at bank shown in the bank statement.		
A cheque from a customer paid into the bank but dishonoured must be corrected by making a debit entry in the bank ledger account.		
An error by the bank must be corrected by an entry in the bank ledger account.		
An overdraft is a debit balance in the bank statement.		

296 The following bank reconciliation statement was prepared by an inexperienced bookkeeper at 31 December 20X5:

	$
Balance per bank statement (overdrawn)	38,640
Add: Lodgements not credited	19,270
	57,910
Less: Unpresented cheques	14,260
Balance per bank ledger account	43,650

What should the bank ledger account balance be when all the above items have been properly accounted for?

A $43,650 overdrawn

B $33,630 overdrawn

C $5,110 overdrawn

D $72,170 overdrawn

297 A bank reconciliation statement for Dallas at 30 June 20X5 is being prepared. The following information is available:

1 Bank charges of $350 have not been entered in the bank ledger account.

2 The bank statement shows a debit balance of $200.

3 Unpresented cheques amount to $1,250.

4 A direct debit of $250 has not been recorded in the ledger accounts.

5 A bank error has resulted in a cheque for $97 being debited to Dallas' account instead of Dynasty's account.

6 Cheques received but not yet banked amounted to $890.

What will be the bank ledger account balance after all necessary adjustments?

A $463 Dr

B $463 Cr

C $63 Cr

D $63 Dr

298 The following information relates to a bank reconciliation:

1 The balance in the bank ledger account before taking the items below into account was $8,970 overdrawn.

2 Bank charges of $550 on the bank statement have not been entered in the bank ledger account.

3 The bank has credited the account in error with $425 which belongs to another customer.

4 Cheque payments totalling $3,275 have been recorded in the bank ledger account but have not been presented for payment.

5 Cheques totalling $5,380 have been correctly entered on the debit side of the bank ledger account but have not been paid in at the bank.

What was the revised balance as shown by the bank statement before taking the items above into account?

A $8,970 overdrawn

B $11,200 overdrawn

C $12,050 overdrawn

D $17,750 overdrawn

299 Setu's bank statement at 31 October 20X8 shows a balance of $13,400. Setu subsequently discovers that the bank has dishonoured a customer's cheque for $300 and has charged bank charges of $50, neither of which is recorded in the bank ledger account.

There are unpresented cheques totalling $1,400 and an automatic receipt from a customer of $195 has been recorded as a credit in Setu's bank ledger account.

What was Setu's bank ledger account balance, PRIOR to correcting the errors and omissions?

A $11,455

B $11,960

C $12,000

D $12,155

300 Wimborne's bank statement shows a balance of $715 overdrawn. The statement includes bank charges of $74 which have not been recorded in the bank ledger account. There are also unpresented cheques totalling $824 and lodgements not yet credited of $337. In addition, the bank statement erroneously includes a dividend receipt of $25 belonging to another customer.

What should be the bank overdraft in the statement of financial position?

A $253

B $1,177

C $1,202

D $1,227

301 The bank ledger account of a business shows a balance of $5,675 overdrawn at 31 August 20X5. It is subsequently discovered that a standing order for $125 has been entered twice, and that a dishonoured cheque for $450 has been debited in the bank ledger account instead of credited.

What is the correct bank balance?

A $5,100 overdrawn

B $6,000 overdrawn

C $6,250 overdrawn

D $6,450 overdrawn

302 An entity's bank ledger account had an opening balance of $485 credit. During the following week, the following transactions took place:

Cash sales $1,450 including sales tax of $150.

Receipts from credit customers of $2,400.

Payments to suppliers of debts of $1,800 less 5% cash discount.

Dishonoured cheques from customers amounting to $250.

What was the resulting balance on the bank ledger account after the transactions had been recorded?

A $1,255 debit

B $1,405 debit

C $1,905 credit

D $2,375 credit

303 The bank statement of a business at 31 October 20X7 showed an overdraft of $800. On reconciling the bank statement, it was discovered that a cheque drawn in favour of Smith for $80 had not been presented for payment, and that a cheque for $130 from a customer had been dishonoured on 30 October 20X7, but that this had not yet been notified to you by the bank.

What is the correct bank balance to be shown in the statement of financial position at 31 October 20X7?

A $1,010 overdrawn

B $880 overdrawn

C $750 overdrawn

D $720 overdrawn

304 Yang Co's bank ledger account at 30 April 20X8 showed a balance at the bank of $2,490. Comparison with the bank statement at the same date revealed the following differences:

	$
Unpresented cheques	840
Bank charges not in bank ledger account	50
Receipts not yet credited by the bank	470
Dishonoured cheque not in bank ledger account	140

What was the correct bank ledger account balance at 30 April 20X8?

A $1,460

B $2,300

C $2,580

D $3,140

305 Your firm's bank ledger account shows a credit bank balance of $1,240 at 30 April 20X9. In comparison with the bank statement, you determine that there are unpresented cheques totalling $450, and a receipt of $140 which has not yet been passed through the bank account. The bank statement shows bank charges of $75 which have not been recorded in the bank ledger account.

What was the balance on the bank statement?

A $1,005 overdrawn

B $930 overdrawn

C $1,475 in credit

D $1,550 in credit

306 Which of the following is not an 'unrecorded difference' when reconciling the balance on the bank ledger account to the amount shown in the bank statement?

A   A standing order

B   Bank interest

C   An uncleared lodgement

D   A BACS receipt

307 An entity has prepared its bank reconciliation at 31 March 20X4 taking the following information into account:

Outstanding lodgements $5,000   Unpresented cheques $2,800

Bank charges included in the bank statement but not recorded in the bank ledger account were $125. The adjusted bank ledger balance per the bank reconciliation was a debit balance of $1,060.

What was the balance as shown on the bank statement at 31 March 20X4?

A $1,140 debit

B $1,140 credit

C $1,265 debit

D $1,265 credit

TRADE PAYABLES ACCOUNT RECONCILIATIONS

308 Ordan received a statement from one of its suppliers, Alta, showing a balance due of $3,980. The amount due according to the payables' ledger account of Ordan was only $230.

Comparison of the statement and the ledger account revealed the following differences:

1   A cheque sent by Ordan for $270 has not been recorded in Alta's statement.

2   Alta has not recorded goods returned by Ordan $180.

3   Ordan made a contra entry, reducing the amount due to Alta by $3,200, for a balance due from Alta in Ordan's receivables ledger. No such entry has been made in Alta's records.

What difference remains between the two entities' accounting records after adjusting for these items?

A $460

B $640

C $6,500

D $100

309 A supplier sent Lee Co a statement showing a balance outstanding of $14,350. Lee Co's records show a balance outstanding of $14,500.

Which of the following reasons could account for this difference?

A   The supplier sent an invoice for $150 which Lee Co has not yet received

B   The supplier has allowed Lee Co $150 settlement discount which Lee Co has not yet accounted for in its accounting records

C   Lee Co has paid the supplier $150 which has not yet been accounted for by the supplier

D   Lee Co has returned goods of $150 which the supplier has not yet accounted for

310 Tarbuck Co received a statement of account from one of its suppliers, showing an outstanding balance due to it of $1,350. On comparison with the payable ledger account, the following was identified:

- The ledger account shows a credit balance of $260.

- The supplier has disallowed a cash discount of $80 due to late payment of an invoice.

- The supplier has not yet allowed for goods returned at the end of the period of $270.

- Cash in transit of $830 has not been received by the supplier.

Following consideration of these items, what was the unreconciled difference between the statement of account from the supplier and Tarbuck Co's payable ledger account?

A $70

B $90

C $430

D $590

311   Who issues a statement of account and why is it issued?

A   A business issues a statement of account to those suppliers it still owes money to, advising them of the amount outstanding

B   A business issues a statement of account to cash customers to advise them how much they have purchased in the previous month

C   A business issues a statement of account to credit customers to advise them how much the customer owes the business

D   A business issues a statement of account to all credit customers and suppliers to advise them of the amount outstanding or due

312   Which of the following statements relating to a statement of account issued by a supplier to a customer is true?

A   The balance on a statement of account will always agree with the payable ledger account balance of the customer

B   The balance on a statement of account will never agree with the payable ledger account balance of the customer

C   The balance on a statement of account will always be higher than the payable ledger account balance of the customer

D   The balance on a statement of account can be agreed or reconciled with the payable ledger account balance of the customer subject to identification of goods in transit, cash in transit, early settlement discount or goods returned

313 **Which of the following would be identified by matching a supplier statement against the transactions within the month?**

   A   Incorrect calculations on invoices

   B   Non-delivery of goods charged

   C   Incorrect trade discounts

   D   Duplication of invoices

314 A supplier issued a statement of account to Spark Co showing a balance outstanding of $2,850 at 28 February 20X3. Spark Co's payables ledger account for that supplier had a balance of $2,925.

   Which of the following reasons could account for this difference?

   A   Spark Co has paid the supplier $75 which has not yet been received and accounted for by the supplier

   B   Spark Co has returned goods of $75 which the supplier has not yet accounted for

   C   The supplier has allowed Spark Co settlement discount of $75 which Spark Co has not yet accounted for in its accounting records

   D   The supplier issued an invoice for $75 that Spark Co has not yet received

315 Rome Co received a statement from one of its suppliers, Alpha, showing a balance due of $3,465 at 30 April 20X4.

   Upon reviewing the payables ledger account and the supplier statement the following differences were identified:

   1   An automated payment for $690 was not recorded on the statement from Alpha.

   2   Rome Co had not recorded an invoice issued by Alpha on 29 April 20X4 for $280.

   What was the payable ledger account balance at 30 April 20X4 for Alpha maintained by Rome Co?

   A $4,435

   B $3,875

   C $2,495

   D $3,055

316 Following a reconciliation of the most recent statement received from a supplier, Omicron, Bologna Co discovered that a purchase invoice from Omega had been allocated to the payable ledger account of Omicron.

   What accounting entries should Bologna Co record to rectify this error?

A	Debit: Payables, and	Credit: Purchases
B	Debit: Purchases, and	Credit: Payables
C	Debit: Payable ledger Omicron, and	Credit: Payable ledger Omega
D	Debit: Payable ledger Omega, and	Credit: Payable ledger Omicron

317 Milan Co received a statement dated 30 November 20X7 from one of its suppliers, Beta, showing a balance due of $4,278.

Upon reviewing the payables ledger account and the supplier statement the following differences were identified:

1   A contra of $784 recently agreed with Beta was not recorded on the statement from Beta.

2   Milan Co had not recorded an invoice issued on 29 November by Beta for $543.

When all transactions have been recorded, what will be the updated balance on the payable ledger account for Beta maintained by Milan Co?

A $5,342

B $4,782

C $3,214

D $3,494

318 Delta issued a statement to one of its customers, Verona Co for the month ended 31 January 20X2. At that date, the payable ledger account for Delta maintained by Verona Co had a balance of $6,045.

A review of Verona Co's payable ledger account for Delta and the supplier statement revealed the following differences:

1   Verona Co had recorded discount received of $25 along with a payment made of $389 which was not recorded on the statement.

2   Verona Co had returned goods which cost $105 which was not yet recorded on the statement.

What was the balance on the statement at 31 January 20X2 issued by Delta?

A $6,564

B $6,539

C $6,434

D $5,526

319 Following a reconciliation of the most recent statement received from a supplier, Kappa, Venice Co discovered that discount received of $22 it had recorded had not been allowed by Kappa.

What accounting entries in the general ledger should Venice Co record to rectify this error?

A   Debit: Payable ledger – Kappa $22, and   Credit: Payables $22

B   Debit: Discount received $22, and   Credit: Payable ledger – Kappa 22

C   Debit: Payables $22, and   Credit: Discount received $22

D   Debit: Discount received $22, and   Credit: Payables $22

320 Zeta issued a statement to one of its customers, Portofino Co for the month of July 20X4. At 31 July 20X4, the payable ledger account for Zeta maintained by Portofino Co had a balance of $7,672.

A review of Portofino Co's payable ledger account for Zeta and the supplier statement revealed the following differences:

1   Portofino Co had not yet recorded a purchase invoice from Zeta for goods which cost $435.

2   Portofino Co made an automated payment of $1,506 on 30 July 20X4 which was not recorded on the statement.

What was the closing balance on the statement issued by Zeta?

A $9,178

B $5,731

C $9,613

D $6,601

321 Genoa Co received a statement for the month ended 30 April 20X3 from one of its suppliers, Theta, showing a balance due of $4,278.

Upon reviewing the payables ledger account and the supplier statement the following differences were identified:

1   A contra of $784 recently agreed with Theta was not recorded on the statement from Beta.

2   Genoa Co had not recorded an invoice issued by Theta for $543.

What was the balance on the payable ledger account for Theta maintained by Genoa Co at 30 April 20X3?

A $4,519

B $5,605

C $3,494

D $2,951

322 Kappa issued a statement to one of its customers, Venice Co for the month ended 31 May 20X8. The payable ledger account for Kappa maintained by Venice Co had a balance of $4,368.

A review of Venice Co's payable ledger account for Kappa and the supplier statement revealed the following differences:

1   Venice Co had recorded discount received of $22 along with an automated bank payment made of $389. Only the bank payment was recorded on the statement. Discussion with Kappa identified that the payment was received late and that the discount would not be granted.

2   Venice Co had returned goods which cost $532 which was not yet recorded on the statement.

What was the closing balance at 31 May 20X8 on the statement issued by Kappa?

A $4,922

B $4,408

C $3,858

D $3,814

323 Lecce Co received a statement dated 30 September 20X5 from one of its suppliers, Rho, showing a balance due of $7,278.

Upon reviewing the payables ledger account and the supplier statement the following differences were identified:

1   A contra of $2,471 recently agreed with Rho was not recorded on the statement from Rho.

2   Lecce Co had not recorded a credit note issued by Rho on 29 September for $832.

What is the payable ledger account balance at 30 September 20X5 for Rho as maintained by Lecce Co?

A $3,168

B $6,446

C $4,807

D $5,639

324 Parma Co received a statement for the month ended 31 March 20X3 from one of its suppliers, Sigma, showing a balance due of $4,684.

Upon reviewing the payables ledger account and the supplier statement the following differences were identified:

1   Parma Co had not recorded an invoice issued by Sigma for $584, and nor had it recorded a credit note issued by Sigma for $276.

2   An automated bank payment of $1,342 made recently was not recorded on the statement from Sigma.

When all transactions have been recorded, what will be the updated payable ledger account balance for Sigma maintained by Parma Co at 31 March 20X3?

A $3,034

B $3,342

C $3,650

D $2,482

325 Omega issued a statement to one of its customers, Turin Co for the month ended 31 October 20X9. At that date, the payable ledger account for Omega maintained by Turin Co had a balance of $1,213.

A review of Turin Co's payable ledger account for Omega and the supplier statement revealed the following differences:

1   Turin Co had not recorded an invoice for $241 or a credit note for $92 recently issued by Omega.

2   Turin Co agreed a contra with Omega of $421 which was not yet recorded on the statement.

What was the balance on the statement issued by Omega for the month ended 31 October 20X9?

A $792

B $1,362

C $1,783

D $941

326 Tau Co issued a statement to one of its customers, Ancona Co for the month ended 28 February 20X5. At that date, the payable ledger account for Tau Co maintained by Ancona Co had a balance of $4,575.

A review of Ancona Co's payable ledger account for Tau and the supplier statement revealed the following differences:

1   Ancona Co had not recorded a credit note for $18 recently issued by Tau Co.

2   An invoice on the statement from Tau Co for $875 related to another customer and had been included in in error.

What was the original balance on the statement issued by Tau Co for the month ended 31 October 20X9?

A $4,557

B $5,432

C $4,593

D $3,682

327 Omicron issued a statement to one of its customers, Bologna Co for the month ended 28 February 20X5 with a closing balance of $8,314.

A review of Bologna Co's payable ledger account for Omicron and the supplier statement revealed the following differences:

1   Bologna Co made an automated payment of $2,546 on 27 February 20X5 which was not recorded on the statement issued by Omicron.

2   An invoice on the payable ledger account for Omicron for $1,456 related to another supplier and had been recorded in Omicron's payable ledger account in error.

What was the initial payable ledger account balance for Omicron as maintained by Bologna Co for the month ended 28 February 20X9?

A $7,224

B $5,768

C $4,678

D $6,134

328 The payables account for the year ended 31 May 20X7 in Lisbon Co's general ledger is presented below.

Payables

	$		$
Contra with receivables	3,925	Balance	37,500
Bank	340,750	Purchases	357,500
Discount received	1,325		
Returns outwards	11,235		
Balance	37,765		
	395,000		395,000

What numerical value should be included in the statement of financial position as at 31 May 20X7 within liabilities?

A $37,500

B $37,765

C $395,000

D $357,500

329 Phi issued a statement to one of its customers, Trento Co for the month of August 20X4. At 31 August 20X4, the payable ledger account for Phi maintained by Trento Co had a balance of $6,727.

A review of Trento Co's payable ledger account for Phi and the supplier statement revealed the following differences:

1   Trento Co had not yet recorded a purchase invoice of $534 from Phi.

2   Trento Co made an automated payment of $1,605 on 30 August 20X4 which was not recorded on the statement.

What was the closing balance on the statement issued by Phi?

A $7,798

B $8,332

C $8,866

D $5,122

PREPARING A TRIAL BALANCE

TRIAL BALANCE

330 **Which of the following are limitations of the trial balance?**

1   It does not include all final figures to be included in the financial statements.

2   It does not identify all errors of commission.

3   It does not identify in which accounts errors have been made.

A   1 and 2 only

B   2 and 3 only

C   1, 2 and 3

D   1 and 3 only

331 **Identify whether each of the following statements is true or false.**

	True	False
The trial balance provides a check that no errors exist in the accounting records of a business.		
The trial balance is one of the financial statements prepared annually by an entity for its shareholders.		

332 Harsha extracted the following balances from the business accounting records:

	$
Property, plant and equipment	209,000
Inventory	4,600
Payables	6,300
Receivables	5,900
Bank overdraft	790
Loan	50,000
Capital	100,000
Drawings	23,000
Sales	330,000
Purchases	168,200
Sales returns	7,000
Discounts received	?
Sundry expenses	73,890

What was the balance on the discounts received account?

$ _____

333 Kayak Co had the following year-end adjustments to a set of draft financial statements:

- Closing inventory of $45,700 was to be recorded.

- Depreciation at 20% straight line was to be charged on assets which had a cost of $470,800.

- An Irrecoverable debt of $230 was to be written off.

- Deferred income of $6,700 was to be recorded.

What is the impact on Kayak Co's net assets of these adjustments?

A $55,390 increase

B $55,390 decrease

C $41,990 decrease

D $41,990 increase

334 **What is the most important reason for producing a trial balance prior to preparing the financial statements?**

A   It confirms the accuracy of the general ledger accounts

B   It provides all the figures necessary to prepare the financial statements

C   It shows that the ledger accounts contain debit and credit entries of an equal value

D   It enables the accountant to calculate any adjustments required

335 The following is an extract from the trial balance of Gardeners:

	$	$
Non-current assets	50,000	
Inventory	2,600	
Capital		28,000
Receivables and payables	4,500	5,000
Allowance for receivables		320
Cash	290	
Purchases and revenue	78,900	120,000
Rental expense	3,400	
Sundry expenses	13,900	
Bank interest		270
	153,590	153,590

The following items have not yet been accounted for:

- Rent of $200 was prepaid.

- Inventory valuation at the end of the accounting period was $1,900.

- The allowance for receivables should be amended to $200.

What was the operating profit for the year?

$ _____

336 The following is the extract of Jehan's trial balance as at 31 December 20X7:

The policy of the business is to charge depreciation at 10% per annum on a straight-line basis.

	DR	CR
	$	$
Plant and machinery	50,000	
Plant and machinery accumulated depreciation		15,000

What is the depreciation charge to Jehan's statement of profit or loss for the year ended 31 December 20X7 and the closing carrying amount as at 31 December 20X7?

	Depreciation charge	Carrying amount
	$	$
A	3,500	31,500
B	5,000	30,000
C	5,000	45,000
D	3,500	30,000

337 The following is the extract of Jordan's trial balance as at 31 December 20X7:

	DR
	$
Rent	22,000
Insurance	30,000

The following notes have been provided:

(i)   The monthly rent charge is $2,000.

(ii)   The annual insurance charge for the above year is $28,000.

What is the charge for rent and insurance for the year and the closing accrual and prepayment?

		Charge for the year		Closing balance
		$		$
A	Rent	22,000	Rent prepayment	2,000
	Insurance	28,000	Insurance prepayment	2,000
B	Rent	22,000	Rent accrual	2,000
	Insurance	30,000	Insurance prepayment	2,000
C	Rent	24,000	Rent accrual	2,000
	Insurance	28,000	Insurance prepayment	2,000
D	Rent	24,000	Rent accrual	2,000
	Insurance	30,000	Insurance accrual	2,000

338 The following is the extract of Joginder's trial balance as at 31 December 20X7:

	DR	CR
	$	$
Receivables	29,600	
Allowance for receivables		3,100
Irrecoverable debts	1,600	

The following notes are provided.

(i)   Additional irrecoverable debts of $3,000 were identified at the year end.

(ii)   It has been decided to make an allowance for receivables of $2,660 on the adjusted receivables at the year end.

What was the total irrecoverable debts expense (irrecoverable debts and allowances for receivables) for the year ended 31 December 20X7 and the closing net receivables balance as at 31 December 20X7?

	Irrecoverable debts expense	Net receivables
	$	$
A	4,160	23,940
B	5,040	23,940
C	2,560	21,830
D	4,000	19,800

339 The following is the extract of Kadal's trial balance as at 31 December 20X7:

	DR	CR
	$	$
Motor vehicles	50,000	
Motor vehicles accumulated depreciation		21,875

The policy of the business is to charge depreciation at 25% per annum on a reducing balance basis.

What is the statement of profit or loss depreciation charge for the year ended 31 December 20X7 and the closing carrying amount as at 31 December 20X7?

Calculations to be rounded to the nearest $.

	Depreciation charge	Carrying amount
	$	$
A	12,500	15,625
B	7,031	42,969
C	12,500	37,500
D	7,031	21,094

340 The following is the answer to a trial balance exercise prepared by a new office junior. When the errors are corrected, the trail balance will agree.

	Dr	Cr
	$	$
Premises and accumulated depreciation	500,000	120,000
Opening inventory		23,000
Share capital	200,000	
Retained earnings		105,000
Receivables	43,500	
Payables		35,900
Carriage in	1,500	
Allowance for receivables		3,400
Bank overdraft	1,010	
Revenue		486,690
Purchases	359,700	
Sales returns	10,300	
Sundry expenses	14,000	
Difference		356,020
	_____	_____
	1,130,010	1,128,510
	_____	_____

After correcting the trial balance, what will be the total of debit and credit columns?

$ [   ]

CORRECTION OF ERRORS

341 A business produced draft financial statements for the year ended 31 December 20X7 that showed a profit for the year of $78,500. Subsequent investigation of the accounting records revealed the following:

1 Closing inventories, which cost $120,000 and had a net realisable value of $112,000, were shown at cost in the financial statements.

2 A motor vehicle, purchased for $30,000 during the year, had been posted to the motor expenses account with no entry made in the asset register. Motor vehicles held at the year-end were depreciated at the rate of 25% per annum on cost, with a full year's charge in the year of acquisition.

What will be the revised profit for the year after taking account of the above?

$ [   ]

342 A draft statement of profit or loss for the year ended 31 March 20X8 presented a profit for the year of $65,800. Subsequently, the following errors were discovered:

1   A $2,000 receipt from a credit customer was omitted from the general ledger

2   A sales invoice for $8,000 was incorrectly raised at an amount of $9,000

3   A $400 supplier invoice for IT services was incorrectly posted to the depreciation charge general ledger account

What will be the revised profit for the year after taking account of the above?

A $64,800

B $66,400

C $66,800

D $67,800

343 The draft financial statements of Haseen's business for the year ended 31 July 20X0 show a profit of $54,250 prior to the correction of the following errors:

1   Cash drawings of $250 have not been accounted for.

2   Debts amounting to $420, which were provided against in full during the year, should have been written off as irrecoverable.

3   Rental income of $300 has been classified as interest income.

4   On the last day of the accounting period, $200 in cash was received from a credit customer, but no accounting entries have been made.

What is Haseen's profit for the year ended 31 July 20X2 after the correction of the errors?

A $53,580

B $53,830

C $54,250

D $55,830

344 The bookkeeper of High Hurdles was instructed to make a contra entry for $270 between the payables and receivables accounts in the general ledger. The bookkeeper recorded the transaction by debiting receivables and crediting payables with $270.

Which of the following statements is correct?

A   Unless the error is corrected, profit will be over-stated by $540

B   Unless the error is corrected, net assets will be over-stated by $270

C   Unless the error is corrected, net assets will be over-stated by $540

D   The errors should be corrected, but neither the profit nor the net assets are over-stated

345 At 30 September 20X8, the following items had been omitted from the financial statements and require inclusion in MCD Co's financial statements:

1   On 1 September 20X8, MCD Co received $5,000 as a deposit for goods which were despatched to the customer on 15 October 20X8.

2   On 1 August 20X8, MCD Co paid an insurance premium of $5,000 for the six-month period commencing 1 July 20X8.

3   On 1 April 20X8, MCD Co raised a five-year bank loan of $12,000 which is repayable in a single capital sum at the end of the loan term. Interest is payable on the loan annually in arrears at 5% per annum.

For these items, what was the effect of these transactions total figures included in the MCD Co's statement of financial position at 30 September 20X8?

A	Current assets	$17,000	Current liabilities	$2,800
B	Current assets	$19,500	Current liabilities	$10,300
C	Current assets	$14,500	Current liabilities	$5,300
D	Current assets	$7,500	Current liabilities	$5,300

346 The statement of profit or loss for a business for the year ended 31 July 20X8 showed an operating profit of $57,400. It was later discovered that a suite of office furniture purchased on 1 February 20X8 at a cost of $15,500 had been charged to the office expenses account. The suite of office furniture had an estimated useful life of ten years with an estimated residual value of $1,500. Depreciation is charged on a monthly basis, commencing with the month of purchase.

What was the operating profit for the year ended 31 July 20X8 after adjusting for this error?

$	

347 **Which of the following items is an error of principle?**

A   A gas bill credited to the gas account and debited to the bank account

B   The purchase of a non-current asset credited to the asset account and debited to the payables account

C   The purchase of a non-current asset debited to the purchases account and credited to the payables account

D   The payment of wages debited and credited to the correct accounts, but using an incorrect monetary amount.

348 Tirath, who is registered to account for sales tax, received a purchase invoice from a credit supplier for $750, inclusive of sales tax at 20%. When processing the invoice, Tirath recorded only the invoice total and did not account for sales tax.

What adjustment must Tirath make to correctly account for sales tax?

A	Dr Payables $150	Cr Sales tax $150
B	Dr Sales tax $125	Cr Purchases $125
C	Dr Sales tax $150	Cr Purchases $150
D	Dr Payables $125	Cr Sales tax $125

349 Maxi, who is registered to account for sales tax, received a purchase invoice from a credit supplier for $3,300 plus sales tax at 20%. When processing the invoice, Maxi recorded only the gross invoice amount and did not account for sales tax.

What adjustment must Maxi make to correctly account for sales tax?

A   Dr Sales tax $550   Cr Purchases $550

B   Dr Payables $550   Cr Sales tax $550

C   Dr Payables $660   Cr Purchases $660

D   Dr Sales tax $660   Cr Purchases $660

350 Aztec Co revalued its land on 30 June 20X6 from $60,000 to $85,000. The entry in the non-current asset account was correctly accounted for and the other accounting entry recorded in retained earnings.

What adjustment must Aztec Co make to correctly account for this transaction?

A   Dr Retained earnings $25,000   Cr Share premium $25,000

B   Dr Retained earnings $25,000   Cr Revaluation surplus $25,000

C   Dr Retained earnings $85,000   Cr Revaluation surplus $85,000

D   Dr Retained earnings $25,000   Cr Share capital $25,000

351 When recording the purchase of goods from a credit supplier, Lime Co posted the gross cost of $1,500 to the purchases and payables general ledger accounts. Both the supplier and Lime Co are registered to account for sales tax at the rate of 20%.

What journal adjustment should Lime Co make to correct this error?

A   Dr   Purchases $300, and   Cr   Sales tax $300

B   Dr   Sales tax $250, and   Cr   Purchases $250

C   Dr   Sales tax $300, and   Cr   Purchases $300

D   Dr   Purchases $250, and   Cr   Sales tax $250

352 Peach Co returned faulty goods to a supplier and received a credit note from the supplier. When recording the credit note in the accounting system, Peach Co omitted to account for sales tax and, instead posted the gross amount of $1,296 to the returns outwards account. Both Peach Co and the supplier are registered to account for sales tax at the rate of 8%.

What journal adjustment should Peach Co make to correct this error?

A   Dr   Returns outwards $96, and Cr   Payables $96

B   Dr   Sales tax $96, and   Cr   Payables $96

C   Dr   Returns outwards $96, and Cr   Sales tax $96

D   Dr   Sales tax $96, and   Cr   Returns outwards $96

353 When recording a contra entry for $2,000 in the general ledger, Lemon Co correctly recorded the entry in the payables account and recorded the other entry in the allowance for receivables account. Both Lemon Co and the other party are registered to account for sales tax at the rate of 20%.

What journal adjustment should Lemon Co make to correct this error?

A	Dr	Receivables	$2,000, and	Cr	Allowance for receivables	$2,000
B	Dr	Receivables	$2,400, and	Cr	Receivables	$2,400
C	Dr	Allowance for receivables $2,400, and		Cr	Receivables	$2,400
D	Dr	Allowance for receivables $2000, and		Cr	Receivables	$2,000

354 When recording a purchase invoice for the repair of a laptop from a credit supplier, Orange Co recorded it as an addition to non-current assets. The cost of the repair was $500, on which sales tax was charged at 15%. Orange Co is registered to account for sales tax.

What journal adjustment should Orange Co make to correct this error?

A	Dr	Repairs	$500, and	Cr	Non-current assets $500
B	Dr	Repairs	$575, and	Cr	Non-current assets $575
C	Dr	Non-current assets $500, and		Cr	Repairs $500
D	Dr	Non-current assets $575, and		Cr	Repairs $575

355 When recording a customer (sales) invoice, Date Co recorded the net amount as $1,000 instead of $100. Date Co is registered to account for sales tax at 10%.

What journal adjustment should Date Co make to correct this error?

A	Dr	Receivables	$990	Cr	Sales	$990
B	Dr	Sales	$990	Cr	Receivables	$990
C	Dr	Receivables	$990	Cr	Sales	$900
				Cr	Sales tax	$90
D	Dr	Sales	$900	Cr	Receivables	$990
	Dr	Sales tax	$90			

356 Tangerine Co made a sale to a credit customer for $500 plus sales tax at 40% which was recorded correctly in the general ledger. The customer subsequently returned half of the goods as they were damaged upon receipt and a credit note was issued for that amount. The entry for the credit note in the receivables account was made correctly and the other entry was made for the same amount in the returns inwards account.

What journal adjustment should Tangerine Co make to correct this error?

A	Dr	Returns inwards $50, and	Cr	Sales tax	$50
B	Dr	Sales tax	$50, and	Cr	Returns inwards	$50
C	Dr	Sales tax	$100, and	Cr	Returns inwards	$100
D	Dr	Returns inwards $100, and	Cr	Sales tax	$100

SUSPENSE ACCOUNTS

357 Consider the following statements relating to suspense accounts:

State whether each statement is true or false.

	True	False
A separate suspense account should be opened for each error in the general ledger		
A suspense account can be opened to complete the recording of a transaction in the general ledger whilst more information is obtained about it		

358 Savvy Co had a suspense account balance of $1,300 in its general ledger. This balance related to the accounting for an increase in the allowance for receivables. The increase in the allowance had been correctly recorded in the allowance for receivables account but the other accounting entry was posted to the suspense account pending the junior accountant making further enquiries.

What accounting entries are required to clear the suspense account?

A	Dr Irrecoverable debts expense $1,300	Cr Suspense $1,300
B	Dr Receivables $1,300	Cr Suspense $9,000
C	Dr Suspense $1,300	Cr Receivables $1,300
D	Dr Suspense $1,300	Cr Irrecoverable debts expense $1,300

359 The trial balance of Duha Co included a suspense account balance of $5,850 for a transaction that had not been fully and properly accounted for. It related to a payment made to modify a machine which resulted in it becoming more productive. The machine is now able to produce 300 widgets per week, rather than its previous capability of 200 widgets. The bank payment had been correctly accounted for and the other part of the double-entry had been posted to suspense account.

What accounting entries are required to clear the suspense account?

A	Dr Non-current assets – cost $5,850	Cr Suspense $5,850
B	Dr Machine repairs $5,850	Cr Suspense $5,850
C	Dr Suspense $5,850	Cr Machine repairs $5,850
D	Dr Suspense $5,850	Cr Non-current assets – cost $5,850

360 The trial balance of Adelaide Co included a suspense account balance of $20,000 relating to the issue of shares during the year. Adelaide Co made an issue of 10,000 equity shares with a nominal value of $1 each at a price of $3 per share. The cash receipt had been correctly accounted for, along with the accounting entry to increase the nominal value of issued share capital. However, the entry to record the difference between the proceeds received and the nominal value of shares issued was posted to the suspense account.

What accounting entries are required to clear the suspense account?

A	Dr Suspense $20,000	Cr Share premium $20,000
B	Dr Share premium $10,000	Cr Suspense $10,000
C	Dr Share premium $20,000	Cr Suspense $20,000
D	Dr Suspense $20,000	Cr Revaluation surplus $20,000

361 The junior accountant at Magadan Co was asked to process a transaction to record the unexpected receipt of $1,500 from a credit customer whose debt had been written off as irrecoverable several months previously. The cash receipt was correctly accounted for, but as the junior accountant was unsure of the other accounting entry required, recorded that in a suspense account.

What accounting entries are required to clear the suspense account?

A	Dr Suspense $1,500	Cr Allowance for receivables $1,500
B	Dr Allowance for receivables $1,500	Cr Suspense $1,500
C	Dr Suspense $1,500	Cr Irrecoverable debts $1,500
D	Dr Suspense $1,500	Cr Receivables $1,500

362 Seattle Co has an accounting policy of revaluation of its buildings and to account for the annual transfer of 'excess depreciation' of $3,250. An inexperienced member of staff was unsure how to record this transaction in the general ledger. The accounting entry in revaluation surplus account was correctly accounted for, and the other accounting entry was posted to suspense account, pending clarification from a colleague.

What accounting entries are required to clear the suspense account?

A	Dr Suspense $3,250	Cr Depreciation expense $3,250
B	Dr Buildings – asset $3,250	Cr Suspense $3,250
C	Dr Suspense $3,250	Cr Accumulated depreciation $3,250
D	Dr Suspense $3,250	Cr Retained earnings $3,250

363 Consider the following statements relating to suspense accounts:

State whether each statement is true or false.

	True	False
A suspense account needs to be opened to correct a transaction account which was posted to the general ledger using the correct monetary amount but the wrong general ledger accounts		
A suspense account needs to be opened to record the removal of a duplicated transaction in the general ledger		

364 Pahal's trial balance includes a temporary suspense account with a balance of $280 relating to settlement discount on early payment of an amount due to a credit supplier. The accounting entry in the payables' account had been correctly recorded in the general ledger but the junior accountant was unsure where to record the other half of the transaction and posted it to suspense account pending further guidance.

What are the accounting entries required to clear the suspense account?

A   Debit: Suspense, and   Credit: Sales

B   Debit: Discount received, and   Credit: Suspense

C   Debit: Suspense, and   Credit: Discount received

D   Debit: Sales, and   Credit: Suspense

365 Georgie is preparing the general ledger journal entry to write off an irrecoverable debt. Georgie knows that the debit entry should be made in the receivables expense account and posted the other part of the transaction to a temporary suspense account pending further enquiries.

Into which general ledger account should Georgie have posted the credit entry?

A   Sales account

B   Bank account

C   Receivables account

D   Receivables allowance account

366 Daz is preparing the general ledger journal entry to record discount received. The transaction was properly recorded in the payables account, with the other entry recorded in a temporary suspense account to clarify how it should be recorded in the general ledger.

What accounting entries should be made to clear the suspense account and record the transaction correctly?

A   Debit Receivables, and Credit Suspense

B   Debit Discount received, and Credit Suspense

C   Debit Suspense, and Credit Purchases

D   Debit Suspense, and Credit Discount received

367 Jamie's Cars has a balance on its suspense account of $324 debit.

Which TWO of the following errors could, on its own, explain this?

1   Rent paid of $162 credited to the rent account, but correctly recorded in cash

2   Omitting interest paid of $324 from the trial balance

3   Cash sales of $162 debited to the sales account, but correctly recorded in cash

4   An invoice for materials for $324 debited to wages, but correctly recorded in trade payables

A   1 and 2

B   1 and 4

C   2 and 3

D   3 and 4

PREPARING BASIC FINANCIAL STATEMENTS

STATEMENT OF FINANCIAL POSITION AND STATEMENT OF PROFIT OR LOSS AND OTHER COMPREHENSIVE INCOME

368 Shakur had net assets of $19,000 at 30 April 20X7. During the year to 30 April 20X7, Shakur introduced $9,800 additional capital into the business and the profit for the year was $8,000. During the year ended 30 April 20X7 Shakur withdrew $4,200.

What was the balance on Shakur's capital account at 1 May 20X6?

A $5,400

B $13,000

C $16,600

D $32,600

369 **Which TWO of the following statements are advantages of a bonus issue of shares?**

	Selection
It is the cheapest way for a company to raise finance through the issuing of shares	
It makes the shares in a company more marketable	
The total of retained earnings and other components of equity of the company will increase	
Share capital is brought more into line with assets employed in the company	

370 The following information relates to Minnie's hairdressing business in the year ended 31 August 20X7:

	$
Expenses	7,100
Opening inventory	1,500
Closing inventory	900
Purchases	12,950
Gross profit	12,125
Inventory drawings of shampoo	75

What was the revenue earned by the business for the year ended 31 August 20X7?

A $32,700

B $25,600

C $25,675

D $25,750

371 Astral Co has a debit balance relating to income tax of $500 included in its trial balance extracted at 30 June 20X4. Astral Co estimated that its liability for income taxes payable for the year ended 30 June 20X4 was $8,000.

What amounts should be included in Astral Co's financial statements for the year ended 30 June 20X4?

	Statement of profit or loss	**Statement of financial position**
A	$8,000	$8,000
B	$8,500	$8,000
C	$7,500	$8,500
D	$8,000	$7,500

372 **Which of the following would change the capital of a business?**

A   Making an automated bank payment to a supplier

B   Purchasing raw materials on credit

C   Purchasing non-current assets on credit

D   Paying wages in cash

373 A draft statement of financial position has been prepared for Lollipop, a sole trader. It has now been discovered that a loan due for repayment by Lollipop 14 months after the reporting date was included in trade payables.

What will be the effect of the necessary adjustment?

A   No effect on net current assets

B   Increase net current assets

C   Reduce net current assets

D   Increase current assets but reduce net current assets

374 The profit of a business may be calculated using which of the following formulae?

    A   Opening capital – drawings + capital introduced – closing capital

    B   Closing capital + drawings – capital introduced – opening capital

    C   Opening capital + drawings – capital introduced – closing capital

    D   Closing capital – drawings + capital introduced – opening capital

375 Which accounting concept requires that amounts of goods taken from inventory by the proprietor of a business are treated as drawings?

    A   Accruals

    B   Prudence

    C   Separate entity

    D   Substance over form

376 Calculate the amount that will be included in other comprehensive income of Zappa Co for the year ended 30 June 20X4 based upon the following information.

There was a revaluation surplus of $70,000 arising on revaluation of land and buildings during the year. The depreciation charge for the year relating to buildings was $20,000. Zappa Co does not make an annual transfer of 'excess depreciation' between revaluation surplus and retained earnings. During the year, there was a gain on disposal on disposal of motor vehicles of $1,000.

$

377 The following information is available about Samim's business at 30 September 20X6:

	$
Motor van	14,000
Loan (repayable in 4 equal annual instalments starting 1 January 20X7)	100,000
Receivables	23,800
Bank balance (a debit on the bank statement)	3,250
Accumulated depreciation	7,000
Payables	31,050
Inventory	12,560
Petty cash	150
Rent due	1,200
Allowance for receivables	1,500

What are the correct figures for current assets and current liabilities?

	Current assets $	Current liabilities $
A	35,010	34,300
B	38,260	32,250
C	38,260	57,250
D	35,010	60,500

378 The following transactions relate to Max's business:

1 May	Purchase of goods for resale on credit	$300
2 May	Max injects long term capital into the business	$1,400
3 May	Payment of rent made	$750
5 May	Max withdraws cash from the business	$400
7 May	Goods which had cost $600 were sold on credit	1,200

At the start of the week, the assets of the business were $15,700 and liabilities amounted to $11,200.

At the end of the week, what was the amount of Max's capital?

A $5,350

B $1,400

C $850

D $1,000

379 **Calculate the total amount that will be charged as an expense in the statement of profit or loss of Clapton Co or the year ended 30 September 20X6 based upon the following information.**

Clapton Co incurred development expenditure during the year of $50,000. The amortisation charge on intangible assets for the year was $15,000. During the year, there was a loss on disposal on disposal of plant and equipment of $3,000.

> $ [   ]

380 On 1 January 20X8 Baker Co revalued its property to $100,000. At the date of the revaluation, the asset was accounted for at a cost of $80,000 and had accumulated depreciation $16,000. The property had a useful life of 50 years from the date of purchase and no residual value.

What amount of 'excess depreciation' could be transferred from revaluation surplus to retained earnings at 31 December 20X8 as a result of accounting for the revaluation?

> $ [   ]

381 **In which TWO financial statements, presented in accordance with IFRS Accounting Standards, would you expect to find dividends paid?**

	Selection
Statement of profit or loss and other comprehensive income	
Statement of financial position	
Statement of cash flows	
Statement of changes in equity	

382 On 1 January 20X8 Hendrix Co revalued its property to $200,000. Up to the date of the revaluation, the asset had been accounted for at a cost of $160,000 and had accumulated depreciation $40,000. The property had a useful life of 50 years from the date of purchase and no residual value.

What are the accounting entries required to record the property revaluation in the accounting records?

	Debit	$	Credit	$
A	Non-current asset – property	$200,000	Revaluation surplus	$200,000
B	Revaluation surplus	$80,000	Non-current asset – property	$40,000
			Accumulated depreciation	$40,000
C	Non-current asset – property	$40,000	Revaluation surplus	$40,000
D	Non-current asset – property	$40,000	Revaluation surplus	$80,000
	Accumulated depreciation	$40,000		

383 Brown Co had $100,000 $0.50 shares and $400,000 8% irredeemable preference shares in issue. A dividend of 3 cents per equity share and half of the preference dividend was paid during the year.

Which of the following statements is/are true?

1   An equity dividend of $3,000 was paid during the year.

2   A preference dividend of $16,000 was accrued at the year end.

A   1 only

B   2 only

C   Neither 1 nor 2

D   Both 1 and 2

384 **Where in the financial statements should income tax expense for the current period and a gain on revaluation of a non-current asset in the year, be separately presented?**

	Income tax expense	Gain on revaluation
A	Statement of profit or loss and other comprehensive income	Statement of cash flows
B	Statement of changes in equity	Statement of profit or loss and other comprehensive income
C	Statement of profit or loss and other comprehensive income	Statement of profit or loss and other comprehensive income
D	Statement of cash flows	Statement of cash flows

385 The following information is relevant to Wimbledon:

	$
Opening inventory	12,500
Closing inventory	17,900
Purchases	199,000
Selling expenses	35,600
General and administrative expenses	78,800
Audit fee	15,200
Carriage in	3,500
Carriage out	7,700
Depreciation	40,000

Depreciation is to be allocated in the ratio 70:30 between the factory and the office. All office expenses are classified as general and administrative expenses.

What was Wimbledon's cost of sales?

A $233,600

B $221,600

C $225,100

D $237,100

386 At 1 October 20X6, Ozber Co's capital structure was as follows:

	$
Equity shares, $0.25	100,000
Share premium	30,000

On 10 January 20X7, Ozber Co made a 1-for-4 rights issue at $1.15 to raise finance for expansion. The issue was fully taken up. This was followed by a 1-for-10 bonus issue on 1 June 20X7.

What was the balance on the share premium account after these transactions?

A $17,500

B $21,250

C $107,500

D $120,000

387 The following information is available about dividends on L Co's equity shares:

Sept 20X5	Final dividend for the year ended 30 June 20X5 paid (declared August 20X5)	$100,000
March 20X6	Interim dividend for the year ended 30 June 20X6 paid	$40,000
Sept 20X6	Final dividend for the year ended 30 June 20X6 paid (declared August 20X6)	$120,000

What figures, if any, should be presented in L Co's statement of profit or loss and other comprehensive income for the year ended 30 June 20X6 and its statement of financial position at that date?

	Statement of profit or loss and other comprehensive income	Statement of financial position
A	$160,000 deduction	$120,000
B	$140,000 deduction	$0
C	$0	$120,000
D	$0	$0

388 **Classify each of the following statements as either true or false.**

	True	False
An entity may make a rights issue if it wished to raise more equity capital.		
A rights issue might increase the share premium account whereas a bonus issue is likely to reduce it.		
A rights issue will always increase the number of shareholders in an entity whereas a bonus issue will not.		
A bonus issue will result in an increase in the market value of each share		

389 Florabundi Co's trial balance at 31 December 20X8 included a credit balance of $3,400 on its income tax payable account, having already settled the tax liability for the year ended 31 December 20X7 during the year. Florabundi Co estimated that its income tax expense on profits for the year ended 31 December 20X8 at $67,900.

What amounts should be included in Florabundi Co's financial statements for the year ended 31 December 20X8 in respect of tax?

	Statement of profit or loss	Statement of financial position
A	$67,900 tax expense	$67,900 taxes payable
B	$64,500 tax expense	$64,500 taxes payable
C	$64,500 tax expense	$67,900 taxes payable
D	$71,300 tax expense	$67,900 taxes payable

390 Classify the following assets and liabilities as current or non-current in Albatross Co's financial statements.

	Current	Non-current
A sale has been made on credit to a customer. They have agreed to terms stating that payment is due in 12 months' time.		
A bank overdraft facility of $30,000 is available under an agreement with the bank which is available for the next three years.		
Albatros Co purchases a small number of shares in another entity which it intends to trade.		
A bank loan has been taken out with a repayment date 5 years hence.		

391 Extracts from the accounting records of Andrat Co relating to the year ended 31 December 20X6 are as follows:

Revaluation surplus	$230,000
Equity interim dividend paid	$12,000
Profit before income taxes	$178,000
Estimated liability for income tax payable for year	$45,000
8% $1 Redeemable preference shares	$100,000
Under provision for tax in previous year	$5,600
Proceeds of issue of 2,000 $1 equity shares	$5,000
Final equity dividend proposed	$30,000

What was the total of equity reported in Andrat Co's statement of changes in equity at 31 December 20X6?

A $312,400

B $356,000

C $348,000

D $350,400

392 Which of the following statements is/are true in relation to a preference share?

1   They carry voting rights.

2   Their dividend is paid out in priority to an equity dividend.

3   Their dividend is related to profits.

A   1, 2 and 3

B   1 and 2 only

C   2 and 3 only

D   2 only

393 Bangeroo Co, issues 100,000 3% $1 redeemable preference shares during the year ended 30 September 20X8 at 98 cents per share.

What are the correct accounting entries to account for this transaction?

		Debit		Credit
		$		$
A	Cash	$98,000	Liability	$98,000
B	Cash	$98,000	Share capital	$100,000
			Share premium	$2,000
C	Cash	$98,000	Share capital	$98,000
D	Cash	$98,000	Share capital	$100,000
	Statement of profit or loss	$2,000		

394 **Which of the following items in the statement of financial position change immediately following a bonus issue of shares?**

A   Share capital and Cash

B   Share capital and Retained earnings

C   Share premium and Cash

D   Share premium and Retained earnings

395 Argonaut Co issued $400,000 12% loan notes for $380,000 on 1 August 20X6.

What accounting entries are required in the year ended 30 September 20X6?

A	Dr Bank	$400,000	And	Dr Interest	$7,600
	Cr Non-current liabilities	$400,000		Cr Current liabilities	$7,600
B	Dr Bank	$380,000	And	Dr Interest	$8,000
	Cr Non-current liabilities	$380,000		Cr Current liabilities	$8,000
C	Dr Bank	$400,000	And	Dr Interest	$8,000
	Cr Non-current liabilities	$400,000		Cr Current liabilities	$8,000
D	Dr Bank	$380,000	And	Dr Interest	$7,600
	Cr Non-current liabilities	$380,000		Cr Current liabilities	$7,600

396 **A company's equity reserves would decrease if it did which one of the following?**

A   Sets aside profits to pay future dividends

B   Transfers amounts into a 'general reserve'

C   Issues shares at a premium

D   Pays a dividend

397 Radar Co has accounted for the revaluation of buildings in its financial statements for the year ended 31 December 20X4. The increase in carrying amount of the property was $50,000, with a depreciation charge for the year of $13,000. Radar Co accounts for excess depreciation and this has been calculated at $2,000.

For each of the following items, identify where in the statement of profit or loss and other comprehensive income each item would be included, or if it would be omitted completely from that statement.

A   Profit or loss

B   Other comprehensive income

C   Omitted from the statement of profit or loss and other comprehensive income

	Choice: A, B or C
Excess depreciation on revaluation	
Increase in carrying amount of a property	
Depreciation charge	

398 Saturn Co disposed of a property that had been revalued in an earlier accounting period. The details relating to this property are as follows:

	$000
Carrying amount at disposal date	150
Disposal proceeds	165
Revaluation surplus at disposal date	15

How should the property disposal be accounted for in Saturn's financial statements?

A   Gain on disposal of $15,000 included in profit or loss for the year only.

B   Gain on disposal of $30,000 included in profit or loss for the year only.

C   Gain on disposal of $15,000 included in profit or loss for the year and revaluation gain of $15,000 included in other comprehensive income for the year.

D   Gain on disposal of $15,000 included in profit or loss for the year and a transfer within the statement of changes in equity of $15,000 from revaluation surplus to retained earnings.

399 Details of two of Eman's transactions in the year ended 31 August 20X7 were as follows:

1   Eman sold a machine to a customer, Pitt, on 28 August 20X7. Pitt is responsible for installation and operation of the machine following delivery.

2   Eman sold several food mixers to Damon, on credit. Damon collected the food mixers from Eman on 26 August 20X7. Damon has not yet paid for the goods purchased.

For which of the transactions should revenue be recognised?

A   1 only

B   2 only

C   Both 1 and 2

D   Neither 1 nor 2

400 Starstruck Co estimated its liability for income taxes payable for the year ended 30 September 20X6 at $15,000. The income tax expense presented in the statement of profit or loss for the year ended 30 September 20X6 was $14,200.

Which of the following statements is true?

A   The difference between the expense in the statement of profit or loss and the liability in the statement of financial position is the result of an adjustment for an under provision in the prior year.

B   The difference between the expense in the statement of profit or loss and the liability in the statement of financial position is the result of an adjustment for an overprovision in the prior year.

C   It is not possible to state whether the difference between the expense in the statement of profit or loss and the liability in the statement of financial position is due to an underprovision or overprovision in the prior year.

D   There is no relationship between the amounts included in the statement of financial position and statement of profit or loss relating to income tax.

401 Kaplin Co publishes study materials and runs courses for students studying for professional accountancy examinations. Details of two transactions that occurred in December 20X8 were as follows:

1   Ten students enrolled on a course due to commence in January 20X9 at a price of $1,000 per student and each student paid their fees in advance. If sold separately, the study materials would be sold for $200 and the course of ten lectures would be sold for a total of $800. The study materials are issued on the first day of the course.

2   Kaplin Co sold study materials to 40 self-study students at a price of $400 per student who will receive no further support with their studies, which were delivered to students prior to 31 December 20X8.

What revenue should Kaplin Co recognise in the financial statements for the year ended 31 December 20X8?

$

402 Vostok sells computer games and is the sole distributor of a new game 'Avalanche'. Customer demand for the new game has resulted in lots of advance orders pending release of the game later in the year. At 31 July 20X2, Vostok had received customer orders and deposits received amounting to $500,000. Vostok anticipates that all orders will be despatched to customers by 1 December 20X2.

What revenue can Vostok recognise in the financial statements for the year ended 31 July 20X2?

$

403 Spotless Co provides contract cleaning services in commercial office premises. Spotless Co charges each business an annual fee of $1,200, based upon providing an agreed level of service each month. In one office block there are 12 businesses which use Spotless Co to provide cleaning services. At 1 April 20X5 four businesses had paid one month in advance and two customers were in one month in arrears. With effect from 31 August 20X5, one customer terminated its agreement with Spotless Co, whilst two additional contracts were signed to take effect from 1 December 20X5. At 31 March 20X6, the same four businesses had paid one month in advance and two customers were in arrears by one month. Each annual service contract is regarded as a contract which gives rise to obligations which are satisfied over a period of time.

What revenue can Spotless Co recognise in the financial statements for the year ended 31 March 20X6?

$ [   ]

404 At 1 January 20X8, Clarinet Co had an estimated liability for income taxes payable of $2,350. This liability was settled by a payment of $2,050 made In March 20X8. Due to challenging trading conditions, Clarinet Co made a loss for the year ended 31 December 20X8 and expects to recover a repayment of income taxes of $2,120 during 20X9.

What amounts should be included in Clarinet Co's financial statements for the year ended 31 December 20X8 for income tax?

	Statement of profit or loss	Statement of financial position
A	$2,420 tax expense	$1,820 taxes receivable
B	$2,120 tax income	$2,120 taxes payable
C	$2,420 tax income	$2,120 taxes receivable
D	$1,820 tax expense	$2,120 taxes receivable

405 Banjo Co estimated that its liability for income taxes payable for the year ended 30 June 20X5 was $16,940. This liability was settled in February 20X6 by a payment of $17,500. Having made a trading loss for the year ended 30 June 20X6, Banjo Co estimated that it would receive a $4,500 repayment of income taxes in the next accounting period.

What amounts should be included in Banjo Co's financial statements for the year ended 30 June 20X6 for income taxes?

	Statement of profit or loss	Statement of financial position
A	$3,940 tax income	$4,500 taxes receivable
B	$4,500 tax income	$4,500 taxes payable
C	$3,940 tax expense	$4,500 taxes payable
D	$5,060 tax income	$4,500 taxes receivable

406 Which ONE of the following statements provides the definition to explain the principle of aggregation when preparing financial statements?

    A   Aggregation is the adding together of assets, liabilities, equity or cash flows that share characteristics and are included in the same classification

    B   Aggregation is the adding together of assets, liabilities, income and expenses or cash flows that share characteristics and are included in the same classification

    C   Aggregation is the adding together of assets, liabilities, equity, income and expenses that share characteristics and are included in the same classification

    D   Aggregation is the adding together of assets, liabilities, equity, income and expenses or cash flows that share characteristics and are included in the same classification

DISCLOSURE NOTES

407 Which of the following should be disclosed in the notes to the financial statements relating to intangible assets?

    1   Accumulated amortisation charges at the start and at the end of the reporting period.

    2   A reconciliation of the movement in the net carrying amount of intangible assets for the reporting period.

    3   A statement from the directors, explaining whether or not they believe that capitalised development costs will be recovered at some future date.

    A   1 only

    B   2 only

    C   1 and 2

    D   2 and 3

408 Which of the following would be a suitable accounting policy note for disclosure in the financial statements relating to intangible assets?

    A   The entity has some intangible assets accounted for using the cost model and other intangible assets accounted for using the valuation model, based upon the judgement of the directors. All intangible assets are written off over their useful lives to the business.

    B   The entity accounts for intangible assets using the cost model. All intangible assets are amortised over their useful lives to the business, between five and fifteen years, on a straight-line basis.

    C   The entity accounts for intangible assets using the valuation model, based upon a valuation estimated by the directors. All changes in the carrying valuation from one reporting date to the next are accounted for in the statement of profit or loss.

    D   The entity uses the same accounting policy for tangible and intangible non-current assets.

409 **Which of the following would be a suitable accounting policy note for disclosure in the financial statements relating to land and buildings?**

A Land and buildings are accounted for at cost and are written off over their useful life of 50 years on a straight-line basis.

B Land and buildings are accounted for at cost and are not depreciated as the directors believe that the market value of land and buildings will increase over time.

C Land and buildings are accounted for at cost, and the buildings are written off over their useful life of 50 years on a straight-line basis.

D The entity uses the same accounting policy for land and buildings as it does for intangible assets.

410 **Which of the following would be a suitable accounting policy note for disclosure in the financial statements relating to inventory?**

A Inventory is valued at the lower of total cost and total net realisable value.

B Inventory is valued at the lower of cost and net realisable value for each separate product or item.

C Inventory is valued at the higher of cost and net realisable value for each separate product or item.

D Inventory is valued at cost for each separate product or item.

411 **Is the following statement true or false?**

Non-adjusting events can be ignored when preparing the annual financial statements and supporting disclosure notes.

A True

B False

412 **When dealing with non-adjusting events what information should be disclosed in the notes to the financial statements?**

1 The nature of the event.

2 The names of those with responsibility for the event.

3 The geographical location of the event.

4 An estimate of the financial effect of the event.

A 1 and 2

B 1, 3 and 4

C 2, 3 and 4

D 1 and 4 only

413 In relation to non-current assets, identify for each of the following items whether it should be disclosed in the notes to the financial statements.

	Disclosed	Not disclosed
Reconciliation of carrying amounts of non-current assets at the beginning and end of period.		
Useful lives of assets or depreciation rates used.		
Increases in asset values as a result of revaluations in the period.		
Depreciation expense for the period.		

414 IFRS 18 *Presentation and Disclosure in Financial Statements* requires certain items to be presented in the statement of profit or loss for the year.

Which THREE of the following items must be presented in the statement of profit or loss for the year, classifying expenses by function?

	Selection
Revenue	
Closing inventory	
Interest expense	
Dividends paid	
Income tax expense	
Depreciation expense for the year	

415 Which of the following statements is true in relation to disclosure requirements?

- A Disclosure requirements consist only of monetary disclosures
- B Disclosure requirements consist only of narrative disclosures
- C Disclosure requirements consist of both monetary and narrative disclosures
- D Disclosure notes do not form part of the annual financial statements

416 When considering disclosures required in the financial statements relating to property, plant and equipment, is the following statement true or false?

The estimated useful lives of the property plant and equipment and the depreciation rates used must be disclosed in the notes to the financial statements.

- A True
- B False

417 Which of the following is NOT required to be disclosed in respect of a provision?

- A The nature of the obligation.
- B Expected timing of any payment.
- C The name of the party to whom the obligation is owed.
- D The nature of any uncertainties which may affect the amount to be paid.

418 When considering disclosures required in the financial statements in relation to provisions, is the following statement true or false?

An entity need only state the carrying amount of the obligation at the beginning and end of the accounting period, without providing a reconciliation of the movement in the provision during the year.

A   True

B   False

419 In relation to non-current assets, which of the following items must be disclosed in the notes to the financial statements in accordance with IFRS Accounting Standards?

1   The depreciation charge on property, plant and equipment for the year.

2   The amortisation charge on intangible assets for the year.

3   The date of any revaluation of property plant and equipment made during the accounting year.

4   Whether an independent valuer was used in the revaluation of property, plant and equipment during the accounting year.

A   1, 2 and 3 only

B   2, 3 and 4 only

C   1, 3 and 4 only

D   1, 2, 3 and 4

420 How are intangible assets presented in the statement of financial position?

A   Cost only without any recognition of amortisation or impairment

B   Cost or valuation – amortisation – impairment = Carrying amount

C   The amortisation amount only

D   At the disposal proceeds value

421 X Co had the following disclosure note in respect of provisions for a warranty scheme:

	Warranty provision $
Brought forward balance	5,000
Increase in provision	1,000
Payments for warranty repairs	(2,500)
Carried forward balance	3,500

What is the warranty expense that should be shown in the statement of profit or loss?

A   Debit of $1,000

B   Credit of $1,000

C   Credit of $1,500

D   Debit of $1,500

422 The following disclosure note for property, plant and equipment has been drafted:

	Land and buildings	Fixtures and fittings	Plant and equipment
	$000	$000	$000
Cost b/fwd	5,000	1,200	620
Additions			55
Revaluations	1,000		
Cost/valuation c/fwd	6,000	1,255	690
Acc. Depreciation b/fwd	500	240	93
Charge for the year	333	157	70
Acc. Depreciation c/fwd	833	397	163

There have been no disposals of any property, plant and equipment during the year.

Which of the following items should be included to complete the property, plant and equipment disclosure note?

1   The date of the revaluation

2   Whether an independent valuer had been used

3   The historical carrying amount of the item of land and buildings that would have been included had they not been revalued

4   The total carrying amount of each class of asset at the beginning and end of the accounting period

A   1 and 4 only

B   1, 2 and 3 only

C   4 only

D   1, 2, 3 and 4

EVENTS AFTER THE REPORTING PERIOD

423   What should be disclosed in the notes to the financial statements in respect of a material non-adjusting event?

A   The nature of the event and the estimated financial effect

B   A letter from the solicitor

C   Nothing

D   Where the event took place

424 Ribblesdale Co has prepared financial statements for the year ended 30 September 20X8. The financial statements were approved by the directors on 12 January 20X9 and issued to the shareholders on 20 February 20X9.

State whether each of the following items are adjusting or non-adjusting events after the reporting period.

	Adjusting	Non-adjusting
A flood on 3 October 20X8 that destroyed a relatively small quantity of inventory which had cost $1,700.		
A credit customer with a balance outstanding at 30 September 20X8 was declared insolvent on 20 December 20X8.		
Inventory valued at a cost of $800 at 30 September 20X8 was sold for $650 on 11 November 20X8.		
A dividend on equity shares of 4 cents per share was declared on 1 December 20X8.		

425 **Which of the following statements are correct based upon the requirements of IAS 10** *Events after the Reporting Period*?

1   Details of all adjusting events must be disclosed in the notes to the financial statements.

2   A material loss arising from the sale, after the reporting date of inventory valued at cost at the statement of financial position date must be reflected in the financial statements.

3   If the market value of property, plant and equipment falls materially after the reporting date, the details must be disclosed in the notes.

4   Events after the reporting period are those that occur between the statement of financial position date and the date on which the financial statements are approved.

A   1 and 2

B   1, 3 and 4

C   2 and 3 only

D   2, 3 and 4

426 Brakes Co had a reporting date of 30 September 20X8. The financial statements for that year were approved by the directors on 14 December 20X8 and issued to the shareholders on 17 January 20X9. Details of several events which occurred after the reporting date of 30 September 20X8 are as follows:

1   On 13 December 20X8 a fire destroyed all inventory on the premises and the directors consider that Brakes Co is no longer a going concern.

2   A credit customer with an outstanding balance at 30 September 20X8 was declared bankrupt on 12 December 20X8.

3   An equity dividend of 6 cents per share was declared on 1 December 20X8.

4   Inventory valued at a cost of $800 at the year-end was sold for $650 on 11 November 20X8.

Which of the above would NOT result in the adjustment of amounts recognised in the financial statements of Brake Co?

A   2 and 3

B   3 only

C   3 and 4

D   1 and 3

427 Viola Co has an accounting year-end of 31 January 20X4.

Which of the following events, which occurred before the financial statements were approved, should be classified as adjusting events in accordance with IAS 10 *Events after the Reporting Period*?

1   Viola Co paid an equity dividend of $10,000 on 28 February 20X4. The dividend had been proposed by the directors on 20 January 20X4.

2   Notification of a compensation claim from a customer was received on 15 February 20X4 which related to a faulty product sold by Viola Co in January 20X4.

3   Viola Co received notification on 5 February 20X4 that a major credit customer was insolvent.

A   1, 2 and 3

B   2 and 3

C   1 and 3

D   2 only

428 Between the financial year end of 30 November 20X8 and 31 January 20X9, the date that the financial statements were approved by the directors, the following information was received:

1 A customer had commenced legal action against the company for providing faulty products in December 20X8

2 An ex-employee was suing them for unfair dismissal in November 20X8

The company's legal team have advised them that both claims are likely to succeed. Both claims are material in relation to the financial statements.

How will these two legal claims be reported in the financial statements for the year ended 30 November 20X8?

A Only claim 1 should be provided for and claim 2 does not need to be provided for or disclosed

B Both claims should be provided for

C Neither claim should be provided for or disclosed

D Claim 1 should be disclosed and claim 2 should be provided for

REVENUE FROM CONTRACTS WITH CUSTOMERS

429 Rajesh runs a business selling computers to individuals. The terms of sale are primarily cash on delivery with large customers allowed 14 days credit.

Which of the following transactions should be recognised as revenue in Rajesh's financial statements?

A Rajesh has sold a delivery van to a relative and has received payment in cash

B A customer has promised to place an order next week for a new computer and has paid a refundable deposit of $100

C A competitor has run out of a particular item has asked Rajesh to fulfil a sale to a customer and Rajesh has delivered the goods

D Rajesh has received payment from a customer for a delivery of 20 computers that took place two weeks ago

430 Rep Co is preparing its financial statements for the year ended 30 September 20X4. During that year, Rep Co acted as an agent on behalf of Zip Co and arranged a sale of goods on 1 August 20X4 at a price of $80,000. Rep Co is entitled to 10% commission upon receipt of cash from the customer. The customer paid for the goods on 28 September 20X4.

How much revenue can be recognised by Rep Co in its statement of profit or loss for the year ended 30 September 20X4?

$ [   ]

431 Loc Co sells machines and also offers installation and technical support services. The selling price of each product is as follows.

Sale price of machine $750

Installation $100

One year service support agreement $120

Cox Co purchased a machine, along with the installation service and the service agreement on 1 October 20X5. The machine was delivered and installed on 1 October 20X5 and the service support agreement also commenced from that date.

How much can Loc Co recognise as revenue for the year ended 31 December 20X5?

$ [   ]

432 **Which ONE of the following items has been included correctly in Hat Co's revenue for the year ended 31 March 20X5?**

A   Hat Co negotiated a sale at a value of $200,000 on behalf of a client, Res Co, one of its clients. Hat Co is entitled to 10% commission on the agreed sale price and has recognised revenue of $200,000 in its financial statements.

B   Hat Co entered into a contract to supply consultancy services to Cap Co for a three-year term for a total fee of $300,000. The contract commenced on 1 July 20X4, and Hat Co recognised revenue of $100,000 on this transaction in its financial statements.

C   On 1 November 20X4 Hat Co purchased goods at a cost of $50,000 and sold those goods to Far Co for $75,000 on 20 January 20X5. Hat Co recognised revenue of $75,000 on this contract in its financial statements.

D   On 1 December 20X4 Hat Co purchased goods at a cost of $25,000 and sold those goods to Ber Co for $50,000 on 10 January 20X5. Hat Co recognised revenue of $25,000 on this contract in its financial statements.

433 **Which ONE of the following items is not part of the 'five step' approach for revenue recognition as outlined in IFRS 15 *Revenue from Contracts with Customers*?**

A   Allocate the total price between the separate performance obligations in the contract

B   All contracts must be in writing

C   Recognise revenue when a performance obligation is satisfied

D   Identify the contract

434 **Identify whether each of the following items is an acceptable basis for recognition of revenue in the financial statements of an entity.**

	True	False
On any reasonable basis		
At a point in time		
Annually		
Over a period of time		

435 Which ONE of the following items complies with the revenue recognition requirements of IFRS 15 *Revenue from Contracts with Customers* for inclusion in Archer Co's revenue for the year ended 30 September 20X8?

A   During the year, Archer Co issued a free sample of a product to a new customer. The normal selling price of the product is $1,000. Archer Co included revenue of $1,000 in its financial statements relating to this transaction.

B   During the year, Archer Co sold an annual magazine subscription for to Arrow Co valued at £3,000. The first issue was sent to Arrow Co on 1 November 20Z7. Archer Co included revenue of $3,000 in its financial statements for the year.

C   On 1 December 20X7, Archer Co supplied goods to Bow Co with a list price of $5,000. The transaction was subject to trade discount of 10%. Archer Co recognised revenue of $4,500 in its financial statements for the year.

D   On 1 February, Archer Co sold goods to Quiver Co with a list price of $10,000. Quiver Co was offered any early settlement discount of 2% if the amount due was paid within 14 days of receipt of the goods. At the point when making the sale, Quiver Co was not expected to take advantage of the early settlement discount terms. Archer Co initially recorded revenue of $9,800 in its accounting records relating to this transaction.

STATEMENTS OF CASH FLOWS

436 Extracts from the financial statements of Deuce Co with a reporting date of 31 December show the following balances:

	20X9	**20X8**
Equity shares, $1	300,000	120,000
Share premium	260,000	100,000

On 1 January 20X9, a bonus issue of 1 share for every 12 at 31 December 20X8 was made and loan notes of $300,000 were issued at par. Interest of $12,000 was paid during the year.

What is the net cash inflow from financing activities?

A $480,000

B $468,000

C $640,000

D $628,000

437 Nobus Co is producing its statement of cash flows for the year ended 31 December 20X5. The accountant has identified the following cash flows:

	$
Interest paid	20,000
Interest received	13,000
Proceeds of share issue	120,000
Loan repaid	140,000
Dividends paid	600,000

What is the net cash flow from investing activities?

$	Inflow/outflow*	* delete which does not apply

438 **Which of the following items could be presented in a statement of cash flows?**

1   A bonus issue of shares.

2   A rights issue of shares.

3   The revaluation of non-current assets.

4   Dividends paid.

A   1, 2, 3 and 4

B   1, 3 and 4 only

C   2 and 4 only

D   3 only

439 A draft statement of cash flows shows the following:

	$m
Operating profit	22
Depreciation	8
Increase in inventories	(4)
Decrease in receivables	(3)
Increase in payables	(2)
Cash from operating activities before income taxes	21

Which TWO of the following corrections need to be made to the calculation of cash from operating activities before income taxes?

	Selection
Depreciation should be deducted, not added	
Increase in inventories should be added, not deducted	
Decrease in receivables should be added, not deducted	
Increase in payables should be added, not deducted	

440 **Where, in an entity's financial statements presented in according with IFRS Accounting Standards, should you find the proceeds from the disposal of non-current assets during the year?**

A   Statement of cash flows and Statement of financial position

B   Statement of changes in equity and Statement of financial position

C   Statement of profit or loss and other comprehensive income and Statement of cash flows

D   Statement of cash flows only

441 A business's bank balance increased by $750,000 during the previous financial year. During that same period it issued shares, raising $1.1 million, repaid a loan of $750,000 and paid income taxes of $100,000. It purchased property, plant and equipment for $200,000 and charged depreciation of $100,000. Receivables and inventory increased by $575,000.

What was the operating profit for the year?

A $1,175,000

B $1,275,000

C $1,325,000

D $1,375,000

442 The following amounts have been prepared for inclusion in the statement of cash flows of Bamboo Co:

Interest and dividends paid	$87,566
Increase in payables	$13,899
Decrease in inventories	$8,900
Redemption of loans	$300,000
Increase in receivables	$6,555
Decrease in cash and cash equivalents	$3,211
Depreciation charge	$10,600
Payments to acquire non-current assets	$47,999
Proceeds from sale of non-current assets	$13,100

What is the net cash from operating activities?

A $331,688

B $338,110

C $425,676

D $419,254

443 A business had non-current assets with a carrying amount of $50,000 at the start of the financial year. During the year it sold assets that had cost $4,000 and had been depreciated by $1,500. Depreciation for the year was $9,000. The carrying amount of assets at the end of the financial year was $46,000.

How much cash was invested in non-current assets during the year?

A $4,000

B $7,500

C $9,000

D $10,000

444 State whether each of the following statements relating to a statement of cash flows prepared using the 'direct method' is true or false?

	True	False
A statement of cash flows prepared using the 'direct method' produces a different figure for investing activities in comparison with that produced if the indirect method is used.		
A bonus issue of shares does not feature in a statement of cash flows.		
The amortisation charge for the year on intangible assets will appear as an item under 'Cash flows from operating activities' in a statement of cash flows.		
Loss on the sale of a non-current asset will appear as an item under 'Cash flows from investing activities' in a statement of cash flows.		

445 A Co made an operating profit for the year of $20,750, after accounting for depreciation of $1,250. During the year, the company purchased non-current assets for $8,000 and paid income taxes of $2,000. At the end of the year, receivables had increased by $1,000, inventories decreased by $1,800 and payables increased by $350, as compared to the prior year end.

What was A Co's increase in cash and bank balances during the year?

A $10,650

B $10,850

C $12,450

D $13,150

446 A statement of cash flows prepared in accordance with the indirect method reconciles operating profit to net cash from operating activities.

Which of the following is a list of items that would all be ADDED to operating profit?

A   Decrease in inventory, depreciation charge, profit on sale of non-current assets

B   Increase in payables, decrease in receivables, profit on sale of non-current assets

C   Loss on sale of non-current assets, depreciation charge, increase in receivables

D   Decrease in receivables, increase in payables, loss on sale of non-current assets

447 In relation to statements of cash flows, state whether each of the following statements is true or false.

	True	False
The direct method of calculating net cash from operating activities leads to a different figure from that produced by the indirect method, but this is balanced elsewhere in the statement of cash flows.		
An entity making high profits must necessarily have a net cash inflow from operating activities.		
Profits and losses on disposals of non-current assets are classified as investing activities in the statement of cash flows.		

448 The movement on the plant and machinery account for X Co is shown below:

Cost b/f	**$10,000**
Additions	$2,000
Disposals	($3,000)
Cost c/f	**$9,000**
Depreciation b/f	**$2,000**
Charge for the year	$1,000
Disposals	($1,500)
Depreciation c/f	**$1,500**
Carrying amount b/f	$8,000
Carrying amount c/f	$7,500

The profit on the sale of the machine was $500. What figures would be presented in the statement of cash flows of X Co classified as 'Investing activities'?

A Movement on plant account $500 and profit on disposal of $500

B Movement on plant account $500 and proceeds on sale of plant $2,000

C Purchase of plant $2,000 and profit on disposal of $500

D Purchase of plant $2,000 and proceeds on sale of plant $2,000

449 Which of the following is NOT an advantage of the statement of cash flows?

A It highlights the effect of non-cash transactions

B It helps an assessment of the liquidity off a business

C The numbers within it cannot be manipulated through the adoption of beneficial accounting policies

D It helps users to estimate future cash flows

450 Grainger makes all sales for cash and is preparing its statement of cash flows using the direct method. Grainger has compiled the following information:

Cash sales		$212,500
Cash purchases		$4,600
Cash expenses		$11,200
Payables at start and at the end of the year	$12,300	and $14,300
Credit purchases		$123,780
Wages and salaries due at start and at the end of the year	$1,500	and $2,300
Wages and salaries expense		$34,600
Inventory at start and at the end of the year	$23,000	and $17,800

What is the cash generated from operations by Grainger?

A $35,520

B $46,320

C $74,920

D $41,120

451 Howard Co provided the following extracts from the statement of financial position for the years ended 31 December:

	20X6	20X7
	$000	$000
Retained earnings	72,000	82,000
10% Loan notes	30,000	40,000
Income taxes payable	12,000	15,000
Dividends payable	1,200	1,600

Dividends payable were declared **before** the year end. There was no adjustment for under/over provision for tax in the year ended 31 December 20X7. No interim dividends were paid during the year. The additional 10% loan notes were issued on 1 January 20X7.

What is Howard Co's operating profit for the year ended 31 December 20X7?

A $29,600

B $27,200

C $30,600

D $102,600

452 In the year ended 31 May 20X2, Galleon purchased non-current assets at a cost of $140,000, financing them partly with a new loan of $120,000. Galleon also disposed of non-current assets with a carrying amount of $50,000, making a loss of $3,000. Cash of $18,000 was received from the disposal of investments during the year.

What is Galleon's net cash inflow or outflow from investing activities to include in the statement of cash flows?

$	Inflow/Outflow*	* delete which does not apply

453 The following is an extract from the financial statements of Pompeii at 31 October:

	20X7	**20X6**
	$000	$000
Equity and liabilities:		
Share capital	120	80
Share premium	60	40
Retained earnings	85	68
	265	188
Non-current liabilities: Bank loan	100	150
	365	338

What was Pompeii's net cash inflow or outflow from financing activities to include in the statement of cash flows for the year ended 31 October 20X7?

$		Inflow/Outflow*	* delete which does not apply

454 Carter Co has non-current assets with a carrying amount of $2,500,000 on 1 December 20X7. During the year ended 20 November 20X8, the following occurred:

1 Depreciation of $75,000 was charged to the statement of profit or loss.

2 Land and buildings with a carrying amount of $1,200,000 were revalued to $1,700,000.

3 An asset with a carrying amount of $120,000 was disposed of for $150,000.

The carrying amount of non-current assets at 30 November 20X8 was $4,200,000.

What amount should be shown for the purchase of non-current assets in the statement of cash flows of Carter Co for the year ended 30 November 20X8?

$		Inflow/Outflow*	* delete which does not apply

455 Which THREE of the following items would you expect to see included within the operating activities section of a statement of cash flows prepared using the DIRECT method?

	Selection
Payments to suppliers	
Increase or decrease in receivables	
Receipts from customers	
Increase or decrease in inventories	
Increase or decrease in payables	
Payments to employees	

456 When comparing two statements of cash flows, one prepared using the direct method and the other prepared using the indirect method, the only differences relate to the presentation of items within 'cash flows from operating activities'.

Is this statement true or false?

A   True

B   False

457 When preparing a statement of cash flows using the direct method in accordance with IAS 7 *Statement of Cash Flows*, the depreciation charge for the year is an adjustment to operating profit 'cash flows from operating activities'.

Is this statement true or false?

A   True

B   False

INCOMPLETE RECORDS

458 The following information is available about the transactions of Razil, a sole trader who does not keep proper accounting records:

	$
Opening inventory	77,000
Closing inventory	84,000
Purchases	763,000
Gross profit margin	30%

Based on this information, what was Razil's revenue for the year?

A $982,800

B $1,090,000

C $2,520,000

D $1,080,000

459 On 1 September 20X8, Buj had inventory of $380,000. During the month, sales totalled $650,000 and purchases $480,000. On 30 September 20X8 a fire destroyed some of the inventory. The undamaged goods were valued at $220,000. The business makes all sales with a standard gross profit margin of 30%.

Based upon this information, what was the cost of the inventory destroyed in the fire?

A $185,000

B $140,000

C $405,000

D $360,000

460 You have been provided with the following incomplete and incorrect extract from the statement of profit or loss of a business that trades at a mark-up of 25% on cost:

	$	$
Revenue		174,258
Less: Cost of goods sold:		
Opening inventory	12,274	
Purchases	136,527	
Closing inventory	X	(X)
Gross profit		X

You discover that the revenue figure should have been $174,825 and that purchase returns of $1,084 and sales returns of $1,146 have been omitted.

What should be the amount for closing inventory?

$ [   ]

461 A fire in the offices of Lewis has destroyed most of the accounting records. The following information has been retrieved:

	$
Sales	630,000
Opening inventory	24,300
Closing inventory	32,750
Opening payables	29,780
Closing payables	34,600

Gross profit for the period should represent a mark-up of 40%.

What was the total cash paid to suppliers in the year?

A $463,270

B $381,630

C $391,270

D $453,630

462 Pioneer's annual inventory count took place on 6 January 20X6. The value of inventory on this date was $32,780. During the period from 31 December 20X5 to 6 January 20X6, the following information is available:

Sales $8,600, and   Purchases $4,200

The value of inventory at 31 December 20X5 was $34,600.

What is the gross margin of Pioneer?

A   70%

B   72%

C   30%

D   43%

463 Fatin has a mark-up of 25% on cost of sales. The following information is also available:

	$
Receivables at start of year	6,340
Receivables at end of year	5,200
Cash at start of year	620
Cash at end of year	500
Total cash payments	16,780

The only receipts during the year consisted of cash and cheques received from customers.

What is Fatin's gross profit for the year?

A $3,880

B $3,152

C $3,560

D $3,104

464 During September, Edel had sales of $148,000, which made a gross profit of $40,000. Purchases amounted to $100,000 and opening inventory was $34,000.

What was the value of closing inventory?

A $24,000

B $26,000

C $42,000

D $54,000

465 Which of the following gives a gross profit mark-up of 40%?

A   Sales are $120,000 and gross profit is $48,000

B   Sales are $120,000 and cost of sales is $72,000

C   Sales are $100,800 and cost of sales is $72,000

D   Sales are $100,800 and cost of sales is $60,480

466 Many of the accounting records of G have been destroyed by fire. The following information is available for the period under review.

1   Sales totalled $480,000.

2   Opening inventory at cost was $36,420, and closing inventory was $40,680.

3   Trade payables at the start and end of the year were $29,590 and $33,875.

4   Gross profit for the period should represent a mark-up on cost of 50%.

What was the total of cash paid to suppliers for the period under review?

A $239,975

B $315,715

C $319,975

D $328,545

467 Pike runs an angling shop. Pike spends a lot of time fishing and consequently maintained no accounting records in the year ended 31 August 20X5. Pike knows that $6,800 cash was taken out of the business during the year plus bait which cost the business $250. Pike can also remember putting $20,000 lottery winnings into the business in March.

Pike knows that at the last year end the business had assets of $40,000 and liabilities of $14,600. Pike has also calculated that the assets of the business at 31 August 20X5 were $56,000, and there were liabilities totalling $18,750.

What profit or loss did Pike made in the year?

A $1,100 profit

B $1,100 loss

C $1,350 profit

D $1,350 loss

468 Taman makes and sells handmade pottery. Taman keeps all finished items in a storeroom at the back of the pottery workshop on the banks of the River Flow. In August 20X5, freak weather conditions led to extensive flooding, and Taman lost pottery which had cost $3,400 and had a retail value of $5,750.

Taman was insured for loss of inventory due to flooding.

What double entry is required to record the loss of inventory?

	Debit	Credit
A	Expense (P/L) $5,750	Cost of sales (P/L) $5,750
B	Current asset (SFP) $5,750	Cost of sales (P/L) $5,750
C	Expense (P/L) $3,400	Cost of sales (P/L) $3,400
D	Current asset (SFP) $3,400	Cost of sales (P/L) $3,400

469 A fire in the offices of Oyez Media on 22 March 20X6 destroyed various accounting records. From the records that were salvaged, the following credit sales information relating to the period from 31 December 20X5 until 22 March 20X6 are available:

1	Cash received from credit customers	$76,100
2	Contra entries with credit suppliers	$3,400
3	Discounts allowed to credit customers	$5,200 (not expected to be taken when invoice first issued)
4	Interest charged on overdue accounts	$3,200

On 31 December 20X5, trade receivables amounted to $65,800 and on 22 March 20X6 they were $69,400.

What is the credit sales figure for the period from 31 December 20X5 until 22 March 20X6?

$ _____

PREPARING SIMPLE CONSOLIDATED FINANCIAL STATEMENTS

470 At 1 January 20X4 Yogi acquired 80% of the share capital of Bear for $1,400,000. At that date, the share capital of Bear consisted of 600,000 equity shares of $0.50 each and other components of equity were $800,000. The fair value of the non-controlling interest was valued at $300,000 at the date of acquisition.

In the consolidated statement of financial position of Yogi and its subsidiary Bear at 31 December 20X8, what amount should appear for goodwill?

A $600,000

B $300,000

C $800,000

D $Nil

471 At 1 January 20X8 Tom Co acquired 80% of the share capital of Jerry Co for $100,000. At that date the share capital of Jerry Co consisted of 50,000 equity shares of $1 each and other components of equity were $30,000. At 31 December 20X9, the other components of equity of Tom Co and Jerry Co were as follows:

Tom Co $400,000

Jerry Co $50,000

In the consolidated statement of financial position of Tom and its subsidiary Jerry at 31 December 20X9, what amount should appear for group reserves?

A $400,000

B $438,000

C $416,000

D $404,000

472 At 1 January 20X6 Fred Co acquired 75% of the share capital of Barney Co for $65,000. At that date the share capital of Barney Co consisted of 20,000 equity shares of $1 each and other components of equity were $40,000. The fair value of the non-controlling interest was valued at $20,000 at 1 January 20X6.

In the consolidated statement of financial position of Fred Co and its subsidiary Barney Co at 31 December 20X9, what amount should appear for goodwill?

A $45,000

B $15,000

C $25,000

D $5,000

473 At 1 January 20X6 Gary Co acquired 60% of the share capital of Barlow Co for $35,000. At that date the share capital of Barlow Co consisted of 20,000 equity shares of $1 each and other components of equity were $10,000. At 31 December 20X9, the other components of equity of Gary Co and Barlow Co were as follows:

Gary Co $40,000

Barlow Co $15,000

At the date of acquisition the fair value of the non-controlling interest was valued at $25,000.

In the consolidated statement of financial position of Gary Group at 31 December 20X9, what amount should appear for non-controlling interest?

A $25,000

B $27,000

C $28,000

D $31,000

474 At 1 January 20X8 Williams acquired 65% of the share capital of Barlow for $300,000. At that date the share capital of Barlow consisted of 400,000 equity shares of $0.50 each and other components of equity were $60,000. At 31 December 20X9, the other components of equity of Williams and Barlow were as follows:

Williams $200,000

Barlow $75,000

The fair value of the non-controlling interest was valued at $50,000 at the date of acquisition.

In the consolidated statement of financial position of Williams Group at 31 December 20X9, what amount should appear for non-controlling interest?

A $55,250

B $50,000

C $76,250

D $5,250

475 Salt owns 70% of Pepper and sold goods to Pepper valued at $1,500 at a mark-up of 20%. 40% of these goods were sold on by Pepper to external parties at the year end.

What is the provision for unrealised profit (PURP) adjustment in the group financial statements?

A $100

B $150

C $240

D $120

476 The following are extracts from the statements of financial position of Dora and Diego:

	Dora	Diego
Current assets	$000	$000
Inventory	200	100
Receivables	540	160
Cash	240	80
Current liabilities		
Payables	320	180

Dora's statement of financial position includes a receivable of $40,000 due from Diego.

In the consolidated statement of financial position what will be the correct amounts for receivables and payables?

	Payables	Receivables
A	$460,000	$660,000
B	$306,000	$660,000
C	$294,000	$694,000
D	$294,000	$654,000

477 Stress acquired 100% of the equity shares of Full on 1 October 20X7 when Full's retained earnings were $300,000. Full's statement of financial position at 30 September 20X9 was as follows:

Assets	$000	Equity and liabilities	$000
Property, plant and equipment	1,800	Share capital	1,600
Current assets	1,000	Retained earnings	500
		Current liabilities	700
	2,800		2,800

On 1 October 20X7 the fair value of land included within Full's non-current assets was $400,000 greater than the carrying amount. Stress had non-current assets at 30 September 20X9 at a carrying amount of $2.2m.

What is the total amount for non-current assets that will appear on the consolidated statement of financial position at 30 September 20X9?

$ _____

The following data relate to questions 478 to 480.

Hard acquired 80% of the equity shares of Work on 1 April 20X8. The summarised statement of profit or loss for the year-ended 31 March 20X9 is as follows:

	Hard	Work
	$000	$000
Revenue	120,000	48,000
Cost of sales	84,000	40,000
Gross profit	36,000	8,000
Other operating expenses	12,000	400
Operating profit	24,000	7,600
Interest income	150	–
Profit before financing and income taxes	24,150	7,600
Interest expense	–	400
Profit before income taxes	24,150	7,200
Income tax expense	6,000	1,200
Profit (for the year)	18,150	6,000

During the year Hard sold Work some goods for $24m, these had originally cost $18m. At the year-end Work had sold half of these goods to third parties.

Note: in the exam, all questions will be independent, and not based on a common scenario.

478 **What is the provision for unrealised profit (PURP) adjustment for the year-ended 31 March 20X9?**

    A $1,000,000

    B $6,000,000

    C $3,000,000

    D $7,000,000

479 **What is the total share of group profit attributable to non-controlling interest?**

    A $1,200,000

    B $4,800,000

    C $3,630,000

    D $1,440,000

480 **What is the total amount for revenue and cost of sales to be shown in the consolidated statement of profit or loss for the year-ended 31 March 20X9?**

	Sales	Cost of sales
A	$144,000,000	$100,000,000
B	$168,000,000	$97,400,000
C	$192,000,000	$100,600,000
D	$144,000,000	$103,000,000

The following data relate to questions 481 and 482

Really acquired 75% of the equity shares of Hard on 1 January 20X9 when Hard had retained losses of $112,000. On 31 December 20X9, Really acquired 30% of the equity shares of Work when Work had retained earnings of $280,000. The summarised statements of financial position for the year-ended 31 December 20X9 were as follows:

	Really	Hard
Non-current assets	$000	$000
Property, plant and equipment	1,918	1,960
Investment in Hard	1,610	
Investment in Work	448	
	3,976	1,960
Current assets		
Inventory	760	1,280
Receivables	380	620
Cash	70	116
	5,186	3,976
Equity		
Equity shares, $1	2,240	1,680
Retained earnings	2,464	1,204
	4,704	2,884
Current liabilities		
Payables	300	960
Income taxes payable	182	132
	5,186	3976

Note: in the exam, all questions will be independent, and not based on a common scenario.

481 **What is the amount for property, plant and equipment to be included in the consolidated statement of financial position?**

$\boxed{\text{\$}}$

482 **What is the amount for retained earnings to be included in the consolidated statement of financial position?**

A $3,959,200

B $3,451,000

C $3,735,200

D $3,740,800

483 **Which of the following statements is most likely to indicate an investment by one entity in another which should be recognised and accounted for as an associate?**

A Ownership of 100% of the equity shares of another entity

B Ownership of over 50% and less than 100% of the equity shares of another entity

C Ownership of between 20% and 50% of the equity shares of another entity

D Ownership of less than 20% of the equity shares in another entity

484 IFRS 10 Consolidated Financial Statements specify three necessary elements to determine whether one entity controls another.

Which of the following is not one of the three necessary elements to determine whether one entity has control of another?

A Power over the other entity

B Exposure or rights to variable returns from involvement in the other entity

C The ability to use power over the other entity to affect the amount of investor returns

D The ability to exercise significant influence over another entity

485 **Which of the following would normally indicate that one entity has significant influence over the activities of another?**

A Ability to appoint the majority of the board of directors of that other entity

B Ability to appoint at least one person to the board of directors of that other entity

C Ability to request that a director is appointed to the board of directors of that other entity

D Ability to submit requests regarding corporate policy to the board of directors of that other entity

486 **Which of the following would normally indicate that one entity has control over the activities of another?**

    A   Ownership of some equity shares in another entity

    B   Ownership of up to 20% of the equity shares of another entity

    C   Ownership of over 50% of the equity shares of another entity

    D   Ownership of between 20% and 50% of the equity shares of another entity

487 **Which of the following would normally indicate that one entity has control of another?**

    A   Ownership of the majority of the equity shares of that other entity

    B   Ownership of between 20% and 50% of the equity shares of that other entity

    C   Ownership of less than 20% of the equity shares of that other entity

    D   Ownership of some of the shares of that other entity – the precise percentage of shares held is not relevant

488 **Which of the following would normally indicate that one entity has significant influence over the activities of another entity?**

    A   Ownership of some equity shares in another entity

    B   Ownership of up to 20% of the equity shares of another entity

    C   Ownership of over 50% of the equity shares of another entity

    D   Ownership of between 20% and 50% of the equity shares of another entity

489 Entity A acquired 60% of the issued equity shares of entity B by exchanging three shares in entity A for every two shares acquired in entity B. At that date, entity B had 100,000 equity shares. At the date of acquisition, the fair value of an equity share in entity A was $3.50 and the fair value of an equity share in entity B was $2.00. The nominal value per share of both entities was $1.00 per share.

What was the fair value of consideration paid by entity A to gain control of entity B?

    A $80,000

    B $90,000

    C $180,000

    D $315,000

490 Entity C acquired 80% of the issued equity shares of entity D by paying cash of $3.00 per share plus exchanging three shares in entity C for every five shares acquired in entity D. At that date, entity D had issued 250,000 equity shares. At the date of acquisition, the fair value of an equity share in entity C was $3.50 and the fair value of an equity share in entity D was $2.00. The nominal value per share of both entities was $1.00 per share.

What was the fair value of consideration paid by entity C to gain control of entity D?

    $ [_____]

491 Entity X acquired 60% of the issued equity shares of entity Z on 1 October 20X3. During the year ended 31 December 20X3, X and Z had revenue of $2 million and $1.5 million respectively. During the post-acquisition period, X made sales to Z of $0.1 million.

What is the group revenue figure for the year ended 31 December 20X3?

A $2.275 million

B $2.375 million

C $3.4 million

D $3.5 million

492 Entity T acquired 80% of the issued equity shares of entity S on 1 July 20X6. The revenue for the year ended 31 March 20X7 for entity T and entity S was $5 million and $3 million respectively. During the post-acquisition period, S made sales to T of $0.5 million.

What is the group revenue figure for the year ended 31 March 20X7?

A $6.75 million

B $7.25 million

C $7.5 million

D $8.0 million

493 Entity F acquired 80% of the issued equity shares of entity G on 1 July 20X6. The cost of sales for the year ended 31 March 20X7 for entity F and entity G were $10 million and $4 million respectively. During the post-acquisition period, F made sales to G of $1.6 million. The intra-group sales were made at a mark-up of 25%. At the year end, one quarter of the goods sold by F to G remained within G's inventory.

What was the group cost of sales figure for the year ended 31 March 20X7?

A $12.480 million

B $12.320 million

C $11.480 million

D $11.320 million

494 On 1 June 20X5 Hightown acquired control of Southport. During the year ended 30 September 20X5, Hightown and Southport had cost of sales of $10 million and $6 million respectively. During the post-acquisition period, Hightown had sales to Southport of $1.8 million. These sales had been made at a mark-up of 20% and at the year end, one third of the goods remained within Southport's inventory.

What was the group cost of sales figure for the year ended 30 September 20X5?

$ [   ]

495 On 1 July 20X4 Lion paid $20 million to acquire 70% of the issued equity capital of Tiger. For the year ended 31 December 20X4, Tiger had earned $2 million profit. Tiger had retained earnings of $10 million at 1 January 20X4. At the date of acquisition, Tiger had issued equity capital of $8 million and the fair value of the non-controlling interest at that date was $6 million.

What was goodwill on acquisition of Tiger for inclusion in the Lion consolidated financial statements for the year ended 31 December 20X4?

$ [   ]

496 Pole acquired 80% of the issued equity shares of Rod for $43 million on 1 March 20X8. Rod had retained earnings of $15 million at 1 July 20X7 and made a profit of $6 million for the year ended 30 June 20X8. At the date of acquisition, Rod had equity shares of $25 million and the fair value of the non-controlling interest was $10 million. On 1 March 20X8 the fair value of land and buildings owned by Rod was $1 million in excess of their carrying amount.

What was goodwill on acquisition of Rod for inclusion in the Pole consolidated financial statements for the year ended 30 June 20X8?

A $4.0 million

B $8.0 million

C $16.0 million

D $20.0 million

497 Plank acquired 60% of the issued equity shares of Splinter on 1 January 20X2. On that date, Plank paid $3 cash per share acquired and issued two shares (nominal value $1 per share) in exchange for each Splinter share acquired. At the date of acquisition, Splinter had ten million equity shares of $1 nominal value in issue, plus a share premium account balance of $10 million and had retained earnings of $50 million. The fair value of the non-controlling interest in Splinter at the date of acquisition was $14 million. The fair value of an equity share in Plank and Splinter were $4.50 and $1.50 respectively at 1 January 20X2.

What was goodwill on acquisition of Splinter for inclusion in the consolidated financial statements of Plank for the year ended 31 December 20X2?

$ [   ]

498 On 1 October 20X5, Luton acquired 75% of the issued equity capital of Bedford. In exchange for gaining control of Bedford, Luton made immediate cash payment of $4.50 per share acquired and also issued one new share for each share acquired. At the date of acquisition, Bedford had 15 million equity shares of $1 nominal value and a share premium account balance of $5 million. On 1 October 20X5, Bedford had retained earnings of $76.875 million and the fair value of the non-controlling interest in Bedford was $27 million. Bedford had a factory that had a fair value of $2 million in excess of its carrying amount at the date of acquisition. The fair value of a $1 equity share of Luton at the date of acquisition was $5.00 per share.

What was goodwill on acquisition of Bedford for inclusion in the consolidated financial statements of Luton for the year ended 30 September 20X6?

A $35 million

B $37 million

C $39 million

D $40 million

499 On 1 January 20X6, Hyndland acquired 90% of the issued equity capital of Shawfield. In exchange for gaining control of Shawfield, Hyndland made immediate cash payment of $3 per share acquired and also issued one new share of $0.5 nominal value per share for each share acquired. At the date of acquisition, Shawfield had 200,000 equity shares of $1 nominal value, a share premium account balance of $100,000 and retained earnings of $590,000. On 1 January 20X6, the fair value of the non-controlling interest in Shawfield was $75,000. In addition, at the date of acquisition, Shawfield had several items of property plant and equipment which together had a fair value of $90,000 and a carrying amount of $70,000. The fair value of a $0.5 equity share of Hyndland at 1 January 20X3 was $2.00 per share. There has been no impairment of goodwill.

What was goodwill on acquisition of Shawfield for inclusion in the consolidated financial statements of Hyndland for the year ended 30 September 20X6?

$

500 On 1 July 20X5, Huyton acquired 60% of the equity shares of Speke. For the year ended 31 December 20X5, Huyton and Speke made profits of $600,000 and $400,000, respectively. During the post-acquisition period, Huyton sold goods to Speke which included a profit element of $20,000. At the year-end, one quarter of the goods sold by Huyton to Speke remained in Speke's inventory.

What was the non-controlling interest share of the group profit for the year ended 31 December 20X5?

A $75,000

B $80,000

C $120,000

D $160,000

501 Honey Co acquired 75% of Bee Co on 1 April 20X3, paying $2 for each equity share acquired. The fair value of the non-controlling interest at 1 April 20X3 was $300. Bee Co's individual financial statements as at 30 September 20X3 included:

Statement of financial position:	$
Equity	
Share capital ($1 each)	1,000
Retained earnings	710
	1,710

Statement of profit or loss:	
Profit (for the year)	250

Profit accrued evenly throughout the year.

What was goodwill on acquisition at 1 April 20X3?

A $715

B $90

C $517

D $215

502 Panther acquired 80% of the equity shares in Seal on 31 August 20X2. The statements of profit or loss for Panther and Seal for the year ended 31 December 20X2 were as follows:

	Panther	Seal
	$	$
Revenue	100,000	62,000
Cost of sales	25,000	16,000

During October 20X2, sales of $6,000 were made by Panther to Seal. None of these items remained in inventory at the year-end.

What is the consolidated revenue for Panther Group or the year ended 31 December 20X2?

$

503 Tulip acquired 70% of the equity shares of Daffodil on 1 March 20X2. The following extracts are from the individual financial statements of profit or loss for each entity for the year ended 31 August 20X2:

	Tulip	Daffodil
	$	$
Revenue	61,000	23,000
Cost of sales	(42,700)	(13,800)
Gross profit	18,300	9,200

What should be the consolidated gross profit for the year ended 31 August 20X2?

$

504 Venus acquired 75% of Mercury's 100,000 $1 equity shares on 1 November 20X4. The consideration comprised $2 cash per share plus one share in Venus for every share acquired in Mercury.

Shares in Venus have a nominal value of $1 and a fair value of $1.75. The fair value of the non-controlling interest was $82,000 and the fair value of the net assets acquired was $215,500.

What should be recorded as goodwill on acquisition of Mercury in the consolidated Mercury Group financial statements?

$ _____

505 **Which of the following investments of Coffee should be equity accounted in the consolidated financial statements?**

1   40% of the non-voting preference share capital in Tea Co

2   18% of the equity share capital in Café Co with two of the five directors of Coffee Co on the board of Café Co

3   50% of the equity share capital of Choc Co, with five of the seven directors of Coffee Co on the board of Choc Co

A   1 and 2

B   2 only

C   1 and 3

D   2 and 3

506 **Are the following statements about accounting for associates true or false?**

	True	False
Equity accounting will always be used when an investing entity holds between 20% – 50% of the equity shares in another entity.		
Dividends received from an investment in associate will be presented as investment income in the consolidated financial statements.		

507 Companies Co has several subsidiaries and has invested in an associate for the first time in the current year.

Identify whether each of the following statements regarding associates are true or false.

		True	False
1	Goodwill in associates is presented separately on the consolidated statement of financial position		
2	Associates are accounted for using equity accounting		
3	An associate's total profit for the year is presented in the consolidated statement of profit or loss		
4	The group share of an associate's assets and liabilities are consolidated on a line-by-line basis		

INTERPRETATION OF FINANCIAL STATEMENTS

The following data relate to questions 508 to 519. Barnstorm Co case-study.

Note: The following questions, based upon the financial statements of Barnstorm Co presented below are designed as a revision aid to test your knowledge of definitions and calculations of accounting ratios. You will not necessarily be required to state the ratio definition and calculate the ratio for two years in the real exam.

You should calculate all ratios to two decimal places.

The financial statements of Barnstorm Co for the year ended 31 July 20X4, with comparatives, are presented below.

Statement of profit or loss and other comprehensive income – year ended 31 July 20X4.

	20X4	20X3
	$000	$000
Revenue	1,391,820	1,159,850
Cost of sales	(1,050,825)	(753,450)
Gross profit	340,995	406,400
Operating expenses	(161,450)	(170,950)
Profit before financing and income taxes	179,545	235,450
Interest expenses	(10,000)	(14,000)
Profit before income taxes	169,545	221,450
Income tax expense	(50,800)	(66,300)
Profit (for the year)	118,745	155,150
Other comprehensive income:		
Revaluation surplus on land and buildings	10,000	
Total comprehensive income (for the year)	128,745	155,150

Statement of financial position at 31 July 20X4

	20X4	20X3
	$000	$000
Non-current assets		
Property, plant and equipment	559,590	341,400
Current assets		
Inventories	109,400	88,760
Receivables	419,455	206,550
Bank		95,400
	1,088,445	732,110

Equity

Equity shares, $1	140,000	100,000
Share premium	40,000	20,000
Revaluation reserve	10,000	
Retained earnings	406,165	287,420
	596,165	407,420

Non-current liabilities

10% Bank loan 20X7	61,600	83,100

Current liabilities

Payables	345,480	179,590
Bank overdraft	30,200	
Income taxes payable	55,000	62,000
	1,088,445	732,110

Note: in the exam, all questions will be independent, and not based on a common scenario.

508 **Calculate the return on capital employed for the year ended 31 July 20X4, together with the comparative for the prior year.**

20X4	
20X3	

509 **Calculate the gross profit margin for the year ended 31 July 20X4, together with the comparative for the prior year.**

20X4	
20X3	

510 **Calculate the operating profit margin for the year ended 31 July 20X4, together with the comparative for the prior year.**

20X4	
20X3	

511 **Calculate the asset turnover for the year ended 31 July 20X4, together with the comparative for the prior year.**

20X4	
20X3	

512 Calculate the current ratio for the year ended 31 July 20X4, together with the comparative for the prior year.

20X4	
20X3	

513 Calculate quick 'acid test' ratio for the year ended 31 July 20X4, together with the comparative for the prior year.

20X4	
20X3	

514 Calculate the inventory holding period for the year ended 31 July 20X4, together with the comparative for the prior year.

20X4	
20X3	

515 Calculate the receivables collection period for the year ended 31 July 20X4, together with the comparative for the prior year.

20X4	
20X3	

516 Calculate the payables payment period for the year ended 31 July 20X4, together with the comparative for the prior year.

20X4	
20X3	

517 Calculate the debt-equity ratio for the year ended 31 July 20X4, together with the comparative for the prior year.

20X4	
20X3	

518 Calculate the gearing ratio for the year ended 31 July 20X4, together with the comparative for the prior year.

20X4	
20X3	

519 Calculate interest cover for the year ended 31 July 20X4, together with the comparative for the prior year.

20X4	
20X3	

520 W Co had sales of $20,000 and cost of sales of $15,400.

What W Co's gross profit margin?

A   77%

B   129%

C   43%

D   23%

521 The following extract relates to X Co for the years ended 30 June 20X5 and 20X6:

	20X5	**20X6**
Revenue	20,000	26,000
Cost of sales	(15,400)	(21,050)
Gross profit	4,600	4,950
Less expenses	(2,460)	(2,770)
Profit before financing and income tax	2,140	2,180

What was the operating profit margin for 20X5 and 20X6?

	20X5	**20X6**
A	10.7%	8.38%
B	8.38%	10.7%
C	23.0%	19.0%
D	12.0%	10.0%

522 The following extract relates to Y Co for 20X5 and 20X6:

	20X5	**20X6**
Statement of profit or loss extract	$	$
Revenue	20,000	26,000
Statement of financial position extract		
Receivables	4,400	6,740
Cash	120	960

What was the receivables collection period for 20X5 and 20X6?

	20X5	**20X6**
A	80 days	95 days
B	82 days	108 days
C	75 days	111 days
D	95 days	80 days

523 The following extract of the statement of profit or loss relates to Z Co for the year ended 30 September 20X6:

	20X6
Statement of profit or loss extract	
Gross profit	15,175
Operating expenses	(2,460)
	————
Profit before financing and income taxes	12,715
Interest expenses	(5,000)
	————
Profit before income taxes	7,715
Income tax expense	(1,515)
	————
Profit	6,200
	————

What was interest cover for the year?

A   2.54 times

B   3.03 times

C   1.54 times

D   1.24 times

524 **Given a selling price of $700 and gross profit mark-up of 40%, what is the cost of an item?**

A $280

B $420

C $500

D $980

525 A Co had sales of $220,000 and purchases of $160,000, together with opening inventory and closing inventory of $24,000 and $20,000 respectively.

What was the average inventory holding period?

A   44.5 days

B   22.2 days

C   53.4 days

D   49.0 days

526 **What is the formula for calculating the average inventory holding period in days?**

A   Cost of goods sold divided by average inventories × 365

B   Sales divided by average inventories at cost × 365

C   Sales divided by average inventories at selling price × 365

D   Average inventories at cost divided by cost of goods sold × 365

527 B Co had the following account balances extracted from its statement of financial position:

	$000
Inventory	3,800
Receivables	2,000
Bank overdraft	200
Payables	2,000

What was B Co's current ratio?

A   1.72:1

B   2.90:1

C   2.64:1

D   3.00:1

528 **Which one of the following would increase an entity's gearing ratio?**

A   A decrease in long-term loans that is less than a decrease in equity

B   A decrease in long-term loans that is more than a decrease in equity

C   An increase in interest rates

D   A decrease in interest rates

529 R Co extracted the following details from its statement of financial position:

	$000
Inventory	3,800
Receivables	2,000
Bank overdraft	200
Payables	2,000

What was the quick (acid test) ratio of R Co?

A   2.63 : 1

B   0.9 : 1

C   29.0 : 1

D   1 : 1

530 Extracts from the financial statements of Miller Co for the year ended 31 May 20X2 are shown below:

	$000
Revenue	475
Cost of sales	(342)
	————
Gross profit	133
Operating expenses	(59)
Interest expense	(26)
	————
Profit before income taxes	48
	————

What was Miller Co's interest cover ratio for the year ended 31 May 20X2?

A   2.85

B   1.85

C   5.12

D   0.35

531 The following extracts relate to R Co for the years ended 30 June 20X6 and 20X5:

	20X6	20X5
Statement of profit or loss extract	$	$
Cost of sales	55,000	48,000
	————	————
Statement of financial position extract		
Trade payables	4,400	5,300
Overdraft	120	960

Calculate the payables payment period of R Co for 20X6 and 20X5.

20X6	days
20X5	days

532 An increase in the gearing ratio could be caused by the issue of equity shares for cash during the year.

Is this statement true or false?

A   True

B   False

533 A reduction in the unit purchase cost of raw materials whilst the unit selling price remains unchanged will increase the gross profit margin.

Is this statement true or false?

A   True

B   False

534 The following extracts relate to T Co for the year ended 31 March 20X3 and 20X2:

	20X3	**20X2**
	$	$
Inventory	18,000	16,000
Trade receivables	17,500	21,050
Cash and equivalents	3,095	
	38,595	37,050
Current liabilities		
Trade payables	20,750	18,500
Bank overdraft		500
	20,750	19,000

Calculate the current ratio of T Co for 20X3 and 20X2.

20X3	
20X2	

535 An increase in return on capital could be caused by an increase in long-term loans taken out by the business during the year.

Is this statement true or false?

A   True

B   False

536 The following financial statement extracts relate to MN Co for the year ended 31 January 20X8 and 20X7:

	20X8	**20X7**
Equity share capital	50,000	50,000
Share premium	5,500	5,500
Retained earnings	34,500	24,500
	90,000	80,000
Non-current liabilities		
10% Bank loan	4,500	5,600
Current liabilities		
Bank overdraft	3,000	500

Calculate the debt/equity ratio of MN Co for 20X8 and 20X7.

20X8	
20X7	

537 **Which of the following is likely to increase the trade receivables collection period?**

A Offering credit customers a significant discount for settlement within seven days of receipt of invoice

B Application of effective credit control procedures

C Poor application of credit control procedures by a business

D An increasing volume of credit sales during an accounting period

538 **Which of the following is likely to reduce the trade payables payment period?**

A Offering credit customers a significant discount for settlement within seven days of receipt of invoice

B Paying trade suppliers within seven days of receipt of invoice to obtain a discount

C Buying proportionately more goods on a cash basis, rather than on a credit basis

D Buying an increasing volume of credit purchases during an accounting period

539 **Which of the following is likely to increase the inventory holding period?**

A Building up inventory levels in preparation of a sales and marketing campaign later in the year

B Scrapping of old and obsolete items of inventory

C Only ordering goods from a reliable supplier upon receipt of a customer order

D Implementation of effective goods requisitioning and ordering policies

540 You have been advised that a business has an inventory turnover of 8.49.

What is the average inventory holding period in days?

541 During the year, A Co made a bonus issue of shares to its shareholders.

What is the impact of this upon the gearing ratio?

A The gearing ratio will increase

B The gearing ratio will decrease

C There will be no change to the gearing ratio

D It is not possible to determine the impact on the gearing ratio as there is insufficient information available

542 Which of the following statements could explain why return on capital for an entity increased from 20% in 20X7 to 25% in 20X8?

    1   The entity reduced long-term borrowings during 20X8.

    2   The entity managed to increase in profit margin during 20X8.

    3   The entity made an issue of shares for cash during 20X8 to finance asset expenditure.

    A   1, 2 and 3

    B   2 and 3 only

    C   1 and 3 only

    D   1 and 2 only

543 During the year ended 31 July 20X8, B Co made a rights issue of shares to its shareholders.

What was the impact of this upon the gearing ratio?

    A   It is not possible to determine the impact on the gearing ratio as there is insufficient information available

    B   The gearing ratio increased

    C   The gearing ratio decreased

    D   The gearing ratio remained unchanged

544 In an attempt to increase revenue during the year, C Co offered extended credit terms to its major customers. Whilst many major customers took advantage of the extended credit period, C Co did not increase its volume of sales.

What impact did this have upon the current ratio?

    A   There was no change to the current ratio

    B   It is not possible to determine the impact on the current ratio as there is insufficient information available

    C   The current ratio increased

    D   The current ratio decreased

545 On 1 July 20X5, D Co raised $5 million from an issue of equity shares. D Co then immediately used this cash to repay a loan of $5 million, which was not due for repayment until 30 June 20X9.

What impact did this have upon the debt/equity ratio?

    A   It is not possible to determine the impact on the debt/equity ratio as there is insufficient information available

    B   The debt/equity ratio increased

    C   The debt/equity ratio decreased

    D   There will be no change to the debt/equity ratio

546 XYZ Co has the following working capital ratios:

	20X9	**20X8**
Current ratio	1.2:1	0.9:1
Receivables collection period	60 days	50 days
Payables payment period	45 days	35 days
Inventory holding period	36 days	45 days

Which ONE of the following statements relating to XYZ Co is true?

A   XYZ Co is taking longer to pay suppliers in 20X9 than in 20X8

B   XYZ Co is suffering a worsening liquidity position in 20X9

C   XYZ Co is managing inventory less efficiently in 20X9 in comparison with 20X8.

D   XYZ Co is reiving cash from customers more quickly in 20X9 than in 20X8

547 The following extracts are taken from the financial statements of Companies Co for the year ended 31 December 20X6:

	20X6	20X5
	$	$
Revenue	500,000	450,000
Trade receivables	45,900	51,300

Which of the following conclusions could be drawn from the above information?

1   Credit customers are now taking less time to pay their debts

2   The business has improved its profitability as revenue has increased

3   Trade receivables days have deteriorated

4   The credit control department has been more efficient

A   1 and 4

B   3 and 4

C   1, 2 and 3

D   1, 2 and 4

548 **Which TWO of the following statements about accounting ratios are correct?**

	Selection
Ratios help the user of financial information to focus attention on significant issues	
Ratios are only useful when comparing a business' results from one year to the next	
Ratios provide all the information needed for interpreting company accounts	
Ratios can provide information about the profitability, liquidity, efficiency and position of the company	

549 **Which TWO of the following statements about accounting ratios are correct?**

	Selection
Ratios can be affected by a business' choice of accounting policies	
If there is an increase in any calculated accounting ratio, it is seen as favourable	
Gearing may indicate how risky a business is	
Interest cover will give an investor information about whether a dividend will be paid	

550 Doc Co has decided to revalue its land and buildings, having previously applied the cost model in accordance with IAS 16 *Property, Plant and Equipment*.

What impact will this decision have on Doc Co's current ratio and the gearing ratio?

A Both ratios would remain improve

B The current ratio would deteriorate, and the gearing ratio would increase

C The current ratio would be unchanged, and the gearing ratio would be reduced

D The current ratio would improve, and the gearing ratio would increase

Section 2

MULTI-TASK QUESTIONS – SECTION B

1 **ICE CO**

Task 1

The following is an extract from the trial balance of Ice Co, an entity, as at 31 December 20X1:

	Dr	Cr
	$	$
Revenue		600,000
Inventory valuation at 1 January 20X1	24,000	
Purchases	240,000	
Carriage inwards	2,000	
Carriage outwards	3,000	
General and administrative expenses	180,000	
Selling expenses	75,000	
Returns inwards	500	

Note: Inventory valuation at 31 December 20X1 was $30,000.

Required:

(a) How should the following items be classified in the statement of profit or loss?

(1 mark)

	Cost of sales	Selling expenses	General and administrative expenses
Carriage inwards			
Carriage outwards			

(b) Using the information available, what was Ice Co's gross profit for the year ended 31 December 20X1?

(2 marks)

$ _____

(c) Using the information available, identify the adjustments required to gross profit to calculate Ice Co's draft profit before income taxes.

(2 marks)

		Selected answer
(i)	Gross profit – $30,000 – $180,000 – $75,000	
(ii)	Gross profit – $500 – $2,000 – $180,000 – $75,000	
(iii)	Gross profit – $3,000 – $180,000 – $75,000	

Task 2

You are now advised that, on 1 April 20X1, Ice Co raised loan finance of $100,000 which will be repayable in a single instalment on 31 March 20X5. Interest is payable annually at the rate of 6% in arrears.

(a) **What interest expense should be included in Ice Co's statement of profit or loss in relation to the loan?** **(1 mark)**

$

(b) **How should the loan be classified in the statement of financial position at 31 December 20X1?** **(1 mark)**

		Selected answer
(i)	An equity component	
(ii)	A non-current liability	
(iii)	A current liability	

Task 3

On 21 January 20X2, Ice Co received notification from a customer that they had suffered injury as a result of using one of its products which had been purchased in December 20X1. The customer made a claim for compensation amounting to $5,000 and Ice Co's legal advisors have advised that it is virtually certain that compensation will be required to settle the claim.

How should this matter be reflected in Ice Co's financial statements for the year ended 31 December 20X1? **(2 marks)**

		Selected answer
(i)	It should not be recognised or disclosed in the financial statements for the year ended 31 December 20X1	
(ii)	It should be disclosed only in the financial statements for the year ended 31 December 20X1	
(iii)	It should be recognised as a liability in the financial statements for the year ended 31 December 20X1	

Task 4

Ice Co is considering whether to undertake some work in relation to the land and buildings that it owns.

(a) **State whether each of the following costs should be classified as asset expenditure or treated as an expense.** **(4 marks)**

		Asset/ Expense
(i)	Work to install additional, high-specification, electrical power cabling and circuits so that additional plant and equipment can become operational	
(ii)	Replacement of some loose and damaged roof tiles following a recent storm	
(iii)	Repainting the factory administration office	
(iv)	Modifications to the factory entrance to enable a large item of plant and equipment to be installed	

(b) You have now been provided with an additional extract from Ice Co's trial balance as at 31 December 20X1 as follows:

	$	$
Land and building – cost (Land $70,000)	120,000	
Building – accumulated depreciation at 1 Jan 20X1		20,000
Plant and equipment – cost	120,000	
Plant and equipment – accumulated depreciation at 1 Jan 20X1		15,000

The building is depreciated on a straight-line basis over its estimated useful life of 50 years. The plant and equipment is depreciated on a reducing balance basis at the rate of 15%. There were no purchases or disposals of non-current assets during the year.

Calculate the depreciation charge for the year that should be included as an expense within cost of sales. **(2 marks)**

Building	$
Plant and equipment	$

(Total: 15 marks)

2 WILLOW CO

You have been asked to help prepare the financial statements of Willow Co for the year ended 30 June 20X1.

Task 1

You have discovered that several purchase invoices have not been recorded in the general ledger. The total value of the invoices was $2,300 including sales tax charged at 15%.

(a) **Complete the following table to state the accounting entries required to record the invoices in the general ledger.** **(2 marks)**

	$	Credit/Debit
Bank and cash		
Payables		
Purchases		
Sales tax		
Suspense account		

(b) **Complete the following statement relating to the omitted purchases invoices.**

(1 mark)

This accounting error will/will not* result in the totals of the trial balance failing to agree.

*Delete which does not apply

Task 2

An extract of Willow Co's trial balance as at 30 June 20X1 is shown below.

	Debit	Credit
	$000	$000
Equity shares, $1		72,000
Share premium		13,000
Revaluation surplus at 1 July 20X0		10,000
Retained earnings at 1 July 20X0		12,920
Dividends paid	3,000	

During the year ended 30 June 20X1, Willow Co made a '1 for 5' bonus issue.

Complete the following table to identify the accounting entries required to record the bonus issue. (4 marks)

	$000	Credit/Debit
Bank and cash		
Equity shares		
Retained earnings		
Share premium		

Task 3

Inventory at 30 June 20X1 had been valued at cost at $9,420,000. However, on further investigation, information relating to three specific items was established as follows:

Product	Quantity	Cost per unit	Selling price per unit	Selling expenses
		$	$	$
Standard	70	1,000	1,500	200
Super	50	1,500	1,800	350
Elite	40	2,000	2,500	650

(a) **Calculate the correct total value of each product that should be included in the inventory valuation at 30 June 20X1 in accordance with IAS 2 *Inventories*.** (3 marks)

Standard	$
Super	$
Elite	$

(b) **What adjustment should be made to the inventory valuation stated at cost of $9,420,000 to ensure that it complies with the requirements of IAS 2 *Inventories*?**
(2 marks)

$	Decrease/Increase*

* Delete which does not apply

Task 4

During the year ended 30 June 20X1, Willow Co purchased a licence which enabled it sell a new product 'Supreme' for a five-year period commencing 1 July 20X0. The licence cost $2,000,000 and cannot be renewed at the end of the five-year term.

(a) **A licence is an example of which type of asset?** **(1 mark)**

| Current/Intangible/Tangible* | * Delete which does not apply

(b) **Calculate the amortisation charge for the year ended 30 June 20X1 and the carrying amount of the licence at that date.** **(2 marks)**

Amortisation charge	$
Carrying amount	$

(Total: 15 marks)

3 **CLER CO**

You are helping to prepare the financial statements of Cler Co for the year ended 31 December 20X7. Your initial focus is on accounting for amounts due to the business.

Task 1

One specific receivable for $3,500 is four months old and is now considered to be irrecoverable.

(a) **State the accounting entries required to write-off this amount in the general ledger.** **(1 mark)**

	$	Credit/Debit
Allowance for receivables		
Irrecoverable debts		
Trade payables		
Trade receivables'		

Additionally, it has been agreed with another credit customer who also supplies goods to Cler Co on credit that an amount of $4,750 will offset against their respective receivable and payable balances due to each other.

(b) **Complete the following statement** **(2 marks)**

For Cler Co to record the contra entries in its general ledger, it must credit/debit* the trade payables' account and credit/debit* the trade receivables' account.

* Delete which does not apply

Finally, in relation to amounts due to the business, you have been asked to confirm the accounting entries required to record a sale transaction to a credit customer for goods with a list price of $2,000. The customer is entitled to 10% trade discount and was also offered 5% early settlement discount if payment is received within 10 days of the invoice date. The customer is expected to take advantage of the early settlement discount terms.

(c)   **State the accounting entries required to record this transaction in the general ledger.**
                                                                    (2 marks)

	$	Credit/Debit
Discount received		
Revenue		
Trade payables		
Trade receivables		

Task 2

You are now dealing with the bank reconciliation as at 31 December 20X7 and a colleague has provided you with the following information:

	$
Payments not yet presented	2,400
Automated payments returned unpaid by customer's bank	1,000
Lodgments not yet cleared	3,400
Debit balance per bank statement	1,500

Using the information available to you, complete the bank reconciliation as at 31 December 20X7:   **(4 marks)**

	$	
Debit balance per bank statement	1,500	
Payments not yet presented		
	———	
Sub-total		
Lodgments not yet cleared		
	———	
Balance per bank ledger account		Credit/Debit*
Automated payment returned unpaid by customer's bank		
	———	
Updated balance per bank ledger account		Credit/Debit*
	———	

* Delete as appropriate

Task 3

Inventories at the close of business on 31 December 20X7 were valued at cost of $190,871. Included in this amount was a product at a cost of $4,000 that, due to a change in legislation, no longer meets current safety standards. Cler Co could modify this product at a cost of $1,500 and plans to do so. The product could then be sold for $6,000.

(a)   **At what valuation should inventory be stated in the financial statements at 31 December 20X7?**   **(1 mark)**

$ _____

(b) Complete the accounting policy disclosure note for inventory for inclusion in the financial statements for the year ended 31 December 20X7. **(2 marks)**

Inventory is stated at the higher/lower* of cost and net realisable value/selling price* for each separate item or product.

* Delete as appropriate

(c) Complete the following table to state whether each of the following items should be included as part of the cost of inventory. **(3 marks)**

		Included/Excluded
(i)	Selling expenses	
(ii)	Transport costs from supplier to Cler Co premises	
(iii)	Storage costs	

(Total: 15 marks)

4   CARBON CO

You are helping to prepare the financial statements of Carbon Co for the year ended 31 December 20X5. Your initial focus is on accounting for property plant and equipment.

Task 1

Carbon Co purchased land and buildings at a cost of $4,000,000 (of which the land accounted for $2,500,000) on 1 January 20X2. At that date, it was estimated that the buildings had an estimated useful life of 50 years.

Carbon Co has now decided to account for the land and buildings at their fair value. At 31 December 20X5, the fair value of land and buildings was $6,000,000, of which land accounted for $4,000,000.

(a) State whether each of the following statements relating to accounting for property, plant and equipment is true or false: **(3 marks)**

		True/False
(i)	When an entity does revalue its land and buildings, it is compulsory to make an annual transfer of 'excess depreciation' from revaluation surplus to retained earnings	
(ii)	Any gain on revaluation of property, plant and equipment is presented as operating income in the statement of profit or loss	
(iii)	The revaluation surplus is accounted for as an adjustment to cash inflows from operating activities	

(b) State the accounting entries required to account for the revaluation at 31 December 20X5. **(3 marks)**

	$000	Credit/Debit
Land and buildings		
Depreciation charge for the year		
Accumulated depreciation provision		
Revaluation surplus		

Task 2

At 1 January 20X5, Carbon Co had a credit balance on its income taxes payable account of $2,300,000. For the year ended 31 December 20X5, Carbon Co estimated its liability for income taxes payable to be $2,400,000. During 20X5, the income tax liability for the previous year was settled at $2,350,000.

What was the income tax expense included in the statement of profit or loss for the year ended 31 December 20X5? **(1 mark)**

$ [   ]

Task 3

An extract of Carbon Co's trial balance at 31 December 20X5 is presented below:

	$000
Equity shares, $1	10,000
Retained earnings – 1 January 20X5	25,500

On 1 February 20X5, Carbon Co made a '1-for-four' rights issue at an issue price of $2.50 per share. The rights issue was fully subscribed and taken up by the shareholders.

(a) **How many shares were issued as a result of making the rights issue?** **(1 mark)**

[   ]

(b) **What were the total proceeds raised as a result of making the rights issue? (1 mark)**

$ [   ]

(c) **What was the balance on the share premium account as a result of making the rights issue?** **(1 mark)**

$ [   ]

Task 4

You are preparing Carbon Co's statement of changes in equity for the year ended 31 December 20X5.

Identify whether or not each of the following items would be presented in the statement of changes in equity. **(3 marks)**

	Included/Excluded
Depreciation charge for the year	
Share issue made in the year	
Proposed dividend due to be paid on 26 February 20X6	
Dividend paid on 28 October 20X5	

Task 5

Carbon Co's gross profit margin for the year ended 31 December 20X5 was 28%, in comparison with 24% for the preceding year.

Which one of the following statements could be a plausible reason for the increase in the gross profit margin during 20X5? **(2 marks)**

		Selected answer
(i)	Selling expenses reduced during 20X5	
(ii)	Carbon Co sold more goods during 20X5 due to a successful marketing campaign early in the year	
(iii)	There was a change in the sales mix during 20X5, with Carbon Co selling proportionately fewer of its low-margin goods	

(Total: 15 marks)

5 **HARUMI**

You are helping to prepare the financial statements of Harumi for the year ended 30 April 20X5. Harumi uses a computerised accounting system to record accounting transactions and produce financial information. There are a number of accounting issues to deal with before the financial statements can be finalised.

Task 1

During the year, problems were experienced with goods from a particular supplier. In total, goods which cost $300,000, inclusive of sales tax at 20%, were returned to the supplier.

State the accounting entries required to record the return of goods to the supplier.

(2 marks)

	$000	Credit/Debit
Revenue		
Returns inwards		
Returns outwards		
Sales tax		
Trade payables		
Trade receivables		

Task 2

During the year, Harumi withdrew goods from the business for personal use. The goods cost $15,000 and had a sale value of $20,000.

State the accounting entries required to record withdrawal of goods from the business by Harumi for personal use. **(3 marks)**

	$000	Credit/Debit
Drawings		
Trade payables		
Purchases		
Revenue		

Task 3

During the year, Harumi introduced a system of trade discounts and early settlement discounts for customers to encourage sales.

State whether each of the following statements is true or false. **(3 marks)**

		True/False
(i)	Trade discount allowed to customers should be included as an expense in the statement of profit or loss	
(ii)	Early settlement discount allowed to credit customers is deducted from the invoice value at the point of sale when the customer is not expected to take advantage of the early settlement discount terms offered	
(iii)	Early settlement discount earned from suppliers should be included in the statement of profit or loss	

Task 4

You are now dealing with accruals and prepayments required at 30 April 20X5. You have been advised that the insurance premium of $18,000 paid on 31 December 20X4 was to cover the twelve month period to 31 December 20X5. You have also identified that, following a long-running dispute with a customer, there will be legal fees to pay, amounting to $6,000.

Complete each of the following three statements in relation to the information contained in this Task. **(3 marks)**

Accounting for the insurance accrual/prepayment* will increase/reduce* the profit for the year ended 30 April 20X5.

Accounting for the legal fees accrual/prepayment* will increase/reduce* the profit for the year ended 30 April 20X5.

The net effect on the profit for the year ended 30 April 20X5 as a result of accounting for the accrual and/or prepayment required for insurance and legal fees will be to increase/reduce* profit for the year by $1,500/$3,000/$6,000*.

* Delete as appropriate

Task 5

A colleague has produced the trial balance as at 30 April 20X5 which includes a suspense account. The transaction in question was processed by an inexperienced office junior who is now on long-term sick leave. Several possible reasons have been suggested as the reason for the entry in the suspense account.

Identify whether each of the following items is a potential reason for the suspense account balance. **(4 marks)**

		Relevant/ Not relevant
(i)	The cost of a machine was recorded in the appropriate general ledger accounts but at a cost of $4,280, rather than the correct amount of $8,240	
(ii)	Discounts received were credited to the discounts received account and debited to the suspense account	
(iii)	The total of purchases for March was debited to the trade payables account and credited to the purchases account	
(iv)	A contra had been debited to the payables account and credited to the receivables account	

(Total: 15 marks)

6   FIREWORK CO

The following financial statements and supporting information relate to Firework Co:

Statement of profit or loss and other comprehensive income for the year ended 30 June 20X5

	$000
Revenue	113,250
Less: Cost of sales	77,500
Gross profit	35,750
Less: Selling expenses	3,000
Less: General and administrative expenses	1,000
Operating profit/Profit before financing and income taxes	31,750
Less: Interest expense	750
Profit before income taxes	31,000
Less: Income tax expense	6,000
Profit for the year	25,000
Other comprehensive income:	
Gain on revaluation of property, plant and equipment	2,000
Total comprehensive income (for the year)	27,000

Statement of financial position at 30 June 20X5:

	20X5	20X4
	$000	$000
ASSETS		
Non-current assets		
Property, plant and equipment	110,000	93,000
Current assets		
Inventories	36,000	30,000
Trade receivables	40,000	35,000
Cash and equivalents	Nil	10,000
Total assets	186,000	168,000

EQUITY AND LIABILITIES		
Equity share capital	20,000	15,000
Share premium	8,000	3,000
Revaluation surplus	10,000	8,000
Retained earnings	96,000	85,000
Total equity	134,000	111,000
Non-current liabilities		
Bank loan	7,000	17,000
Current liabilities		
Trade payables	36,500	30,000
Income taxes payable	6,500	10,000
Bank overdraft	2,000	Nil
Total equity and liabilities	186,000	168,000

The following information is relevant to the financial statements of Firework Co:

(i)   During the year ended 30 June 20X5, Firework Co disposed of several items of plant and equipment for sale proceeds of $8,000,000. The loss on disposal of $2,000,000 is included within cost of sales. The depreciation charge for the year was $15,000,000.

(ii)   Firework Co estimated that the liability for income taxes payable on the profit for the year ended 30 June 20X5 was $6,500,000.

Required:

Using the information available, complete the statement of cash flows for Firework Co for the year ended 30 June 20X5 in accordance with the requirements of IAS 7 *Statement of Cash Flows*.   **(Total: 15 marks)**

Firework Co – Statement of cash flows for the year ended 30 June 20X5

	$000	
Cash flows from operating activities		
Operating profit /Profit before income taxes*		
Adjustments for:		
Depreciation		Add/Subtract*
Loss on sale of plant and equipment		Add/Subtract*
Change in inventories		Add/Subtract*
Change in trade receivables		Add/Subtract*
Change in trade payables		Add/Subtract*
	_____	
Cash from operating activities before income taxes	N/A	
Income taxes paid		Add/Subtract*
	_____	
	N/A	
Cash flows from investing activities		
Cash purchase of property, plant and equipment		Add/Subtract*
Disposal proceeds of plant and equipment		Add/Subtract*
	_____	
	N/A	
Cash flows from financing activities		
Repayment of bank loan		Add/Subtract*
Proceeds of share issue		Add/Subtract*
Finance costs paid		Add/Subtract*
Dividend paid		Add/Subtract*
	_____	
	N/A	
Net decrease/increase* in cash and cash equivalents for the year		
Cash and cash equivalents at start of year		Add/Subtract*
	_____	
Cash and cash equivalents at end of year		Net cash/net overdraft*
	_____	

Note: * = delete which does not apply

7   CRACKER CO

The following financial statements and supporting information relate to Cracker Co:

Statement of profit or loss and other comprehensive income for the year ended 31 March 20X1

	$000
Revenue	88,740
Less: Cost of sales	73,750
Gross profit	14,990
Less: Selling expenses	1,200
Less: General and administrative expenses	610
Add: Profit on disposal of plant and equipment	300
Operating profit	13,480
Add: Interest income	320
Profit before financing and income tax	13,800
Less: Interest expense	2,150
Profit before income taxes	11,650
Less: Income tax expense	2,900
Profit for the year	8,750

There were no items of other comprehensive income during the year.

Statement of financial position at 31 March 20X1:

	20X1	20X0
ASSETS	$000	$000
Non-current assets		
Property, plant and equipment	73,000	70,500
Current assets		
Inventories	27,500	25,500
Trade receivables	37,500	33,000
Cash and equivalents	4,250	1,250
Total assets	142,250	130,250

	20X1	**20X0**
EQUITY AND LIABILITIES	$000	$000
Equity share capital	11,000	10,000
Share premium	610	Nil
Retained earnings	74,790	66,040
Total equity	86,400	76,040
Non-current liabilities		
10% Debenture	23,500	20,000
Current liabilities		
Trade payables	29,450	31,900
Income taxes payable	2,900	2,310
Total equity and liabilities	142,250	130,250

Notes:

The following information is relevant to the financial statements of Cracker Co:

(i)   During the year ended 31 March 20X1, Cracker Co disposed of some items of plant and equipment. The carrying amount of these items at the date of disposal was $800,000. The depreciation charge for the year was $500,000.

(ii)   Cracker Co estimated that its liability for income taxes payables on the profit for the year ended 31 March 20X1 was $2,900,000.

Required:

Using the information available, complete the statement of cash flows for Cracker Co for the year ended 31 March 20X1 in accordance with the requirements of IAS 7 *Statement of Cash Flows*.   **(Total: 15 marks)**

Cracker Co – Statement of cash flows for the year ended 31 March 20X1

	$000	
Cash flows from operating activities		
Operating profit /Profit before income taxes*		
Adjustments for:		
Depreciation		Add/Subtract*
Gain/loss * on disposal of plant and equipment		Add/Subtract*
Change in inventories		Add/Subtract*
Change in trade receivables		Add/Subtract*
Change in trade payables		Add/Subtract*
Cash from operating activities before income taxes	N/A	
Income taxes paid		Add/Subtract*
	N/A	

Cash flows from investing activities

Interest income received		Add/Subtract*
Cash purchase of property, plant and equipment		Add/Subtract*
Disposal proceeds of plant and equipment	*Item 1*	Add/Subtract*
	_____	
	N/A	

Cash flows from financing activities

Proceeds of loan raised		Add/Subtract*
Proceeds of share issue	*Item 2*	Add/Subtract*
Finance costs paid		Add/Subtract*
	_____	
	N/A	

Net change in cash and cash equivalents for the year		Decrease/Increase*
Cash and cash equivalents at start of the year		Add/Subtract*
	_____	
Cash and cash equivalents at end of the year		
	_____	

Note: * = delete which does not apply

Item 1: Disposal proceeds of plant and equipment:

Select the correct calculation of the disposal proceeds of plant and equipment (all figures in $000):

		Selected answer
(i)	$800 – $300	
(ii)	$800 + $300	
(iii)	$800	

Item 2: Proceeds of the share issue:

Select the correct calculation of the proceeds of the share issue (all figures in $000):

		Selected answer
(i)	$11,000 – $10,000	
(ii)	$11,000 – $10,000 + $610	
(iii)	$11,000 – $10,000 – $610	

8 SPARKLER CO

The following financial statements and supporting information relate to Sparkler Co:

Statement of profit or loss and other comprehensive income for the year ended 30 September 20X9

	$000
Revenue	94,800
Less: Cost of sales	71,100
	———
Gross profit	23,700
Less: Selling expenses	2,500
Less: General and administrative expenses	1,000
Add: Profit on disposal of plant and equipment	500
	———
Operating profit/Profit before financing and income taxes	20,700
Less: Interest expense	2,700
	———
Profit before income taxes	18,000
Less: Income tax expense	3,500
	———
Profit for the year	14,500
Other comprehensive income:	
Revaluation surplus on property, plant and equipment	3,000
	———
Total comprehensive income for the year	17,500
	———

Statement of financial position at 30 September 20X9:

	20X9	20X8
	$000	$000
ASSETS		
Non-current assets		
Property, plant and equipment	95,000	85,000
Current assets		
Inventories	30,750	36,000
Trade receivables	39,250	45,000
Cash and equivalents	3,000	Nil
	———	———
Total assets	168,000	166,000
	———	———

	20X9	20X8
EQUITY AND LIABILITIES	$000	$000
Equity share capital	30,000	24,000
Share premium	10,000	8,000
Revaluation surplus	3,000	Nil
Retained earnings	60,875	66,500
Total equity	103,875	98,500
Non-current liabilities		
10% Debenture	25,000	20,000
Current liabilities		
Bank overdraft	Nil	4,500
Trade payables	35,000	38,500
Income taxes payable	3,500	4,000
Accrued interest	625	500
Total equity and liabilities	168,000	166,000

The following information is relevant to the financial statements of Sparkler Co during the year ended 30 September 20X9

(a) Sparkler Co disposed of some items of plant and equipment for sale proceeds of $2,000,000. The carrying amount of the items disposed of was $1,500,000.

(b) Sparkler Co purchased property plant and equipment at a cost of $21,000,000. In addition, land and buildings were revalued during the year.

(c) Sparkler Co estimated that its liability for income taxes payable on the profit for the year was $3,500,000.

Required:

Using the information available, complete the statement of cash flows using the indirect method for Sparkler Co for the year ended 30 September 20X9 in accordance with the requirements of IAS 7 *Statement of Cash Flows*. (Total: 15 marks)

Sparkler Co – Statement of cash flows for the year ended 30 September 20X9

	$000	
Cash flows from operating activities		
Operating profit/Profit before income taxes*		
Adjustments for:		
Depreciation		Add/Subtract*
Profit on sale of plant and equipment		Add/Subtract*
Change in inventories		Add/Subtract*
Change in trade receivables		Add/Subtract*
Change in trade payables		Add/Subtract*
	————	
Cash /from operating activities before income taxes	N/A	
Income taxes paid		Add/Subtract*
	————	
Net cash from/used in operating activities	N/A	
Cash flows from investing activities		
Cash purchase of property, plant and equipment		Add/Subtract*
Disposal proceeds of plant and equipment		Add/Subtract*
	————	
Net cash from/used in investing activities	N/A	
Cash flows from financing activities		
Proceeds of loan raised		Add/Subtract*
Proceeds of share issue		Add/Subtract*
Finance costs paid	Item 1	Add/Subtract*
Dividend paid	Item 2	Add/Subtract*
	————	
Net cash from/used in financing activities	N/A	
Net change in cash and equivalents for the year		Decrease/Increase*
Cash and cash equivalents b/f		Add/Subtract*
	———	
Cash and cash equivalents c/f		
	———	

Note: * = delete which does not apply

Item 1: Interest paid:

Select the correct calculation of finance costs paid (all figures in $000):

		Selected answer
(i)	$2,700 – $625 – $500	
(ii)	$2,700 + $500 + $625	
(iii)	$2,700 + $500 – $625	

Item 2: Dividend paid:

Select the correct calculation of dividend paid in the year:

		Selected answer
(i)	Retained earnings b/f + Profit – Retained earnings c/f	
(ii)	Retained earnings b/f + Total comprehensive income – Retained earnings carried forward	
(iii)	Retained earnings b/f – Profit + Retained earnings c/f	

9 OUTFLOW CO

The following financial statements and supporting information relate to Outflow Co:

Statement of profit or loss and other comprehensive income for the year ended 30 April 20X2

	$000
Revenue	34,760
Less: Cost of sales	(33,560)
Gross profit	1,200
Less: Selling and administrative expenses	(4,500)
Operating loss/Loss before financing and income taxes	(3,300)
Less: Interest expense	(1,000)
Loss before income taxes	(4,300)
Income tax income	500
Loss for the year	(3,800)
Other comprehensive income:	
Revaluation surplus on property, plant and equipment	2,000
Total comprehensive income for the year	(1,800)

Statement of financial position at 30 April 20X2:

	20X2	20X1
	$000	$000
ASSETS		
Non-current assets		
Property, plant and equipment – carrying amount	110,000	100,000
Current assets		
Inventories	30,000	33,000
Receivables	48,750	52,000
Income taxes receivable	500	Nil
Total assets	189,250	185,000

EQUITY AND LIABILITIES	$000	$000
Equity shares, $1	44,000	40,000
Share premium	5,000	4,000
Revaluation surplus	22,000	20,000
Retained earnings	72,450	77,250
Total equity	143,450	141,250
Non-current liabilities		
Long-term bank loan	15,500	8,000
Current liabilities		
Bank overdraft	4,000	3,250
Payables	26,300	27,500
Income taxes payable	Nil	5,000
Total equity and liabilities	189,250	185,000

The following information is relevant to the financial statements of Outflow Co for the year ended 30 April 20X2:

(a)   Outflow Co scrapped numerous items of plant and equipment during the year for nil proceeds. The items scrapped were originally purchased for $7,000,000 and they had a carrying amount of $1,000,000 at the date of disposal. The gain or loss on scrapping is included within cost of sales.

(b)   Outflow Co made a depreciation charge for the year of $11,000,000 and several buildings had been revalued during the year.

(c)   Outflow Co estimated that it would receive a tax refund of $500,000 as a result of the loss before income taxes for the year ended 30 April 20X2.

Required:

Using the information available, complete the statement of cash flows using the indirect method for Outflow Co for the year ended 30 April 20X2 in accordance with the requirements of *IAS 7 Statement of Cash Flows*.   **(Total: 15 marks)**

Outflow Co – Statement of cash flows for the year ended 30 April 20X2

	$000	
Cash flows from operating activities		
Operating loss/Loss before income taxes *	( )	
Adjustments for:		
Depreciation		Add/Subtract*
Loss on scrapped assets		Add/Subtract*
Change in inventories		Add/Subtract*
Change in receivables		Add/Subtract*
Change in payables		Add/Subtract*
	———	
Cash from operating activities before income taxes	N/A	
Income taxes paid		Add/Subtract*
	———	
	N/A	
Cash flows from investing activities		
Cash purchase of property, plant and equipment	Item 1	Add/Subtract*
	———	
	N/A	
Cash flows from financing activities		
Proceeds of loan raised		Add/Subtract*
Proceeds of share issue	Item 2	Add/Subtract*
Finance costs paid		Add/Subtract*
Dividend paid		Add/Subtract*
	———	
	N/A	
Net change in cash and cash equivalents in the year		Decrease/Increase*
Cash and cash equivalents b/f		Net cash at bank/Net overdraft*
	———	
Cash and cash equivalents c/f		Net cash at bank/Net overdraft*
	———	

Note: * = delete which does not apply

Item 1: Additions to property, plant and equipment in the year:

Select the correct calculation of the cash paid for property, plant and equipment additions in the year (all figures in $000):

		Selected answer
(i)	$110,000 + $2,000 − $100,000 + $11,000 + $1,000	
(ii)	$110,000 − $100,000 + $11,000	
(iii)	$110,000 − $2,000 − $100,000 + $1,000 + $11,000	

Item 2: Proceeds of the share issue:

Select the correct calculation of the proceeds of the share issue (all figures in $000):

		Selected answer
(i)	$40,000 + 4,000 – $44,000	
(ii)	$44,000 + $5,000 – $40,000 – $4,000	
(iii)	$44,000 – $40,000	

10 PATTY AND SELMA

The statements of profit or loss for two entities, Patty and Selma, for the year ended 31 December 20X1 are presented below:

	Patty	Selma
	$000	$000
Revenue	987	567
Cost of sales	564	336
Gross profit	423	231
General and administrative expenses	223	123
Operating profit/Profit before financing and income taxes	200	108
Interest expense	50	30
Profit before income taxes	150	78
Income tax expense	40	24
Profit for the year	110	54

The following notes are relevant to the preparation of the consolidated financial statements:

(i) Patty acquired a 70% interest in the equity shares of Selma on 1 May 20X1.

(ii) During the post-acquisition period, Patty sold goods to Selma for $120,000 including mark-up on cost of 20%. One quarter of these goods remained in the inventory of Patty at the year end.

(iii) All items of income and expense in Selma's statement of profit or loss account accrued evenly during the year.

Required:

Task 1

Complete the following consolidated statement of profit or loss for the Patty group the year ended 31 December 20X1. **(8 marks)**

	$000	
Revenue		
Cost of sales	Item 1	Add/Subtract*
	———	
Gross profit	N/A	
General and administrative expenses		Add/Subtract*
	———	
Operating profit/Profit before financing and income taxes	N/A	
Interest expense	Item 2	Add/Subtract*
	———	
Profit before income taxes	N/A	
Income tax expense		Add/Subtract*
	———	
Profit for the year	N/A	
	———	
Profit attributable to:		
Owners of Patty	N/A	
Non-controlling interest	Item 3	
	———	
	N/A	
	———	

Note: * = delete which does not apply

Item 1 – Select the correct calculation for cost of sales

	All figures are in $000	Selected answer
(i)	$564 + ($336 × 8/12) – $120 – $5	
(ii)	$564 + ($336 × 8/12) + $120 – $5	
(iii)	$564 + ($336 × 8/12) – $120 + $5	

Item 2 – Select the correct calculation for interest expense

	All figures are in $000	Selected answer
(i)	$50 – ($30 × 8/12)	
(ii)	$50 + ($30 × 8/12)	
(iii)	$50 + $30	

Item 3 – Select the correct formula to calculate the non-controlling interest share of the consolidated profit for the year

		Selected answer
(i)	(NCI% × Subsidiary's profit before income taxes × 8/12) + NCI's share of unrealised profit on inventory	
(ii)	(NCI% × Subsidiary's profit × 8/12) – NCI's share of unrealised profit on inventory	
(iii)	NCI% × Subsidiary's profit × 8/12	

Task 2

State whether each of the following statements is true or false.   **(3 marks)**

		True/False
(i)	Accounting for the acquisition of a subsidiary always includes recognition and accounting for a non-controlling interest	
(ii)	Accounting for the acquisition of a subsidiary can be achieved by using equity accounting	
(iii)	The share capital and share premium account balances of a subsidiary are not included in the consolidated statement of financial position	

Task 3

(a) **Using the individual entity financial statements, calculate the following ratios Patty and Selma for the year ended 31 December 20X1.**   **(2 marks)**

    (i) **Gross profit margin**

Patty	%
Selma	%

    (ii) **Operating profit margin**

Patty	%
Selma	%

    Note: Ratios should be calculated to one decimal place.

You have been advised that the gross profit margin of an entity, Quartz, was **higher** than that for Patty, and that the operating profit percentage of Quartz was **lower** than that for Patty.

(b) **What conclusion could you arrive at regarding the relative financial performance of the two entities?**   **(2 marks)**

		Selected answer
(i)	Patty is relatively better at minimising selling and administrative expenses than Quartz	
(ii)	Quartz is relatively better at minimising selling and administrative expenses than Patty	
(iii)	It is not possible to arrive at a conclusion regarding which entity is relatively better at minimising selling and administrative expenses	

(Total: 15 marks)

11   PENTAGON AND SQUARE

You have been presented with the following information relating to the acquisition of Square by Pentagon:

(i)   Pentagon acquired 75% of the equity shares of Square on 1 January 20X4 for a total consideration of $250,000, $150,000 of which comprised an immediate cash payment. The balance of the consideration paid consisted of a share exchange of four shares in Pentagon for every three shares of Square acquired. At the date of acquisition, the fair value of a Pentagon share was $2.50. The share issue has not yet been accounted for.

(ii)   At the acquisition date, the retained earnings of Square were $120,000 and revaluation surplus was $10,000. The fair value of the non-controlling interest in Square at the date of acquisition was $75,000.

(iii)   The fair values of the net assets of Square at the acquisition date approximated to their carrying amounts, with the exception of a plot of land. This land was recorded in the financial statements of Square at its cost of $100,000 but was estimated to have a fair value of $170,000. This land was still owned by Square at 31 December 20X4.

Extracts from the statements of financial position for Pentagon and Square as at 31 December 20X4 are presented below:

	Pentagon	Square
Equity and liabilities	$	$
Equity		
Equity shares, $1	80,000	40,000
Revaluation surplus	20,000	10,000
Retained earnings	335,000	279,000

Required:

Task 1

(a)   **Calculate the fair value of consideration paid to acquire the shares in Square.**

(1 mark)

	$
Fair value of consideration paid:	N/A
Cash	
Shares issued	Add/Subtract*

Note: * = delete which does not apply

(b)   **State the accounting entries required by Pentagon to record the issue of shares used as part of the consideration to acquire control of Square.** (2 marks)

	$	Credit/Debit
Investment in Square		
Issued share capital		
Retained earnings		
Revaluation surplus		
Share premium		

(c) **Select the correct formula to calculate goodwill arising on the acquisition of Square.**
(1 mark)

		Selected answer
(i)	Fair value of consideration paid Plus: Fair value of non-controlling interest at acquisition Plus: Fair value of net assets at acquisition date	
(ii)	Fair value of consideration paid Less: Fair value of non-controlling interest at acquisition Plus: Fair value of net assets at acquisition date	
(iii)	Fair value of consideration paid Plus: Fair value of non-controlling interest at acquisition Less: Fair value of net assets at acquisition date	

Task 2

In addition to the information provided above, the following information is also relevant to the preparation of the consolidated financial statements at 31 December 20X4.

Assets	Pentagon	Square
Non-current assets	$	$
Property, plant and equipment	205,000	179,000
Investment in Square	150,000	
Current assets		
Inventories	80,000	50,000
Trade and other receivables	60,000	99,000
Cash and cash equivalents		51,000
Current liabilities		
Bank overdraft	12,000	
Trade and other payables	48,000	50,000

During the year ended 31 December 20X4, Pentagon sold goods to Square for $30,000, including a gross profit margin of 30%. One-third of these goods were included in the inventories of Square at 31 December 20X4.

Calculate the amounts that each of the following items should be included in the consolidated statement of financial position as at 31 December 20X4. **(6 marks)**

	$
Property, plant and equipment	
Inventories	
Trade and other receivables	
Cash and cash equivalents	

Task 3

Select the formula which correctly calculates the non-controlling interest to be included in the consolidated statement of financial position as at 31 December 20X4. **(2 marks)**

	All figures are in $	Selected answer
(i)	(25% × $75,000) + (25% × ($279,000 – $120,000))	
(ii)	$75,000 + (25% × ($279,000 + $120,000))	
(iii)	$75,000 + (25% × ($279,000 – $120,000))	

Task 4

(a) **Using the individual financial statements, calculate the quick (acid test) ratio for Pentagon and Square as at 31 December 20X4.** **(2 marks)**

Pentagon	:1

Square	:1

Note: Ratios should be calculated to one decimal place.

(b) **Complete the following statement relating to the quick (acid test) ratio.** **(1 mark)**

The quick (acid test) ratio is a measure of gearing/liquidity/profitability*. A quick (acid test) ratio of 0.75:1 indicates that an entity has a higher/lower* value of current assets than current liabilities. For the purposes of this ratio, inventories are excluded/included* within the definition of current assets.

* Delete which does not apply

(Total: 15 marks)

12 PIKE AND SALMON

Pike acquired 75% of the issued share capital of Salmon on 1 January 20X6 for $8,720,000. In addition, Pike also invested in $1 million of Salmon's 5% loan notes at par value. An extract of the financial statements of Pike and Salmon as at 31 March 20X6 is presented below:

	Pike	Salmon
Equity and liabilities	$000	$000
Equity		
Share capital	9,200	4,800
Retained earnings	12,480	1,290
Total equity	21,680	6,090
Non-current liabilities		
5% loan notes 20X9	16,440	11,180
Current liabilities	2,640	1,410
	40,760	18,680

The following information is relevant to the preparation of the consolidated financial statements:

(i)   At acquisition, the fair value of land owned by Salmon exceeded its cost by $1,000,000. This land was still owned at 31 March 20X6.

(ii)   During the post-acquisition period, Salmon sold goods to Pike for $500,000, on which it earned a margin of 10%. 80% of the goods remained in Pike's inventory at the year end. At 31 March 20X6 Salmon was still owed half of the total amount invoiced to Pike for these goods.

(iii)   The fair value of the non-controlling interest in Salmon at the date of acquisition was $2,400,000.

(iv)   For the year ended 31 March 20X6, Salmon made a profit of $240,000.

Task 1

(a)   Select the formula which correctly calculates Salmon's retained earnings at the date of acquisition.   **(2 marks)**

	All figures are in $000	Selected answer
(i)	$6,090 + $240 + (3/12 × $240)	
(ii)	$1,290 − $240 + (9/12 × $240)	
(iii)	$1,290 − $240 + (3/12 × $240)	

(b)   Select the formula which correctly calculates the fair value of net assets of Salmon at the date of acquisition.   **(2 marks)**

	All figures are in $000	Selected answer
(i)	$4,800 + $1,290 + $1,000	
(ii)	$4,800 − $1,230 + (3/12 × $240) + $1,000	
(iii)	$4,800 + $1,290 − (3/12 × $240) + $1,000	

(c)   Select the formula which correctly calculates goodwill at acquisition.   **(2 marks)**

	All figures are in $000	Selected answer
(i)	$9,720 + $2,400 − $7,030	
(ii)	$8,720 + $2,400 − $7,030	
(iii)	$8,720 + $2,400 − $6,030	

Task 2

(a)   What amount should be included in the consolidated statement of financial position for the 5% Loan notes as at 31 March 20X6?   **(2 marks)**

$ _____

(b)   What amount should be included in the consolidated statement of financial position for retained earnings at 31 March 20X6?   **(2 marks)**

$ _____

You have now been provided with the following additional information relating to Pike and Salmon as at 31 March 20X6:

	Pike	Salmon
	$000	$000
Assets		
Investments at cost		
Non-current assets	26,280	13,670
Current assets	4,760	5,010
Total assets	40,760	18,680

Task 3

Complete the following table to state at what amount each of the following items should be included in the consolidated statement of financial position at 31 March 20X6.

(5 marks)

		$000
(i)	Non-current assets	
(ii)	Current assets	
(iii)	Current liabilities	
(iv)	Non-controlling interest	

(Total 15 marks)

13   PLATE AND SAUCER

The statements of profit or loss for two entities, Plate and Saucer, for the year ended 31 December 20X4 are presented below:

	Plate	Saucer
	$000	$000
Revenue	1,500	700
Less: Cost of sales	775	370
Gross profit	725	330
Less: Administrative expenses	317	135
Operating profit	408	195
Add: Interest income	15	
Profit before financing and income taxes	423	195
Less: Interest expense	60	20
Profit before income taxes	363	175
Less: Income tax expense	96	45
Profit for the year	267	130

The following notes are relevant to the preparation of the consolidated financial statements:

(i)   Plate acquired 70% of the equity shares in Saucer on 1 January 20X1.

(ii) During the year ended 31 December 20X4, Saucer sold goods to Plate for $150,000 making a mark-up on cost of 20%. One fifth of these goods remained in the inventory of Plate at the year end.

(iii) On 1 October 20X4, Plate made a $1 million loan to Saucer. Interest is charged at 6% annually in arrears.

Required:

Task 1

Complete the following consolidated statement of profit or loss for the Plate group for the year ended 31 December 20X4.   **(9 marks)**

	$000	
Revenue		
Cost of sales	Item 1	Add/Subtract*
	———	
Gross profit	N/A	
Administrative expenses		Add/Subtract*
	———	
Operating profit	N/A	
Interest income		Add/Subtract*
	———	
Profit before financing and income tax	N/A	
Interest expense	Item 2	Add/Subtract*
	———	
Profit before income taxes	N/A	
Income tax expense		Add/Subtract*
	———	
Profit for the year	N/A	
	———	
Profit attributable to:		
Owners of Plate	N/A	
Non-controlling interest	Item 3	
	———	
	N/A	
	———	

Note: * = delete which does not apply

Item 1 – Select the formula which correctly calculates cost of sales

	All figures are in $000	Selected answer
(i)	$775 + $370 + 150 – $5	
(ii)	$775 + $370 – $150 + $5	
(iii)	$775 + $370 – $150 – $5	

Item 2 – Select the formula which correctly calculates interest expense

	All figures are in $000	**Selected answer**
(i)	$60 – $20 + ($1,000 × 6% × 9/12)	
(ii)	$60 + $20 – ($1,000 × 6%)	
(iii)	$60 + $20 – ($1,000 × 6% × 3/12)	

Item 3 – Select the formula which correctly calculates the non-controlling interest share of the consolidated profit for the year

		Selected answer
(i)	(NCI% × Subsidiary's profit) – (NCI share of unrealised profit on inventory)	
(ii)	(NCI% × Subsidiary's profit) + NCI share of unrealised profit on inventory	
(iii)	(NCI% × Subsidiary's profit before income taxes) – NCI share of unrealised profit on inventory	

Task 2

Plate is considering the purchase of a shareholding in another entity and, if purchased, this investment would meet the definition of an associate.

Select which one of the following is the correct accounting treatment for an associate in the consolidated statement of financial position. (2 marks)

		Selected answer
(i)	All assets and liabilities of the associate are summed on a line-by-line basis with all other assets and liabilities of the group	
(ii)	The group share of the net assets of the associate are summed on a line-by-line basis with all other assets and liabilities of the group	
(iii)	The investment in the associate is presented as a separate line item in non-current assets	

Task 3

(a) **Using the individual entity financial statements of Plate and Saucer, calculate the operating profit margin for each entity for the year ended 31 December 20X4.** (2 marks)

Plate	

Saucer	

Note: Ratios should be calculated to one decimal place.

(b) **State whether each of the following statements is true or false** (2 marks)

		True/False
(i)	The operating profit margin will be affected by a change in the value of closing inventory, if all other factors remain unchanged	
(ii)	The operating profit margin is not affected by interest expenses incurred during the accounting period	

(Total: 15 marks)

14   PORT AND STARBOARD

The statements of financial position for Port and Starboard as at 31 December 20X6 are presented below:

Assets	Port	Starboard
Non-current assets	$	$
Property, plant and equipment	350,000	265,000
Investments	300,000	–
Current assets		
Inventories	109,000	80,000
Trade and other receivables	79,000	95,000
Cash and cash equivalents	12,000	25,000
Total assets	850,000	465,000
Equity and liabilities		
Equity		
Share capital	80,000	60,000
Share premium	20,000	10,000
Retained earnings	295,000	250,000
Non-current liabilities		
7% Bank loan 20X9	300,000	85,000
Current liabilities		
Trade and other payables	155,000	60,000
Total equity and liabilities	850,000	465,000

The following notes are relevant to the preparation of the consolidated financial statements:

(i)   Port acquired 80% of the equity shares of Starboard for $300,000 on 1 January 20X2. At the acquisition date, the retained earnings of Starboard were $150,000. The fair value of the non-controlling interest in Starboard at the date of acquisition was $80,000.

(ii)   At the date of acquisition, the fair values of the net assets of Starboard approximated their carrying amounts, with the exception of a plot of land. This land was recorded in the financial statements of Starboard at its cost of $150,000 but was estimated to have a fair value of $180,000. This land was still owned by Starboard at 31 December 20X6.

(iii) During the year ended 31 December 20X6, Port sold goods to Starboard for $50,000 making a gross profit margin on the sale of 25%. 60% of these goods had been sold by Starboard by 31 December 20X6. At the reporting date, Starboard still had a payable due to Port for $30,000, and this agreed with the receivable recorded in Port's accounting records.

Required

Task 1:

(a)   Select the formula which correctly calculates goodwill on acquisition of Starboard.

(2 marks)

		Selected answer
(i)	$300,000 + $80,000 – ($60,000 + $150,000 + $30,000)	
(ii)	$300,000 + $80,000 – ($70,000 + $150,000 + $30,000)	
(iii)	$300,000 + $80,000 – ($70,000 + $150,000 – $30,000)	

(b)   Identify which one of the following would be the correct classification for goodwill in the consolidated statement of financial position   (1 mark)

		Selected answer
(i)	A tangible non-current asset	
(ii)	A current asset	
(iii)	An intangible non-current asset	

Task 2

Complete the following table to state at what amount each of the following items should be included in the consolidated statement of financial position at 31 December 20X6.

(5 marks)

		$000
(i)	Property, plant and equipment	
(ii)	Inventories	
(iii)	Trade receivables	
(iv)	Trade and other payables	
(v)	7% Bank loan 20X9	

Task 3

(a)   What amount should be included in the consolidated statement of financial position for the non-controlling interest as at 31 December 20X6?   (2 marks)

$ _____

(b)   What amount should be included in the consolidated statement of financial position for retained earnings as at 31 December 20X6?   (2 marks)

$ _____

Task 4

Port is considering making an investment in another entity, Astern, which would be accounted for as an associate.

Which TWO of the following factors would be relevant when accounting for an associate?
(1 mark)

		Selected answer
(i)	Control of Astern	
(ii)	Exercising significant influence over Astern	
(iii)	Owning the majority of the equity shares of Astern	
(iv)	Owning between 20% and 50% of the equity shares of Astern	
(v)	Accounting for goodwill	
(vi)	Accounting for the non-controlling interest in Astern	

Task 5

State whether each of the following statements is true or false. **(2 marks)**

		True/False
(i)	If the gross profit margin of a business improves, the current ratio will also improve	
(ii)	If a bonus issue of shares is made, this will have no effect on the current ratio	

(Total 15 marks)

15 HIDE AND SEEK

The following statements of profit or loss relate to Hide and its subsidiary Seek for the year ended 30 June 20X6:

	Hide	Seek
	$000	$000
Revenue	200,000	100,000
Less: Cost of sales	110,000	50,000
Gross profit	90,000	50,000
Less: Selling expenses	20,000	10,000
Less: General and administrative expenses	40,000	20500
Operating profit/Profit before financing and income taxes	30,000	20,000
Income tax expense	10,500	6,000
Profit for the year	19,500	14,000

The following notes are relevant to the preparation of the consolidated financial statements for the year ended 30 June 20X6:

(i) Hide acquired 3 million of the $1 equity shares of Seek on 1 April 20X6 when Seek had a total of 4 million equity shares in issue, paying $8 per share.

(ii) At 1 July 20X5, the retained earnings of Seek were $9.5 million and the carrying amounts of the net assets of Seek approximated to their fair values, with the exception of land and buildings, which had a fair value of $2 million in excess of their carrying amount.

(iii) The fair value of the non-controlling interest in Seek at the date of acquisition can be measured by reference to the fair value of a Seek share at 1 April 20X6 which was $4.

(iv) During the post-acquisition period, Seek sold goods to Hide. The goods originally cost $10 million and they were sold to Hide at a mark-up of 25%. By 30 June 20X6, Hide had sold 60% of these goods.

(v) The income and expenses of Seek accrued evenly throughout the accounting period.

Required:

Task 1

Calculate goodwill arising on acquisition of Seek by Hide. **(3 marks)**

	$000
Fair value of consideration paid:	
Cash paid	
	————
Fair value of the NCI at acquisition	
	————
Fair value of net assets at acquisition:	
Share capital	
Retained earnings	Item 1
Fair value adjustment	
	————
	————
Goodwill on acquisition	Item 2
	————

Item 1 – Select the formula which correctly calculates retained earnings of Seek at the date of acquisition

	All figures are in $000	Selected answer
(i)	$9,500 + (3/12 × $14,000)	
(ii)	$9,500 + $14,000	
(iii)	$9,500 + (9/12 × $14,000)	

Item 2 – Select which of the following correctly calculates goodwill

		Selected answer
(i)	Fair value of consideration paid plus fair value of non-controlling interest at acquisition date plus fair value of net assets at acquisition	
(ii)	Fair value of consideration paid plus fair value of non-controlling interest at acquisition date minus fair value of net assets at acquisition	
(iii)	Fair value of consideration paid minus fair value of non-controlling interest at acquisition date + fair value of net assets at acquisition	

Task 2

Prepare the consolidated statement of profit or loss for the Hide group for the year ended 30 June 20X6. **(10 marks)**

Consolidated statement of profit or loss for the year ended 30 June 20X6

	$000
Revenue	
Cost of sales	Item 1
	——————
Gross profit	N/A
Selling expenses	
General and administrative expenses	
	——————
Operating profit/Profit before financing and income taxes	N/A
Income tax expense	
	——————
Profit (for the year)	N/A
	——————
Profit attributable to:	
Owners of Hide	N/A
Non-controlling interest	Item 2
	——————
	N/A
	——————

Item 1 – Select the formula which correctly calculates cost of sales

	All figures are in $000	Selected answer
(i)	$110,000 + (3/12 × $50,000) – $12,500 – $1,500	
(ii)	$110,000 + (3/12 × $50,000) – $12,500 + $1,000	
(iii)	$110,000 + (3/12 × $50,000) + $12,500 + $1,500	

Item 2 – Select which of the following correctly calculates the non-controlling interest share of group profit.

		Selected answer
(i)	Non-controlling interest share of Seek's profit for the year, minus provision for unrealised profit on inventory	
(ii)	Non-controlling interest share of Seek's post-acquisition profit for the year, plus non-controlling interest share of provision for unrealised profit on inventory	
(iii)	Non-controlling interest share of Seek's post-acquisition profit for the year, minus non-controlling interest share of provision for unrealised profit on inventory	

Task 3

Based on the individual financial statements of Hide and Seek, Hide has a lower gross profit margin than Seek.

Which one of the following statements could be a plausible explanation for this situation?

(2 marks)

		Selected answer
(i)	Seek has lower levels of inventory than Hide at the start and end of the reporting period	
(ii)	Seek is able to purchase cheaper materials and has a lower wastage rate of material than Hide	
(iii)	Seek has lower selling expenses and general and administrative expenses than Hide	

(Total: 15 marks)

16 PUSH AND SHOVE

Below are the summarised draft financial statements of Push and Shove:

Statement of profit or loss for the year ended 30 September 20X8 (extract)

	Push	Shove
	$000	$000
Revenue	85,000	42,000
Less: Cost of sales	63,000	32,000
Gross profit	22,000	10,000
Less: Operating expenses	12,000	4,500
Operating profit/Profit before financing and income taxes	10,000	5,500
Less: Interest expense	600	400
Profit before income taxes	9,400	5,100
Income tax expense	2,162	1,000
Profit for the year	7,238	4,100

Statements of financial position as at 30 September 20X8

	Push	Shove
	$000	$000
Assets		
Non-current assets		
Property, plant and equipment	40,600	22,600
Current assets	16,000	6,600
Total assets	56,600	29,200
Equity and liabilities		
Equity shares of $1 each	10,000	4,000
Retained earnings	35,400	16,500
	45,400	20,500
Non-current liabilities:		
10% loan notes	3,000	4,000
Current liabilities	8,200	4,700
Total equity and liabilities	56,600	29,200

The following information is relevant to the preparation of the consolidated financial statements of Push for the year ended 30 September 20X8:

(i) On 1 October 20X7, Push acquired 60% of the equity share capital of Shove in a share exchange of five shares in Push for six shares in Shove. The issue of shares has not yet been recorded by Push. At the date of acquisition shares in Push had a fair value of $6 each.

(ii) At the date of acquisition, the fair values of Shove's net assets were approximately equal to their carrying amounts.

(iii) Push has a policy of accounting for any non-controlling interest at fair value. The fair value of a $1 share in Shove at the date of acquisition was $3.50. Consolidated goodwill was not impaired at 30 September 20X8.

(iv) Sales by Shove to Push during the year ended 30 September 20X8 were $6 million. Shove made a mark-up on cost of 20% on these sales. One quarter of these goods remained in the inventory of Push at the year-end.

(v) At 30 September 20X8, Shove had a receivable due from Push of $1 million. This agreed with the amount payable to Shove in Push's financial statements.

Required:

Task 1

(a)   State the accounting entries required to account for the issue of shares by Push on the acquisition of Shove.   **(2 marks)**

	$000	Credit/Debit
Revaluation surplus		
Issued share capital		
Investment in Shove		
Retained earnings		
Share premium		

(b)   Calculate goodwill on acquisition of Shove   **(3 marks)**

	$000
Fair value of consideration paid	(Item 1)
	_____
Fair value of the NCI at acquisition	
	_____
Fair value of net assets at acquisition:	
Share capital	
Retained earnings	(Item 2)
	_____
	_____
Goodwill on acquisition	(Item 3)
	_____

Item 1 – Select the formula which correctly calculates the fair value of consideration paid

	All figures are in $000	Selected answer
(i)	4,000 × 60% × $6	
(ii)	4,000 × 60% × 5/6 × $1	
(iii)	4,000 × 60% × 5/6 × $6	

Item 2 – Select the formula which correctly calculates retained earnings of Shove at the date of acquisition.

	All figures are in $000	Selected answer
(i)	$16,500	
(ii)	$16,500 − $4,100	
(iii)	$35,400 − $4,100	

Item 3 – Select which of the following correctly calculates goodwill

		Selected answer
(i)	Fair value of consideration paid plus fair value of non-controlling interest at acquisition date plus fair value of net assets at acquisition	
(ii)	Fair value of consideration paid minus fair value of non-controlling interest at acquisition date + fair value of net assets at acquisition	
(iii)	Fair value of consideration paid plus fair value of non-controlling interest at acquisition date minus fair value of net assets at acquisition	

Task 2

Calculate the following figures for inclusion in the consolidated statement of financial position: **(3 marks)**

		$000
(i)	Non-current assets	
(ii)	Current assets	
(iii)	Current liabilities	

Task 3

Select which of the following correctly calculates each of the following items for inclusion in the consolidated statement of financial position: **(4 marks)**

(a) Non-controlling interest at the reporting date

	All figures are in $000	Selected answer
(i)	(4,000 × 40% × $1) + (40% × (4,100 + 250))	
(ii)	(4,000 × 40% × $3.50) + (40% × (4,100 – 250))	
(iii)	(4,000 × 40% × $6) + (40% × (4,100 + 250))	

(b) Retained earnings at the reporting date

	All figures are in $000	Selected answer
(i)	$35,400 – (60% × (4,100 + 250))	
(ii)	$45,400 – (60% × (4,100 – 250))	
(iii)	$35,400 + (60% × (4,100 – 250))	

Task 4

Select which of the following correctly calculates each of the following items for inclusion in the consolidated statement of profit or loss: **(3 marks)**

(a)   Revenue

	All figures are in $000	Selected answer
(i)	$85,000 + $42,000 – $6,000	
(ii)	$85,000 + (40% × ($42,000 – $6,000)	
(iii)	$85,000 + $42,000 + $6,000	

(b)   Cost of sales

	All figures are in $000	Selected answer
(i)	$63,000 + $32,000 – $6,000 – $250	
(ii)	$63,000 + $32,000 – $6,000 + $250	
(iii)	$63,000 + (40% × ($32,000 – $6,000 + $250))	

(Total 15 marks)

Section 3

ANSWERS TO OBJECTIVE TEST QUESTIONS – SECTION A

INTRODUCTION TO FINANCIAL REPORTING

1 C

2 D

3 A

Management require very detailed information in order to make informed decisions with regard to operations (e.g. whether to shut down a particular product line or source new suppliers).

Other parties need far less detail:

- Investors are interested in profitability and the security of their investment.

- The government is interested in profits (for tax purposes) and sales performance (in order to assess how the economy is performing).

- Lenders are interested in whether a business is solvent and able to repay their debt.

4 A

Accounting involves recording transactions as they occur and then summarising them in the form of the financial statements.

Financial accounting describes the production of financial statements for external users.

5 C

6 C

Both financial and management accounts should be equally accurate and reliable.

7 C

8 D

9 B

10 B

Tutorial note:

A sole trader may have employees. A sole trader is fully liable for the debts of the business. A sole trader may have more than one place of business, perhaps with the support of employees or managers acting on their behalf.

11 A

A limited liability company is a separate legal entity and can own assets and incur liabilities in its own name.

12 C

13 A

Equity share capital applies only to limited company financial statements. A sole trader may revalue assets but the surplus would be included in the capital account.

14 B

The dividends paid and share premium ledger accounts apply only to limited company financial statements.

15 D

All of the remaining answers include only part of the full definition of an asset.

16 A

Equity or capital of the business is represented by the net assets of the business.

17

	True	False
Each partner has limited liability for the debts of the partnership		✓
A partner is an employee of the partnership		✓
Each partner is entitled to participate in the management and running of the business	✓	
There must be a formal partnership agreement signed by all partners which specifies the respective rights, duties and obligations of the partners to each other		✓

18

	Limited liability company	Partnership
Owners or investors may receive a return on their investment in the form of a dividend	✓	
The business cannot own assets and incur liabilities in its own name.		✓
Annual financial statements are not subject to external audit		✓
Loans and borrowings for the business may be secured by a floating charge	✓	

19   B

20   D

21   C

22   B

Information is material if omitting, misstating or obscuring it could reasonably be expected to influence decisions that the primary users of general-purpose financial reports make on the basis of those reports, which provide financial information about a specific reporting entity.

23   D

Consistent accounting treatment should be applied to transactions both within an accounting period, and from one accounting period to another.

24   C

25

	Statement of profit or loss	Statement of financial position
Expenses	Correct	
Equity		Correct

26   B

27   A

28   B

Purchases should be recorded when the transaction takes place, which in this case is on receipt of the items. If a business waits until receipt of the invoice to record a purchase, there could be an opportunity for 'window dressing' of the accounts at the end of the year, by asking suppliers not to send in invoices until later.

29   A

30   C

31   C

32   D

Prudence is the exercise of caution when making judgements under conditions of uncertainty. It means that assets and income are not *over*stated (and liabilities and expenses are not understated). It does *not* allow for the overstatement of liabilities or expenses (or the understatement of assets or income). Asymmetry is *not* a qualitative characteristic of useful financial information (even though particular Standards may contain asymmetric requirements).

33   D

If applicable, the going concern concept presumes, but does not guarantee, that a business will continue in operational existence for the foreseeable future.

Commercial substance should always be reflected in financial statements, even where this differs from legal form. A revaluation surplus is not realised. However, it is credited in other comprehensive income in the statement of profit or loss and other comprehensive income and then included in the statement of changes in equity.

34   D

35   D

If a business is a going concern, it is reasonable to assume that non-current assets will be used over their useful lives. It is therefore appropriate to value a non-current asset at cost less accumulated depreciation, which represents the consumption of cost or value so far.

36

	Fundamental qualitative characteristic	Enhancing qualitative characteristic
Comparability		✓
Timeliness		✓
Faithful representation	✓	
Understandability		✓

Faithful representation is a fundamental qualitative characteristic. The other items are enhancing qualitative characteristics.

37

	Yes	No
Relevance		✓
Comparability	✓	
Faithful representation		✓
Verifiability	✓	

38 **B**

39

	Fundamental qualitative characteristic	Enhancing qualitative characteristic
Understandability		Correct
Faithful representation	Correct	

40

	Selected answer
Going concern	
Comparability	Correct
Timeliness	Correct
Relevance	

41

	Selected answer
Relevance	Correct
Reliability	
Faithful representation	Correct
Verifiability	

42 **B**

The **Framework** identifies two fundamental qualitative characteristics, relevance and faithful representation, together with a further four enhancing qualitative characteristics – comparability, verifiability, timeliness and understandability.

43

	Selected answer
Verifiability	Correct
Materiality	
Historical cost	
Understandability	Correct

44 A

45 C

46 B

THE REGULATORY FRAMEWORK

47 D

The directors of a company run the company; however, they are not personally liable for its losses. A sole trader business is owned and operated by the proprietor (sole trader).

Partners are jointly and severally liable for any losses of the business.

A company is owned by the shareholders (members) and run by the directors/management team.

48 B

49 A

50

	True	False
IFRS Accounting Standards are effective only if adopted by national regulatory bodies.	✓	
IFRS Accounting Standards provide guidance on accounting for all types of transaction.		✓

51 B

52 C

53

	True	False
It is a financial reporting standard		✓
It assists in developing IFRS based on consistent concepts	✓	
It assists preparers in developing consistent accounting policies when no Standard applies	✓	
It assists all parties in understanding and interpreting IFRS Accounting Standards	✓	

The Framework is not a Standard itself, although it is used as a reference document when new standards are developed.

54   B

The board of directors are collectively responsible for the preparation of the annual financial statements.

55   C

Disclosure is normally made to the board of directors collectively, although national law or regulation in some countries may require also that disclosure is made to the shareholders of the company.

56

	True?
Directors are collectively responsible for the preparation of the annual financial statements	Yes
Directors are always personally responsible for the financial losses incurred as a result of fraud or error in the company accounting records	
All directors are legally required to hold a professional accounting or business qualification	
Directors are collectively responsible for ensuring that the company maintains adequate accounting records	Yes

Directors may incur personal liability for losses incurred as a result of fraud or error only if they fail to discharge their duties and responsibilities effectively. There is no legal requirement for a director to hold a professional accounting or business qualification.

57   D

The board of directors collectively. The directors may delegate responsibility to another person, such as the external auditor, but they remain responsible for ensuring that that the annual financial statements are distributed to those entitled to receive them.

58   C

It is the system by which companies are directed and controlled in the interests of its shareholders and other stakeholders. Option A is a definition of the Conceptual Framework for financial reporting.

THE USE OF DOUBLE-ENTRY AND ACCOUNTING SYSTEMS

DOUBLE ENTRY BOOKKEEPING

59 **A**

60 **C**

61 **D**

An invoice is raised by a business and issued to a customer. It contains more than the amount due to be paid for goods and services supplied. It will also include the quantity and description of goods, the date of supply and the nett amount, sales tax applied and gross amount due.

62 **D**

A credit note is issued in respect of returned or damaged goods. In these circumstances the amount the customer needs to pay must be reduced. The credit note identifies the amount of the reduction.

63 **B**

The delivery note is sent with the goods to the customer. It lists the contents of the delivery. The other items are used internally for accounting and other purposes.

64 **A**

The remittance advice accompanies the cheque to settle an outstanding amount.

65 **A**

The purchase invoice is received from the supplier and indicates the amount owed for goods or services supplied. It will detail the goods and/or services supplied and contain sales tax details.

66 **B**

The goods received note is an internal document which contains the details of the delivery note but in a standard form used within the business accepting the goods. The next stage is to be charged for the goods and the amount to be paid is detailed on the invoice. The statement follows the invoices and credit notes for the month. The advice note indicates the goods are coming and arrives before the delivery note.

67 **C**

Salal is the purchaser who is being advised of the amount that needs to be paid by the invoice from the supplier. When Salal has paid, the supplier will normally send a receipt to acknowledge payment. A credit note would arise if there was a problem with the paper and Salal returned all or part of it. A goods received note is an internal record of goods delivered.

68   D

The petty cash voucher acts as a source document for petty cash transactions. It is signed by the person making the payment or asking for reimbursement and is commonly authorised by an appropriate person in the organisation. Evidence of the expenditure (such as a till receipt, a rail or bus ticket) is often stapled to the voucher. An invoice is used for credit transactions but not petty cash. Money should not be borrowed from petty cash so no IOU should appear in the petty cash records.

69   B

A paying in slip records the amount paid into the bank account and acts as a source document to update the bank ledger account. Delivery notes and goods received notes details quantities of products and not financial details so are not source documents. A statement is confirmation of transactions and includes details of source documents.

70   B

The computer does not qualify as inventory drawings as it is for the use of Nicky's family member in their role as administrator to the business.

The computer is being transferred from inventory to non-current assets by debiting the non-current assets account. It is no longer part of cost of sales and is removed from cost of sales by a credit.

71   B

Tutorial note:

Drawings, carriage inwards (an expense), prepayments, carriage outwards (expense) and opening inventory are all debit balances. Accruals, rental income and purchase returns are all credit balances.

72   C

73   A

74   D

	$	$
Revenue		256,800
Cost of sales		
Opening inventory	13,400	
Purchases	145,000	
Discount received	(3,900)	
Carriage in	2,300	
Closing inventory	(14,200)	(142,600)
Gross profit		114,200
Operating expenses		(76,000)
Carriage out		(1,950)
Operating profit		36,250

75 $3,150

Bank

	$		$
Balance b/f	1,780	Drawings (4 × $200)	800
Receipt after trade discount	570		
Receipt from customer	400		
Bankings from canteen receipts	1,200	**Balance c/f**	**3,150**
	3,950		3,950

Trade discounts are deducted at source by the seller and only the reduced amount will be payable by the customer. Therefore, the net amount of $570 must have been received during the month.

76 $2,675

Bank

	$		$
Returns of goods purchased for cash	50	Overdraft at start of month	1,340
Rental income	1,300	Payments to credit suppliers	990
Receipts from customers	4,400	Reimbursement of petty cash float	45
		Payment of electricity bill	700
		Balance c/f	**2,675**
	5,750		5,750

77   C

78

	True	False
The journal records all bank and cash transactions		✓
The journal records all accounting transactions		✓
The journal records correction of errors and year-end adjustments made in the general ledger	✓	
The journal records all credit sales transactions		✓

79 B

	Ledger Account	$
Debit	Depreciation expense – motor vehicles	10,000
Credit	Accumulated depreciation – motor vehicles	10,000

80 C

	Ledger Account	$
Debit	Irrecoverable debts expense	4,300
Credit	Receivables	4,300

The irrecoverable debts expense account normally includes irrecoverable debts written off during the year, along with the movement in the allowance for receivables. The movement in the allowance for receivables does not affect the receivables account.

81 D

	Ledger Account	$
Debit	Revenue	2,500
Credit	Disposal of machinery	2,500

82 C

	Ledger Account	$
Debit	Depreciation expense account	3,500
Credit	Accumulated depreciation account – buildings	3,500

83 B

	Ledger Account	$
Debit	Payables	250
Credit	Discount received	250

84 **D**

	Ledger Account	$
Debit	Purchases	6,400
Credit	Payables	6,400

85 **$500**

	$
Revenue	22,000
Purchases	(19,200)
(note: the business does not hold inventory)	
Rent	(5,400)
Bank interest	(825)
Heat and light	(4,475)
	———
Loss for the year	(7,900)
	———

Therefore, closing capital for the accounting period ended 30 April 20X3 =

$12,500 – $7,900 – $4,100 = $500.

86 **D**

87 **A**

88 **B**

The receipt from a credit customer would lead to an increase in cash at bank and a reduction in receivables. The net position is that total assets have not changes. Cash injected into the business would increase assets (cash and bank) and also the owner's capital account. Settlement of the amount due to the supplier would reduce the cash at bank balance. The purchase of a machine would increase assets.

89

	True	False
Business assets will always equal business liabilities		✓
Business assets will always exceed business liabilities		✓
Business assets include proprietor's capital		✓
Business liabilities include proprietor's capital		✓

Tutorial note:

The first two statements ignore proprietor's capital and therefore cannot be true. The other two statements are false as proprietor's capital is neither a business asset nor a business liability.

90   **D**

91   **B**

92   **C**

93   **D**

94   **D**

95   **A**

96   **C**

97

	True/False
With a cloud accounting system, an accountant or auditor can be granted remote access to data and information they require	True
With a cloud accounting system all employees are granted access to all data and information in the system	False

An accountant or auditor can be granted access to the cloud accounting system to enable them to prepare information and documents, such as sales tax returns or the annual financial statements. Not all employees will have access to all parts of the system. For example, access to payroll data and information is likely to be restricted to staff having responsibility for processing and management of the payroll.

98   **D**

Financial records should be maintained to enable the business owner to meet a range of uses, for both internal decision-making and to provide to external interested parties.

99   **D**

Providing information to the general public considers the external perspective of maintaining financial records.

100   **B**

Enabling the proprietor to make investment decisions considers the internal perspective of maintaining financial records.

GENERAL LEDGER ACCOUNTS AND JOURNALS

101

	True	False
The general ledger of a computerised accounting system will permit an unequal value of debits and credits to be posted for an individual transaction		✓
The journal is an integral part of the general ledger		✓
Equity accounts in a general ledger will normally have credit balances	✓	
The payables general ledger account will include accounting entries for irrecoverable debts written off		✓

102 B

$25 + $(7.25 + 12.75 + 15) = $60

Tutorial note:

The petty cash float can always be calculated by adding together the amount in petty cash at the end of the month plus the vouchers evidencing expenditure for the month.

103 $3,004

Receivables

	$		$
Balance b/f	69,472		
Revenue	697,104	Cash received	686,912
		Irrecoverable debts	1,697
		Sales returns (β)	**3,004**
		Balance c/f	74,963
	766,576		766,576

104 B

Tutorial note:

A debit balance on a supplier's account means that the business is owed money by its supplier. This could be explained by the business mistakenly paying an invoice twice. (Alternatively, a business may pay the full invoice amount and then receive a credit note from the supplier following the return of faulty goods.)

105 $38,100

Payables

	$		$
Bank	68,900	Balance b/f	34,500
Discounts received	1,200	Purchases (credit)	78,400
Purchase returns	4,700		
Balance c/f	38,100		
	————		————
	112,900		112,900
	————		————
		Balance b/f	38,100

106 $19,000

Receivables

	$		$
Revenue	250,000	Bank	225,000
Bank: cheque returned	3,500	Sales returns	2,500
		Irrecoverable debts	3,000
		Contra: payables	4,000
		Balance c/f	**19,000**
	————		————
	253,500		253,500
	————		————
Balance b/f	19,000		

107 D

Mehal has received cash (a debit entry) and the credit entry should be made to the payables general ledger account to cancel out the debit entry recorded when the second payment was made in error.

108 A

	Ledger Account	$
Debit	Receivables	12,000
Credit	Revenue	10,000
Credit	Sales tax	2,000

109 B

	Ledger Account	$
Debit	Purchases (100/115 × $1,541)	1,340
Debit	Sales tax (15/115 × $1,541)	201
Credit	Payables	1,541

Tutorial note:

The gross invoice value is credited to the payables general ledger account as that is the total liability due to the supplier. The debit entries comprise the net cost is accounted for as a purchase cost and the related sales tax element, which is recoverable.

110 A

Item B describes a purchase order. Item C describes a supplier statement. Item D describes a remittance advice.

111 C

	Ledger Account	$
Debit	Bank	5,400
Credit	Non-current asset disposal	5,400

112 C

113 D

114 A

115 $12,231 credit

Purchases

	$		$
Purchases – Jan	4,700	Journal 25	1,327
Purchases – Feb	3,387		
Purchases – Mar	5,471	**Balance carried down**	12,231
	────		────
	13,558		13,558
	────		────
Balance brought down	12,231		

116 $35,139 credit

<table>
<tr><td colspan="4" align="center">**Revenue**</td></tr>
<tr><td></td><td>$</td><td></td><td>$</td></tr>
<tr><td>Journal</td><td>854</td><td>Balance brought forward</td><td>18,471</td></tr>
<tr><td></td><td></td><td>Sales – Jun</td><td>4,200</td></tr>
<tr><td></td><td></td><td>Sales – Jul</td><td>5,387</td></tr>
<tr><td>Balance carried down</td><td>35,139</td><td>Sales – Aug</td><td>7,935</td></tr>
<tr><td></td><td>35,993</td><td></td><td>35,993</td></tr>
<tr><td></td><td></td><td>**Balance brought down**</td><td>**35,139**</td></tr>
</table>

117   C

Returns inwards are sales returns from customers. They can be thought of as 'negative sales' or 'negative income', so we debit a returns inwards account. The returns reduce the amount owed by credit customers, so we credit the receivables account (reducing an asset = credit entry).

118   A

Returns outwards are returns made to suppliers, perhaps because goods received were damaged i.e. they are 'negative purchases'. The liability to the supplier must be reduced and the returns outwards account is credited. At the end of the year, the total of returns outwards will be offset against the purchases expense to reduce the net cost of purchases.

119   C

Trade discount should not be recognised in the general ledger accounts. Settlement discount relating to the early payment of amounts due to suppliers is discount received.

120   C

This is a transaction that records an increase in non-current assets (motor vehicle) and an increase in capital.

121   D

Before the debt was written-off it was recognised in receivables (with or without a related allowance for doubtful debts). To remove the debt receivables will be credited and a charge for irrecoverable debts will be recognised in profit or loss.

RECORDING TRANSACTIONS AND EVENTS

SALES, PURCHASES, SALES TAX AND DISCOUNTS

122 $655.50

	$
Price	600.00
Less: trade discount (5% × $600)	(30.00)
	570.00
Add: sales tax at 15% (15% × $570)	85.50
	655.50

Tutorial note:

Sales tax is always charged on the selling price net of trade (bulk purchase) discount given.

123 $75,788

Sales tax

	$		$
		Balance b/f	23,778
Tax on purchases		Tax on sales	
$\dfrac{17.5\%}{117.5\%} \times \$590{,}790$	87,990	17.5% × $800,000	140,000
Balance c/f	**75,788**		
	163,778		163,778
		Balance b/f	75,788

124 $962.50

Sales tax

	$		$
Tax on purchases (input tax)		Tax on sales (output tax)	4,112.50
($18,000 × 17.5%)	3,150.00	($27,612.5 × 17.5/117.5)	
Balance c/f	962.50		
	4,112.50		4,112.50
		Balance b/f	962.50

125 C

	$
Sales net of sales tax	90,000
Purchases net of sales tax	(72,000)
	————
	18,000
	————
Tax payable @ 10%	$1,800

As sales exceed purchases, the excess sales tax is payable to the tax authorities.

126 $5,300

Sales tax

	$		$
Tax on purchases	6,000	Balance b/f	3,400
Bank	2,600	Tax on sales	10,500
Balance c/f	5,300		
	————		————
	13,900		13,900
	————		————
		Balance b/f	5,300

Tax on sales (outputs) = 17.5% × $60,000 = $10,500

Tax on purchases (inputs) = (17.5/117.5) × $40,286 = $6,000

127 B

Revenue is recorded exclusive of sales tax in the statement of profit or loss.

128 B

The receivables account should be debited with the full amount due from the customer, including the tax. The entry in the sales account should be for the sales value excluding sales tax. Sales tax payable to the tax authorities should be credited to the sales tax account (liability = credit balance).

129 A

The receivables account should be credited with the full amount of the sales return, including the tax. The sales returns account should be debited with the value of the returns excluding the sales tax. The sales tax account should be debited with the amount of tax on the returns (since the tax is no longer payable).

130 C

The supplier is owed the full amount of the invoice, including the sales tax, so the credit entry in the payables general ledger account must be $9,200. The non-current asset account is recorded at cost excluding the sales tax. The input tax is recoverable, so debit the sales tax account with $1,200.

131

	True	False
Sales tax is a form of indirect taxation	✓	
If input tax exceeds output tax the difference is payable to the tax authorities		✓
Sales tax is included in the reported sales and purchases of a sales tax registered business		✓
Sales tax cannot be recovered on some purchases	✓	

If input tax (tax on purchases) exceeds output tax (tax on sales), the difference is recoverable from the tax authorities. Sales and purchases are reported net of sales tax. Sales tax cannot be recovered on certain expenses (such as client entertaining) and purchases (such as cars).

132 $578,200

Payables

	$		$
Cash paid	542,300	Balance b/f	142,600
Discounts received	13,200		
Goods returned	27,500		
Balance c/f	137,800	Purchases (β)	578,200
	———		———
	720,800		720,800
	———		———

133 $84,000

Receivables

	$		$
Balance b/f	10,000	Receipts (less cash sales)	80,000
Credit sales (β)	**79,000**		
		Balance c/f	9,000
	———		———
	89,000		89,000
	———		———

Revenue = cash sales $5,000 + credit sales $79,000 = $84,000.

134   C

Cash

	$		$
Balance b/f	300	Bankings	50,000
Proceeds of sale of car	5,000	Wages	12,000
Sales (β)	**81,100**	Drawings	24,000
		Balance c/f	400
	_____		_____
	86,400		86,400
	_____		_____

135   A

The balance on the sales tax account is calculated as:

Credit sales ($121,000/100 × 20) =	$24,200
Credit purchases ($157,110/120 × 20) =	($26,185)
	_____
	($1,985)
	_____

The sales tax on the credit purchases (input tax) exceeds the sales tax on sales (output tax), the balance on the account represents an amount due to Ashvini, therefore is an asset, a debit.

136   A

Carriage inwards is an expense incurred in bringing goods purchased into the business, and carriage outwards is an expense incurred in delivering goods to customers.

137   C

The receivables account should be credited with the full amount of the sales return, including the sales tax. The sales returns (returns inwards) should be debited with the value of the returns excluding the sales tax. The sales tax account should be debited with the amount of tax on the returns (as the output tax will no longer be payable).

138 $920

	$
Price	800
Less: trade discount (8% × $800)	(64)
	_____
	736
Add: sales tax (25% × $736)	184
	_____
	920
	_____

139 C

Trade discount is always deducted when calculating the amount invoiced by the seller. In addition, as Smith was not expected to take account of the early settlement discount terms, the amount of revenue receivable is calculated after deduction of trade discount only at $950 ($1000 × 95%). When Smith subsequently pays early to be eligible for the discount, the accounting entries should reflect that fact and record settlement of the amount outstanding and also reduced revenue.

Debit Bank $912 ($950 × 96%), Debit Revenue $38 ($950 × 4%), and Credit Receivables $950.

140 B

Trade discount is always deducted when calculating the amount invoiced by the seller. In addition, as Jones is expected to take account of the early settlement discount terms, the amount of revenue receivable is calculated after deduction of both trade discount and early settlement discount, a total of $2,280 ($2,500 × 95% × 96%). When Jones subsequently pays early to be eligible for the discount, the accounting entries should reflect the receipt of cash and clearance of the receivable for the amount expected as follows:

Debit Bank $2,280 and Credit Receivables $2,280.

141 D

Trade discount is always deducted when calculating the amount invoiced by the seller. In addition, as Black is expected to take account of the early settlement discount terms, the amount of revenue receivable is calculated after deduction of both trade discount and early settlement discount, a total of $4,104 ($4,500 × 95% × 96%). When Black subsequently pays outside the settlement discount period, the full amount of the receivable $4,275 ($4,500 × 95%) is due. The additional cash received in excess of the receivable amount of $171 is therefore accounted for as a cash sale as follows:

Debit Bank $4,275, Credit Revenue $171 and Credit Receivables $4,104.

142 A

Trade discount is always deducted when calculating the amount invoiced by the seller. In addition, as White is not expected to take account of the early settlement discount terms, the amount of revenue receivable is calculated after deduction of trade discount only, a total of $3,515 ($3,700 × 95%). When White subsequently pays outside the settlement discount period as expected, the full amount of the receivable is due.

Debit Bank $3,515, and Credit Receivables $3,515.

143 B

Trade discount is always deducted and, in addition, as Green is expected to take account of the early settlement discount terms, the amount of revenue receivable is calculated after deduction of trade discount and early settlement discount, a total of $1,276.80 ($1,400 × 96% × 95%). When Green subsequently pays outside the settlement discount period, the full amount of $1,344 ($1,400 × 96%) is due and the additional amount received of $67.20 ($1,344.00 – $1,276.80) is accounted for as a cash sale.

Debit Bank $1,344, and Credit Receivables $1,276.80 and Credit Revenue $67.20.

CASH

144 B

145 $385

	$
Opening float	150
Receipts	
Photocopier use	25
Bank	500
Payments	
Cheque cashed	(90)
Payments (β)	**385**
	———
Closing float	200
	———

146 $70.00

	$
Balance of petty cash in hand	66.00
Add: Sundry purchases	22.00
Loan to sales manager	10.00
Purchase of staff drinks	19.00
Less: Sundry sales receipts	(47.00)
	———
Imprest balance	70.00
	———

147 $32

A total of $35 ($20 + $5 + $10) has been paid out of petty cash and $3 has been received into petty cash. Therefore, the amount required to replenish petty cash to the imprest amount is $32.

INVENTORY

148 $500

The inventory should be valued at the lower of cost and NRV.

Cost is $500 and NRV is ($1,200 – $250) = $950. The correct valuation is therefore $500.

149 B

If prices have fallen during the year, AVCO will give a higher value of closing inventory than FIFO, which values goods for resale at the latest prices. Where the value of closing inventory is higher, profits are higher.

150 A

Opening inventory + units purchased	440
Units sold	(290)
	——
Closing inventory (units)	150
	——
FIFO Closing inventory: 150 units @ $2.78	**$417**
	——

AVCO Weighted average cost	$
100 units @ $2.52	252
140 units @ $2.56	358
200 units @ $2.78	556
——	——
440	1,166
——	——
Average cost per unit	1,166/440 = $2.65
AVCO Closing inventory: 150 units @ $2.65	**$397.50**
FIFO higher by ($417.00 – $397.50)	**$19.50**

Tutorial note:

The periodic weighted requires the total cost of the inventory to be divided by the total units in the period to determine the weighted average cost for the period. This weighted average figure will then be used to value the inventory.

151 $56,640

The number of units held at the year-end is 1,180 (1,200 – 20).

The sale on 31 December provides evidence of a net realisable value $2 below cost. Therefore, each unit should be valued at its net realisable value:

1,180 units × $48 = $56,640.

152

	True	False
Inventory should be valued at the lower of cost, net realisable value and replacement cost.		✓
When valuing work in progress, materials costs, labour costs and variable and fixed production overheads must be included.	✓	
Inventory items can be valued using either first in, first out (FIFO) or weighted average cost.	✓	
An entity's financial statements must disclose the accounting policies used in measuring inventories.	✓	

Tutorial note:

Inventory should be valued at the lower of cost and net realisable value. Replacement cost is irrelevant.

153 C

When inventory is included in purchases at cost and closing inventory is stated at cost, the effect on profit is $0 (the same amount is both a debit and a credit in the statement of profit or loss).

In this case, only the credit is recorded (closing inventory). Therefore, profit is overstated by the cost of the fabric. The inventory valuation is not misstated, as it includes the fabric received on 29 June.

154 A

Tutorial note:

Inventory drawings are credited to purchases in order to remove them from cost of sales, as these goods have not been sold. Inventory is counted and valued at the year-end date.

155 B

Opening inventory must be removed from the statement of financial position inventory account (a credit) and expensed to the statement of profit or loss as part of cost of sales (a debit).

Closing inventory must be debited on to the statement of financial position as an asset and removed from the cost of sales (a credit).

156 $39,900

	$
Value at 7 July 20X6	38,950
Sales since year end (100/125 × $6,500)	5,200
Purchase since year end	(4,250)
	———
Value at 30 June 20X6	39,900
	———

157 $155

	Items	Unit value	
		$	$
Opening inventory	6	15	90
January: purchases	10	19.80	198
	——		——
	16	18	288
February: sales	(10)	18	(180)
	——		——
	6	18	108
March: purchases	20	24.50	490
	——		——
	26	23	598
March: sales	(5)	23	(115)
	——		——
	21	23	483
	——		——
Sales (15 × $30)			450
Cost of sales ($180 + $115)			(295)
			——
Gross profit			155
			——

158 $1,110

Date		Units	Unit value	Inventory value
			$	$
1 October	Opening inventory	60		720
8 October	Purchase 40 units at $15	40		600
14 October	Purchase 50 units at $18	50		900
		——		——
		150	14.80	2,220
21 October	Sold 75 units: cost	(75)	14.80	(1,110)
		——		——
31 October	Closing inventory	75	14.80	1,110
		——		——

159   A

The net realisable value of inventory items is the selling price less the 4% commission payable.

	NRV	Lower of cost or NRV
	$	$
Henry VII	2,784	2,280
Dissuasion	3,840	3,840
John Bunion	1,248	1,248
		─────
		7,368
		─────

160   D

The closing inventory of 12 items (15 – 5 + 10 – 8) comprise

	$
10 items at $3.50 each	35.00
2 items at $3 each	6.00
	─────
Cost on a FIFO basis is	41.00
	─────

161   B

Tutorial note:

If the inventory was not included in the original valuation of closing inventory, closing inventory will be increased by $1,000 (the lower of cost and net realisable value). Since closing inventory is $1,000 higher, cost of sales is $1,000 lower and profit $1,000 higher.

162 $4,700

	Net realisable value	Lower of cost or NRV	Units	Value
	$	$		$
Basic	8	6	200	1,200
Super	8	8	250	2,000
Luxury	10	10	150	1,500
				─────
Total value				4,700
				─────

163   A

When prices are rising, FIFO will give a higher valuation for closing inventory, because the closing inventory will consist of the most recently-purchased items. Higher closing inventory means lower cost of sales and higher profit.

164 C

In contrast, if continuous weighted average cost per unit is calculated, a new cost per unit is calculated each time a purchase is made.

165 A

In contrast, if periodic weighted average cost per unit is calculated, this would be done at the end of the accounting period.

166 $85.00

	Units	Unit cost $	Total cost $
2 Feb	10	5.00	50.00
5 Feb	(6)	5.00	(30.00)
	4		20.00
7 Feb	10	6.50	65.00
	14	6.07	85.00

167 $80.50

Total cost of purchases/total units) = ((10 × $5.00) + (10 × $6.50))/20 units = $5.75 per unit. Closing inventory valuation is therefore 14 units × $5.75 = $80.50.

168 $73.50

Total cost of purchases/total units) = ((4 × $4.00) + (10 × $5.00) + (10 × $6.00))/24 units = $5.25 per unit. Cost of sales is therefore 14 units × $5.25 = $73.50.

169 $71.70

	Units	Unit cost $	Total cost $
1 Apr	4	4.00	16.00
12 Apr	10	5.00	50.00
	14	66.00/14 = 4.71	66.00
15 Apr	(6)	4.71	(28.26)
	8		37.74
17 Apr	10	6.00	60.00
	18	97.74/18 = 5.43	97.74
25 Apr	(8)	5.43	(43.44)
	10		54.30

Cost of sales = $28.26 + $43.44 = $71.70.

170   C

The alternative answers deal with aspects of management accounting. Option C deals with financial accounting and reporting which requires that inventory is quantified and valued at each accounting year end for inclusion in the financial statements.

TANGIBLE NON-CURRENT ASSETS

171   C

Asset register	$	General ledger accounts	$
Carrying amount per question	85,600	Carrying amount per question	130,000
Addition of land	30,000	Disposal at carrying amount	(14,400)
	———		———
	115,600		115,600
	———		———

172   A

			$
1.1.X4	Cost	235,000	
	Depreciation at 30%	(70,500)	
		———	164,500
y/e 31.12.X4	Depreciation at 30%		(49,350)
			———
y/e 31.12.X5	Carrying amount		115,150
	Depreciation at 30%		(34,545)
			———
y/e 31.12.X6	Carrying amount		80,605
			———
	Accumulated depreciation (70,500 + 49,350 + 34,545)		154,395

Therefore

1	Uplift cost account to valuation	Dr Non-current asset $65,000
2	Remove depreciation to date	Dr Accumulated depreciation $154,395
3	Send the balance to the revaluation surplus	Cr Revaluation surplus $219,395

173   D

A non-current asset register is a detailed schedule of non-current assets and is not another name for non-current asset ledger accounts in the general ledger.

174 **$192,600**

			$
Depreciation on additions:	20% × $48,000 × 6/12	=	4,800
Depreciation on disposals:	20% × $84,000 × 9/12	=	12,600
Depreciation on other assets:	20% × (960,000 – 84,000)	=	175,200
			———
			192,600
			———

175 **$50,600**

	$
Cost of plant	48,000
Delivery	400
Modifications	2,200
	———
	50,600
	———

Tutorial note:

The warranty cost cannot be classed as asset expenditure. This is an expense which must be debited to the statement of profit or loss.

176 **B**

		$	$	$
Year 1	Cost less dep'n @ 20%	2,400.00	(480.00)	1,920.00
Year 2	Dep'n (20% × $1,920)		(384.00)	1,536.00
Year 3	Dep'n (20% × $1,536)		(307.20)	1,228.80
Year 4	Sale proceeds			1,200.00
				———
	Loss on disposal			(28.80)
				———

177 **B**

	$	$
Original balance		125,000
Carrying amount of assets sold:		
Proceeds	9,000	
Less: Profit	(2,000)	(7,000)
	———	———
Adjusted balance		118,000
		———

178 $86,000

	$
Purchase cost of machine	80,000
Installation	5,000
Pre-production safety testing	1,000
	86,000

A non-current asset should be measured initially at its cost. 'Cost' means the amounts incurred to acquire the asset and bring it into working condition for its intended use. These include the purchase cost, initial delivery and handling costs, installation costs and professional fees. Costs of testing whether the asset is working properly may be included, but staff training costs cannot be capitalised.

179 A

	$
Cost	5,000
Year 1 (20% × 5,000)	(1,000)
Year 2 (20% × 4,000)	(800)
Year 3 (20% × 3,200)	(640)
Carrying amount at time of disposal	2,560
Sale proceeds	2,200
Loss on disposal	360

180 $4.72 million

	$m
Non-current assets at cost	10.40
Accumulated depreciation	(0.12)
Carrying amount	10.28
Revaluation amount	15.00
Transfer to revaluation surplus	4.72

181 D

Painting and replacing windows are maintenance and repairs, and so are classified as an expense and must be taken to the statement of profit or loss. The purchase of a car for resale means that the car is an item of inventory for the business, not a non-current asset. Legal fees incurred in purchasing a building are included in the cost of the building, and so are part of the non-current asset cost, i.e. asset expenditure.

182 D

Disposals account

	$		$
Cost	12,000	Accumulated depreciation (3 years × 20% × $12,000)	7,200
Profit (β)	200	Proceeds (part exchange allowance)	5,000
	12,200		12,200

183 $510,000

	Cost	Accum dep'n	Carrying amount
	$000	$000	$000
Opening balance	860	397	
Disposal	(80)	(43)	
	780	354	
Purchase	180		
Depreciation (10%)		96	
	960	450	510

184 C

185 $12,500

Depreciation charge 1 Jan – 30 June: 2% × $500,000 × 6/12 = $5,000.

Accumulated depreciation at date of revaluation = $95,000 + $5,000 = $100,000 – i.e. 10 years have passed.

Total estimated useful life is 50 years, with a remaining estimated useful life of 40 years. Thus depreciation for second half of year = $600,000 / 40 years × 6/12 = $7,500. The total depreciation charge for the year = $5,000 + $7,500 = $12,500.

186 D

The reducing balance method charges more depreciation in earlier years than in later years. It is therefore appropriate to use for assets such as motor vehicles that lose a large part of their value in the earlier years of their life.

187 $5,000 LOSS

Annual depreciation = $(40,000 – 10,000)/6 years = $5,000. The machine was used for four years before disposal, giving accumulated depreciation of 4 × $5,000 = $20,000.

When the machine was sold, its carrying amount was $40,000 – $20,000 = $20,000. It was sold for $15,000, giving a loss on disposal of $5,000 as follows:

	$
Disposal proceeds	15,000
Carrying amount at disposal date	20,000
	———
Loss on disposal	5,000
	———

188 D

Do not include the vehicle tax in the cost of the car. Road tax is an expense item.

	$	Acc dep'n $	Proceeds $	Profit $
Cost of asset	10,000			
Depreciation 20X1 (25% × $10,000)	(2,500)	2,500		
Depreciation 20X2 (25% × ($10,000 – $2,500))	(1,875)	4,375		
Depreciation 20X3 (25% × ($10,000 – $4,375))	(1,406)	5,781		
Depreciation 20X4 (25% × ($10,000 – $5,781))	(1,055)	6,836		
	———		———	———
Carrying amount at time of disposal	3,164		5,000	1,836
	———		———	———

189 $3,610

Initial depreciation charge p.a. $\dfrac{\$20,000 - \$500}{10 \, \text{years}} = \$1,950$

Carrying amount at date of change $20,000 – $1,950 = $18,050

New depreciation charge (for y/e 30 June 20X9 onwards) $\dfrac{\$18,050}{5 \, \text{yrs}} = \$3,610$

Note that the revision of estimations takes place in the year ended 30 June 20X9 before the depreciation for that year is charged.

190 $625 PROFIT

The capitalised cost of the truck is $20,000 – the insurance cost is not capitalised but accounted for as an expense in profit or loss. The net cost of the truck is: $17,000 ($20,000 – $3,000) and the annual depreciation charge will be $2,125 ($17,000/8 years).

At the disposal date, the business had owned the truck for exactly five years – therefore accumulated depreciation to disposal date is $10,625, giving a net carrying amount of $9,375 ($20,000 – $10,625). As the trade-in allowance is $10,000, this will result in a profit on disposal of $625.

191 A

The revaluation surplus balance as at 31 October 20X2 is being asked for. When revaluing an asset, it is the carrying amount of the asset which is revalued, rather than the cost, and as the question states there is no annual transfer of the excess depreciation, the balance on the revaluation surplus can be found as: $150,000 – $81,600 = $68,400.

As the revaluation takes place on 1 November 20X1, a whole year's depreciation is calculated on the revalued amount. The new charge will take the revalued amount of $150,000 and depreciate the asset over its remaining useful life. By looking at the accumulated depreciation brought forward you can tell how old the original asset is.

Original depreciation charge: $102,000/50 years = $2,040 per annum and as $20,400 is accumulated depreciation brought forward, then the asset must have already been held for 10 years. Therefore, the remaining useful life is 50 years – 10 years = 40 years. The new depreciation charge should be calculated as: $150,000/40 years = $3,750.

192 Option 1 – Optional and Option 2 – Statement of changes in equity

When an entity has revalued a non-current asset, it is **optional** to account for excess depreciation arising on the revaluation. When excess depreciation is accounted for, the accounting adjustment is reflected in **the statement of changes in equity**.

Tutorial note:

Note that when an entity does decide to account for excess depreciation, it must apply that accounting policy every year and cannot apply the policy in some years and not in others.

193 $5,400

Annual depreciation charge before revaluation: 2% × $480,000 = $9,600

Years since purchase: $480,000 – $384,000 / $9,600 = 10 years

Total estimated useful life is 50 years, with a remaining estimated useful life of 40 years. Thus depreciation following revaluation: $600,000 / 40 = $15,000.

Amount of excess depreciation = $15,000 – $9,600 = $5,400.

194 C

195

	Statement 1	Statement 2
True	✓	
False		✓

IAS 16 *Property, Plant and Equipment* (para 31) states that when the revaluation model is used, revaluations should be made with sufficient regularity to ensure that the carrying amount of the assets remains close to fair value. IAS 16 also states (para 36) that, if one item in a class of assets is revalued, all the assets in that class must be revalued.

196 A

When revaluing an asset, the revaluation surplus can be identified as the difference between the revalued amount and the carrying amount of the asset = $38,400 ($120,000 – $81,600).

As the revaluation takes place on 1 November 20X1, a full year's depreciation is calculated on the revalued amount. The new charge will take the revalued amount of $120,000 and depreciate the asset over its remaining useful life.

Original depreciation charge: $102,000/50 years = $2,040 per annum and as $20,400 is accumulated depreciation brought forward, then the asset must have already been owned for 10 years. Therefore, the remaining useful life is 40 years.

The new depreciation charge should be calculated as: $120,000/40 years = $3,000 per annum. The excess depreciation transfer between accumulated depreciation and revaluation surplus is $960 ($3,000 – $2,040). The balance on revaluation surplus at 31 October 20X2 is $37,440 ($38,400 – $960).

197

	Statement 1	Statement 2
True		
False	✓	✓

IAS 16 requires that, if the revaluation model is adopted, all items of the same class must be accounted for on the same basis. However, it is possible for, e.g. land and buildings to be accounted for using the revaluation model, whilst other classes of property, plant and equipment (e.g. plant and equipment) to be accounted for using the cost model.

The annual transfer of 'excess depreciation' is an accounting policy choice made by an entity when it revalues any class of property, plant and equipment. Note, however, that if this treatment is adopted, it must be applied every year, rather than applied some years and not in other years.

198 $140,000

The profit on disposal is calculated using the carrying amount of the building at the date of disposal (i.e. $450,000 – $310,000). The revaluation surplus does not form part of the calculation of profit or loss on disposal.

199 D

The revaluation surplus does not form part of the calculation of profit or loss on disposal. Instead, it is transferred to retained earnings within equity.

200 $900 LOSS

The cost of the asset is $15,000 – the cost of the maintenance agreement is not capitalised but accounted for as a payment in advance and charged to profit or loss as an expense over three years. The net cost of the asset is: $13,000 ($15,000 – $2,000) and will be depreciated at 20% per annum.

At the disposal date, the business had owned the asset for 3.5 years – therefore accumulated depreciation to disposal date is $9,100, giving a net carrying amount of $5,900 ($15,000 – $9,100). As the trade-in allowance was $5,000, this will result in a loss on disposal of $900.

201 **$752,115**

	$
Property cost	750,000
Legal costs	7,500
Architect's fees	9,200
Alterations to property	25,000
	———
	791,700
Depreciation ($791,700/20 years)	(39,585)
	———
Carrying amount	752,115
	———

The annual maintenance cost is not asset expenditure.

202 **A**

To reverse the original error, the motor vehicles cost account needs to be reduced and the motor expense recorded. Therefore (1) is correct.

The incorrect depreciation adjustment now needs to be reversed. When depreciation is charged this is accounted for as Dr depreciation expense and Cr accumulated depreciation. So, to reverse this entry (4) is correct.

203 **B**

The carrying amount of the asset as at 1 July can be calculated as:

	$
Cost	30,000
Accumulated depreciation ($30,000 × 3/10 years)	(9,000)
	———
Carrying amount	21,000
	———
Reassessing the original useful life as 15 years means there must be 12 years remaining. Therefore, depreciation is $21,000/12	1,750
	———

204 **$10,000**

Depreciation is calculated as: (Revalued amount − Residual value)/Remaining useful life

= ($41,000 − $1,000)/4 years = $10,000

Note that four years remain as the machine was depreciated for three years prior to the revaluation (in the year of acquisition (20X5), and 20X6 and 20X7).

INTANGIBLE ASSETS

205 C

206 A

Tutorial note:

When accounting for intangible assets using the revaluation model, movements in the carrying amount are accounted for in other comprehensive income and other components of equity.

207 B

Answer (A) is not precise enough – there must be an annual impairment review to ensure that the asset is not overstated in the financial statements.

208

	Capitalised	Not capitalised
Employment costs of staff conducting research activities		✓
Cost of constructing a working model of a new product	✓	
Materials and consumables costs associated with conducting scientific experiments		✓
Licence purchased to permit production and sale of a product for ten years	✓	

209 B

When accounting for intangible assets using the cost model, annual impairment charges are accounted for in the statement of profit or loss.

210

	Research expense	Intangible asset
Market research costs	✓	
Patented product design costs		✓
Product advertising	✓	
Employee training costs	✓	

211 A

Tutorial note:

An intangible asset may be internally generated (e.g. development costs) or purchased (e.g. a brand name) – therefore answers B and D are incorrect. Answer C is incorrect as assets can normally be sold.

212

	Written off as an expense	Capitalised as an asset
Project 1 is applying a new technology to the production of heat-resistant fabric. On completion, the fabric will be used in the production of uniforms for the emergency services. Geranium has sufficient resources and the intention to complete the project.		✓
Project 2 is testing whether a particular substance can be used as an appetite suppressant. If this is the case, it is expected be sold worldwide in chemists and pharmacies.	✓	
Project 3 is developing a material for use in kitchens which is self-cleaning and germ resistant. A competitor is currently developing a similar material and, for this reason, Geranium is unsure whether its project will be completed.	✓	

The costs of a development project are capitalised only if:

- The project is separately identifiable.
- Expenditure can be reliably measured.
- It is commercially viable.
- It is technically feasible.
- It is projected to be profitable.
- Resources are available to complete it.

Project 2 falls short of these criteria: it does not appear that the appetite suppressant properties of the substance have yet been confirmed and therefore it is not yet commercially viable.

Project 3 may not be completed and therefore does not meet all six criteria.

The costs of projects 2 and 3 should be expensed to the statement of profit or loss and other comprehensive income.

213 $34,000

	$
Project A	34,000

Project A is a research project and all costs should be written off to the statement of profit or loss and other comprehensive income as incurred.

214 C

The initial capitalised cost of the brand is: $44,880 + $20,400 = $65,280. Therefore, the annual amortisation charge is: 65,280 / 8 = $8,160. The accumulated amortisation balance at 30 April 20X6 is: $20,400 + $8,160 = $28,560.

215 $540,000

The licence will be amortised on a straight-line basis over five years: $3,600,000 × 1/5 = $720,000 per annum. For the year ended 31 March 20X4, this will be pro-rated for nine months: $720,000 × 9/12 = $540,000.

216 D

The initial capitalised cost of the licence is: $17,500 + $12,500 = $30,000. Therefore, the annual amortisation charge is: 30,000 / 6 = $5,000. The accumulated amortisation balance at 31 December 20X6 is: $12,500 + $5,000 = $17,500.

217

	True
Research costs should be expensed to the statement of profit or loss.	✓
All types of goodwill can be capitalised.	
Capitalised development costs that no longer meet the criteria specified by IAS 38 must be written off to the statement of profit or loss.	✓
Capitalised development costs are amortised from the date the assets is available to use or sell.	✓
Research costs written off can be re-capitalised when the developed asset is feasible.	
Only purchased intangibles can be capitalised.	

218 $78,870

	$
Project B	78,870

Project B is a development project. Costs can only be capitalised when the capitalisation criteria are met. Those costs incurred before this was the case cannot be reinstated as an asset.

219 $34,422

	$
Project C ($290,000 + $19,800) × 4/36	34,422

Project C is a development project which has resulted in capitalised expenditure. This asset must be amortised over the 36 months of sales of the product. Amortisation for the current year should be 4 months (1 September to 31 December 20X5).

220 B

221

		Capitalised as intangible asset	Not capitalised as intangible asset
1	$48,000 on staff costs relating to the development of a new product that is expected to generate future economic benefits	✓	
2	$35,000 on advertising a new product which was successfully developed during the year. It is expected that the advertising campaign will generate additional economic benefits for Companies Co		✓
3	$180,000 on laboratory equipment which will be used to build new product prototypes		✓
4	$22,000 on the cost of testing whether a separately acquired intangible asset is functioning properly	✓	

(1) The staff costs can be capitalised as development costs because the product 'is expected to generate future economic benefits (i.e. it can be assumed that all other recognition criteria have been met).

(2) Advertising costs are specifically prohibited from being capitalised as an intangible asset (IAS 38 *Intangible Assets*).

(3) The expenditure relates to laboratory equipment (an item of property, plant and equipment) not the prototype.

(4) Costs of testing should be capitalised as a 'directly attributable cost of preparing the asset for its intended use'.

ACCRUALS AND PREPAYMENTS

222 $453,600

Rental income (property 1 and 2)

	$		$
Balance b/f	5,400	Balance b/f	12,300
Statement of profit or loss		Cash received	
rental income (β)	**453,600**	(280,000 + 160,000)	440,000
Balance c/f	6,700	Balance c/f	13,400
	―――――		―――――
	465,700		465,700
	―――――		―――――
Balance b/f	13,400	Balance b/f	6,700
	―――――		―――――

223 $858,600

Rental income

	$		$
Balance b/f	42,300	Balance b/f	102,600
Statement of profit or loss (β)	**858,600**	Cash received	838,600
Balance c/f	88,700	Balance c/f	48,400
	―――――		―――――
	989,600		989,600
	―――――		―――――

224 A

		$
Statement of profit or loss	9/12 × $10,800	8,100
	3/12 × $12,000	3,000
		―――――
		11,100
		―――――
Statement of financial position prepayment	9/12 × $12,000	9,000

225 D

Statement of profit or loss (5/12 × $24,000) + (7/12 × $30,000) = $27,500

Statement of financial position $7,500 paid on 1 January therefore amount prepaid by tenant is: 2/3 × $7,500 = $5,000. For Vine this is prepaid/deferred income, i.e. income received in advance – a liability.

226 A

Charge to profit or loss = $1,800 × 7/12 = $1,050. Prepayment $1,800 × 5/12 = $750

227 $385

Motor expenses

	$		$
Balance b/f (insurance)	80	Balance b/f (fuel)	95
Cash paid – petrol	95		
– other bills	245	**Statement of profit or loss (β)**	**385**
Balance c/f (petrol)	120	Balance c/f (insurance)	60
	540		540

The insurance prepayment covers 4 months as at the start of September. Therefore there must be a prepayment of 3 months at the end of September.

228 ACCRUAL $560 and EXPENSE IN PROFIT OR LOSS $3,320

The accrual for May and June 20X3 is assumed to be 2/3 × $840 = $560.

Electricity expenses

	$		$
Bank	600	Opening balance b/f	300
Bank (720 + 900 + 840)	2,460		
Closing balance c/f	560	Statement of profit or loss	3,320
	3,620		3,620

229 $12,600

The premium for the year 1 July 20X2 to 30 June 20X3 was $13,200 × 1/1.1 = $12,000

Statement of profit or loss charge:

6 months at $12,000 plus 6 months at $13,200 = $6,000 + $6,600 = $12,600

230 B

The charge in the statement of profit or loss will be the amount of interest incurred from 1 January (when the loan was taken out) to 30 September (the year end) i.e. 9/12 × 12% × $100,000 = $9,000. This represents three interest payments.

However, as only two interest payments were made (1 April and 1 July) the third payment due to be made on 1 October, which relates to the three months to 30 September, will be accrued: 3/12 × 12% × $100,000 = $3,000.

231 C

	$
Prepayment brought forward at the start of the year	10,000
Payment during the year	36,000
	46,000
Less: Prepayment carried forward at the year end (7 months, therefore $36,000 × 7/12)	(21,000)
Charge for insurance in the statement of profit or loss	25,000

232 B

Accrued income is income not yet received for a service already provided (income received in arrears). The correct double entry to record accrued income is:

Dr Accrued income (statement of financial position), Cr Income (statement of profit or loss) which will increase profit.

233 C

The meter rental charge covers the period 1 Oct – 31 Dec and has been paid before the year end. Therefore, there is a prepayment of two months rental as follows: ($60 × 2/3) = $40.

The usage charge is paid in arrears and has been paid up to 30 Sept – therefore an accrual of one month is required as follows: ($135 × 1/3) = $45.

RECEIVABLES

234 B

Receivables account

	$		$
Balance b/f (W)	13,150	Cash	115,500
Sales	125,000	Irrecoverable debts	7,100
		Balance c/f	15,550
	138,150		138,150

	b/f	c/f
	$	$
Gross receivables	13,150	15,550
Allowance	(1,150)	(2,100)
Net receivables	12,000	13,450

235 D

Receivables

	$		$
Balance b/f	34,500	Cash received	247,790
Credit sales (β)	278,090	Contra	1,200
		Irrecoverable debts	18,600
		Balance c/f	45,000
	312,590		312,590
Balance b/f	45,000		

Total sale = Credit sales + Cash sales = $278,090 + $24,000 = $302,090

Note: Discounts received are relevant to the payables ledger account.

The double-entry for the increase in allowance for receivables is:

Dr Irrecoverable debts expense	12,500
Cr Allowance for receivables	12,500

236 B

Receivables

	$		$
Balance b/f	84,700	Contra with payables	5,000
Credit sales	644,000	Irrecoverable debts	4,300
		Cash received from credit customers	625,780
		Balance c/f	93,620
	728,700		728,700

The double entry for a contra is Dr payables Cr receivables.

Discounts received are relevant to payables not receivables. Cash sales should not feature in the receivables account.

The correct double entry for the increase in the allowance for receivables is Dr irrecoverable debts expense and Cr allowance for receivables.

237 A

	$	Allowance $	Expense $
Receivables balance (draft)	58,200		
Irrecoverable debts	(8,900)		8,900
	49,300		
Specific allowance: Carroll	(1,350)	1,350	
Jay	(750)	750	
Mai	(1,416)	1,416	
Allowance c/f		3,516	
Allowance b/f		5,650	
Decrease in allowance		2,134	(2,134)

Total expense = $8,900 – $2,134 = $6,766

238 B

The write off of debts will reduce the gross receivables balance by $72,000 to $766,000.

The allowance is to be adjusted to $60,000 (hence an adjustment of $12,000).

The net balance is therefore $766,000 less $60,000, i.e. $706,000.

239 A

Year-end receivables	5% × $7,000,000	=	$350,000
Year-end allowance for receivables	4% × $350,000	=	$14,000
Allowance at start of year	100/120 × $14,000	=	$11,667
Increase in allowance		=	$2,333

Irrecoverable debts expense

	$		$
Write off of irrecoverable debts	3,200	Recovery of irrecoverable debts	450
Increase in allowance	2,333	Statement of profit or loss (β)	5,083
	5,533		5,533

240 B

Receivables

	$		$
Balance b/f	10,000	Receipts	90,000
Sales	100,000	Contra with payables	800
Irrecoverable debts recovered	1,000	Balance c/f	20,200
	———		———
	111,000		111,000
	———		———

241 C

When a debt is written off as irrecoverable, the transaction is recorded as:

Dr Irrecoverable debts account (expense) and Cr Receivables.

Any subsequent change to the allowance for receivables should be dealt with as a separate matter.

242 A

Receivables

	$		$
Balance b/f	37,500	Contra with payables	15,750
Sales (credit)	357,500	Irrecoverable debts written off	10,500
		Bank (β)	329,750
		Balance c/f	39,000
	———		———
	395,000		395,000
	———		———

Cash sales do not affect receivables. Discounts received affect payables, not receivables.

The allowance for receivables does not affect the amount of receivables, but specific irrecoverable debts written off do affect receivables.

243 A

Receivables (5% of $2 million) = $100,000. Required specific allowance for receivables = $4,000. Current allowance for receivables = $4,000 × ¾ = $3,000. Increase in allowance = $1,000. An increase in the allowance for receivables reduces profits.

244 A

	$
Irrecoverable debts written off (800 + 550)	1,350
Irrecoverable debt recovered	(350)
Reduction in allowance for receivables	(200)
	———
Charge to statement of profit or loss	800
	———

245 B

The allowance for receivables will reduce the carrying amount of receivables. An increase in an allowance for receivables will therefore reduce net current assets.

246 A

	Receivables	Allowance	P&L
	$	$	$
Balance brought forward	230,000	11,700	
Write off irrecoverable debts	(11,429)		11,429
Reduction in allowance		(10,270)	(9,999)
	———	———	
Balance carried forward	218,571	1,430	
			———
Net charge to P&L			1,159
			———

247 D

Tutorial note:

In comparison with making cash sales, the provision of credit will not improve the cash flow position of the business, rather it may result in a deterioration of cash flow. This is particularly true as some customers will be late in paying and others will not pay at all.

248 C

Tutorial note:

An aged receivables analysis is a list of how much each credit customer owes and how old their debt is. It enables the credit control function to identify which customers to follow up and contact, and also helps in the calculation of the allowance for receivables at the year-end. Separate information should be maintained of credit approval of customers, together with agreed limits.

249 $6,966

	$	$
Balance on the receivables' account:	425,700	
Less: irrecoverable debts	(8,466)	8,466
	417,234	
Specific allowance required	(2,400)	2,400
Irrecoverable debt recovered		(2,000)
		8,866

The question states that the allowance for receivables at 1 April 20X3 was $1,900. The receivables expense for the year ended 31 March 20X4 is therefore $8,866 – $1,900 = $6,966.

250 C

> **Tutorial note:**
>
> *Selling goods on credit incurs a risk to the entity as the customer may not pay within the credit period. Even if the customer does make payment, there is a cost incurred in providing credit to the customer and the entity should ensure that such costs are incurred only for appropriate customers who are expected to pay within the agreed credit period.*

251 D

> **Tutorial note:**
>
> *When a debt is regarded as irrecoverable, it is removed from receivables and written off as an expense. Therefore, the best accounting treatment is to record the credit entry in the ledger account in which the original debt was made i.e. the irrecoverable debt expense account.*

252 B

253 C

254 D

255 D

256 **$34,500**

	$
Opening balance as at 1 January 20X6	24,500
Cash received	(102,300)
Discounts allowed	(3,100)
Interest on overdue payments	1,600
Contra agreement	(8,200)
Credit sales	133,700
Returns inwards	(5,000)
Irrecoverable debt	(6,700)
	————
Closing balance as at 31 December 20X6	**34,500**
	————

Note that the discount allowed must be deducted from the opening receivables balance as the sale was originally recorded at its gross amount (discount was not expected to be taken when the invoice was first issued). If the discount was expected to be taken when the invoice was first issued, no adjustment to the receivables balance would be required as the receivable would have been recorded net of the discount.

PAYABLES, PROVISIONS AND CONTINGENCIES

257 **B**

258 **B**

259 **A**

260 **C**

The maximum possible contra is $850, as anything in excess of this result in Zed Co's payable ledger account balance with G Co into a debit balance.

261

	Selection
Discount allowed	
Returns inwards	
Discount received	✓
Irrecoverable debts	
Returns outwards	✓

262 **D**

263 $367,300

	$
Trade payables b/f 1 May 20X4	130,000
Purchases for the year (β)	**367,300**
Payment made	(340,000)
Contra with trade receivables' ledger	(3,800)
Discount received	(3,500)
	———
Trade payables c/f 30 April 20X5	150,000
	———

264

	Provision required	Provision not required
A retail outlet has a policy of providing refunds over and above the statutory requirement to do so. This policy is well publicised, and customers have made use of this facility in the past.	✓	
A customer has made a legal claim against an entity, claiming that faulty goods sold to them caused damage to their property. The entity's lawyers have advised that the claim will possibly succeed and, if it does, compensation of $10,000 will be payable.		✓

Tutorial note:

Based upon the stated and publicised policy it would appear probable that customers who return goods in accordance with the policy will expect to receive a refund – this requires a provision. The outcome of the legal claim has been assessed as only possible (rather than probable) that there will be an outflow of economic benefits. This does not require a provision, only a disclosure note of the contingent liability.

265 A

266 A

Warranties meet the criteria required to recognise a provision; a provision should be made for the best estimate of the obligation. The likelihood of a liability arising for Q Co as a result of the guarantee is assessed as possible. A provision cannot be recognised in the financial statements unless the likelihood is probable.

267 C

A is incorrect – a contingent asset is only recognised and accounted for if it is virtually certain to arise.

B is incorrect as only contingent assets which are regarded as probable are disclosed in the notes to the financial statements.

D is incorrect as a contingent liability which is regarded as probable must be recognised and accounted for in the financial statements.

268 D

A is incorrect – a contingent asset is only recognised and accounted for if it is virtually certain to arise.

B is incorrect as contingent assets can be recognised if they are virtually certain.

C is incorrect as a contingent liability which is regarded as remote can be ignored when preparing the financial statements.

For the same reason, D is correct as contingent liabilities which are regarded as remote can be ignored when preparing the financial statements.

269 B

(1) is incorrect – a provision may be classified as a non-current liability when the probable outflow of economic benefits is expected to occur more than 12 months from the reporting date.

(2) is correct as normally a liability can be precisely quantified whereas quantification of a provision requires estimation and judgement.

(3) is correct – there is a future probable outflow of economic benefits, but the exact amount and/or date of the outflow is still to be confirmed.

270 C

Tutorial note:

IAS 37 requires that a provision should be recognised when it is probable that there will be a future outflow of economic benefits as a result of a past event.

Based upon the licence terms, damage has already been caused which will cost $5 million to rectify in 20X7 or later. This should be recognised and classified as a non-current liability. If damage has not yet been caused, there is not yet an obligation to rectify it. Therefore at 31 August 20X4 no provision can be made for expected future damage.

271 D

IAS 37 requires that a provision should be recognised when it is probable that there will be a future outflow of economic benefits as a result of a past event. Therefore, a provision to settle customer claims should be recognised. As it is only probable that the counter-claim against Bottler will succeed, it cannot be recognised in the statement of financial position – it is disclosed in the notes to the financial statements.

272 C

An increase in the provision from $10,000 to $13,000 requires that a charge is made in profit or loss and that the provision balance within current liabilities is increased by the same amount.

273 B

Tutorial note:

IAS 37 requires that a provision should be recognised when it is probable that there will be a future outflow of economic benefits as a result of a past event. Contingent liabilities that are regarded as possible, rather than probable, should be the subject of a disclosure note in the financial statements.

274

	Yes	No
A manufacturer gives warranties to its customers. The terms of the warranty require the company to repair any defects in its products that arise within two years of the date of sale. The company expects that around 2% of sales each year will result in claims under the warranty.	✓	
A coal-mining company operates in a country where there is no legislation requiring the company to repair environmental damage. The company causes environmental damage but has a widely publicised policy of repairing this damage.	✓	

The first situation is an example of a legal obligation. The warranty gives rise to a legal obligation, at the point of sale, to repair any defects within two years.

The second situation is an example a constructive obligation. The coal-mining company has widely publicised that it will repair any environmental damage, raising a valid expectation of a third party.

CAPITAL STRUCTURE AND FINANCE COSTS

275

	True	**False**
A rights issue capitalises retained earnings or other components of equity, which can be a disadvantage, as this can reduce the amount available for future dividends.		✓
A rights issue is offered to the company's existing shareholders and is usually at a discounted price compared to the nominal value of a share.		✓

As 'capitalisation' describes a bonus issue, the first statement must be incorrect. A rights issue raises cash resources at an issue price less that market value. A rights issue is offered to existing shareholders and does bring in cash but at a discounted price compared to the market value of a share, not its nominal value.

276

	Selection
Bank	✓
Retained earnings	
Interest expense	
Equity	
Long-term debt	✓

On issue of redeemable preference shares, the two items affected would be the bank ledger account to record the receipt of cash and secondly, long-term debt. This is because, although legally they are shares, in substance redeemable preference shares are more like debt (as they have fixed return and are repayable/redeemable at a future date).

277 D

Opening retained earnings + profit – prior year final dividend = closing retained earnings

Opening retained earnings = $79,285 – $12,200 – $320,568

Opening retained earnings = $253,483

278 $15,000

	$
Profit for the year	36,000
Dividend	(21,000)
Added to retained earnings	15,000

You should recognise that it is the profit for the period less any dividend paid that is added to the retained earnings balance. Accounting for the revaluation does not affect retained earnings for the year – this is recognised in other comprehensive income and presented as a revaluation surplus within other components of equity.

279 B

280 D

281 C

Tutorial note:

A rights issue is an issue of shares for cash. It is usually made at less than full market price to encourage current shareholders to take up the share issue.

282 C

A bonus issue of shares is a free issue of shares to current shareholders on a pro-rata basis in relation to their current shareholding.

283

	True	False
Dividends paid by an entity are excluded from the statement of changes in equity		✓
Dividends received by an entity are included in the statement of changes in equity.		✓
Dividends received by an entity are excluded from the statement of changes in equity.	✓	
Dividends paid by an entity are included in the statement of changes in equity.	✓	

Dividends received are accounted for in the statement of profit or loss as income. Dividends paid are accounted for in the statement of changes in equity.

284 C

Tutorial note:

Dividends are paid from retained earnings. They must not be accounted for as an expense in the statement of profit or loss.

285 D

Debit / Credit	Ledger Account	$
Debit	Bank (20,000 × $1.75)	35,000
Credit	Share capital ($20,000 × $1)	20,000
Share premium	Share premium ($20,000 × $0.75)	15,000

286 B

The accounting entries would be:

Dr Share premium $31,250, and Cr Share capital (250,000/4) = 62,500 × $0.50 = $31,250

287 B

A limited company may choose to (or not) revalue its land and buildings. A limited company may (or may not) make a share issue at a premium. When a share issue is made, the company must receive at least the nominal value of the shares issued, although often it will receive a premium in excess of the nominal value.

288 D

Redeemable preference shares have the characteristics of a liability as they will be redeemed at some future date which will require an outflow of economic benefits. They should be classified as a liability, rather than equity.

289 C

Total comprehensive income for the period is the profit or loss plus other comprehensive income (OCI) = -$87,455 (loss) + $145,000 (increase in revaluation surplus) = $57,555.

Dividends are not deducted from profit for the year (nor OCI) as they are distributions of profit to the owners of the business (shareholders). Dividends are deducted from retained earnings and disclosed in the statement of changes in equity.

290 B

A bank loan and redeemable preference shares are non-current liabilities which are included in the statement of financial position. A dividend received is a source of income recognised in the statement of profit or loss. A dividend paid is a deduction from retained earnings which will be included in the statement of changes in equity.

291 A

The existing loan note of $300,000 was in issue between 1 April 20X8 and 1 January 20X9 (i.e. nine months). The new loan note of $300,000 began on 1 June 20X8 and was still in issue at the reporting date of 31 March 20X9 (i.e. 10 months).

	$
1 April 20X8 – 31 December 20X8	
($300,000 × 6% × 9/12)	13,000
1 June 20X8 – 31 March 20X9	
($500,000 × 9% × 10/12)	37,500
	51,000

292 B

The missing profit figure can be calculated as follows:

	$
Retained earnings at 31 March 20X5	119,460
Ordinary dividend (200,000 × $0.25)	(50,000)
Bonus issue	(25,000)
Profit for the year (β)	**101,250**
Retained earnings at 31 March 20X6	145,710

Note that redeemable preference dividends are interest expense in the statement of profit or loss (i.e. included in the balancing profit figure).

RECONCILIATIONS

BANK RECONCILIATIONS

293 D

	$		$
Bank balance per question (credit)	(1,350)	Balance per bank statement (β)	(1,707)
Standing order not recorded	(300)	Unpresented cheques	(56)
		Uncleared lodgements	128
		Bank error	(15)
Revised bank balance	(1,650)	Revised bank balance	(1,650)

On the bank statement the overdrawn balance is shown as a debit (i.e. from the bank's perspective they are owed money).

294 B

Note that the ledger account balance shows an overdraft, however the bank statement shows a positive balance:

	Bank statement	Ledger account
	$	$
Balance per question	250	(190)
Unpresented cheques	(150)	
Misposting of cash receipt		260
Bank interest		30
	——	——
	100	100
	——	——

295

	True	False
When preparing a bank reconciliation, unpresented cheques must be deducted from a balance of cash at bank shown in the bank statement.	✓	
A cheque from a customer paid into the bank but dishonoured must be corrected by making a debit entry in the bank ledger account.		✓
An error by the bank must be corrected by an entry in the bank ledger account.		✓
An overdraft is a debit balance in the bank statement.	✓	

Item 1 – unpresented cheques are those issued by a business but not yet banked by the recipient. They should be deducted from the balance shown on the bank statement to reflect the true bank balance.

Item 2 – a dishonoured cheque is recorded by crediting the bank ledger account. The cheque would previously have been debited to the bank ledger account when received. The credit is the reversal of that entry.

Item 3 – a bank error should be corrected by amendment to the balance per the bank statement.

Item 4 – from the bank's perspective an overdraft means that they are owed money by the customer. Hence it is shown as a debit (an asset to the bank) in the bank statement.

296 B

	$
Balance per bank statement (overdrawn)	(38,640)
Add: Lodgement not credited	19,270
	(19,370)
Less: Unpresented cheques	(14,260)
Balance per bank ledger account	(33,630)

297 B

	$
Balance per bank statement (overdrawn)	(200)
Unpresented cheques	(1,250)
Error	97
Uncleared lodgements	890
Revised balance = revised bank ledger account balance	(463)

298 B

	$		$
Bank ledger account	(8,970)	Bank statement balance (β)	(11,200)
Bank charges	(550)	Unpresented cheques	(3,275)
		Uncleared lodgements	5,380
		Bank error	(425)
Revised bank balance	(9,520)	Revised bank balance	(9,520)

299 B

Cash at bank

	$		$
Original balance (β)	11,960	Dishonoured cheque	300
Error: receipt recorded as payment (2 × $195)	390	Bank charges	50
		Balance c/f (= revised bank ledger account balance)	12,000
	12,350		12,350

	$
Bank statement balance	13,400
Unpresented cheques	(1,400)
Revised bank ledger account balance	12,000

300 D

	$	
Balance per bank statement	(715)	
Less: Unpresented cheques	(824)	
Add: Outstanding lodgements	337	
	(1,202)	
Less: Bank error	(25)	
Statement of financial position/bank ledger account balance	(1,227)	(overdraft)

301 D

Bank

	$		$
Reversal of standing order (entered twice)	125	Draft balance	5,675
Revised balance	6,450	Dishonoured cheque	900
	6,575		6,575

The dishonoured cheque for $450 should have been credited to the bank balance. Instead it was debited. The bank balance is therefore too high by $900.

302 B

Bank

	$		$
Cash sales	1,450	Balance b/f	485
Cash receipts	2,400	Payments to suppliers (95% × $1,800)	1,710
		Dishonoured cheques	250
		Balance c/f	1,405
	3,850		3,850

303 B

	$
Balance per bank statement	(800)
Unpresented cheque	(80)
Revised bank balance	(880)

The dishonoured cheque requires adjustment in the bank ledger account. After this adjustment, the bank ledger account balance will be the revised bank balance to be shown in the statement of financial position.

304 B

Bank

	$		$
Draft balance	2,490	Bank charges	50
		Dishonoured cheque	140
		Revised balance	2,300
	2,490		2,490

305 A

Bank

	$		$
		Draft balance	1,240
Revised balance	1,315	Bank charges	75
	1,315		1,315

	$
Balance per bank statement (β)	(1,005)
Unpresented cheques	(450)
Uncleared lodgements	140
Revised bank ledger account balance	(1,315)

306 C

An unrecorded difference is a transaction that is reflected on the bank statement but has not yet been recorded in the bank ledger account – usually because the accountant is not aware of the transaction until advised by the bank. Examples include direct debits, standing orders, bank charges, bank interest, dishonoured cheques and direct credits. Uncleared lodgements and unpresented cheques are examples of timing differences – amounts which have been recorded in the bank ledger account but have not yet 'cleared' the bank.

307 A

	$
Adjusted bank ledger account balance per bank reconciliation	1,060
Outstanding lodgements	(5,000)
Unpresented cheques	2,800
Balance overdrawn at the bank	(1,140)

On the bank statement an overdraft will appear as a debit balance.

PAYABLES ACCOUNT RECONCILIATIONS

308 D

	Payables' ledger $	Supplier statement $
Per question	230	3,980
Cheque (1)		(270)
Goods returned (2)		(180)
Contra (3)		(3,200)
Revised balance	230	330

Difference $100 (330 – 230)

309 B

	Lee's records $
Per question	14,500
Unrecorded discount	(150)
Revised balance = supplier statement	14,350

Lee Co believes that the amount owed is $150 more than the supplier has stated. Items A, C and D would result in a different outcome.

310 B

	$		$
Balance per payable ledger	260	Balance per supplier's statement	1,350
Cash discount disallowed	80	Less: Goods returned	(270)
		Less: Cash in transit	(830)
Adjusted payable ledger	340	Revised balance	250

Unreconciled difference = ($340 – $250) = $90

311 C

312 D

313 D

314 C

If Spark had paid the supplier, it's payable account balance would be lower than that of the supplier. Similarly, the return of goods to the supplier would reduce the supplier account balance by $75. If the supplier had issued an invoice for $75, the balance on the supplier statement would be higher by an additional $75. If the supplier has granted settlement discount to Spark Co, which Spark Co has not yet accounted for, this would explain the difference.

315 C

	$
Alpha – statement balance	3,465
Automated payment not recorded by Alpha	(690)
Invoice not recorded by Rome Co	(280)
	———
Payable ledger account balance	2,495
	———

316 C

There is no error in the general ledger. The error lies in the coding and allocation of the purchase invoice to the wrong payable ledger account.

317 D

	$
Beta – statement balance	4,278
Contra not recorded by Beta	(784)
	———
Updated payable ledger balance	3,494
	———

318 A

	$
Payable ledger account balance for Delta	6,045
Payment and discount not recorded on Delta statement	414
Goods returned not on Delta statement	105
	———
Balance per statement issued by Delta	6,564
	———

319 D

The general ledger account for payables needs to be increased by $22 to reflect the fact that discount received previously recorded was not confirmed by the supplier. The opposite entry in the general ledger is to reduce discount received by $22. Remember that the payable ledger accounts of individual suppliers do not form part of the double-entry recording process in the general ledger.

320 C

	$		$
Zeta – statement balance	9,613	Payable ledger balance	7,672
Automated payment not recorded by Zeta	(1,506)	Invoice not recorded by Portofino Co	435
	_____		_____
	8,107		8,107
	_____		_____

321 D

	$
Balance per statement issued by Theta	4,278
Contra not yet recorded on statement	(784)
Invoice not yet recorded by Genoa Co	(543)
	_____
Balance per Genoa Co payable ledger account for Theta	2,951
	_____

322 A

	$
Payable ledger account balance for Kappa	4,368
Discount not granted by Kappa	22
Goods returned not on Kappa statement	532
	_____
Balance per statement issued by Kappa	4,922
	_____

323 D

	$		$
Rho – statement balance	7,278	Payable ledger balance	5,639
Contra not yet recorded by Rho	(2,471)	Credit note not yet recorded by Lecce Co	(832)
	_____		_____
	4,807		4,807
	_____		_____

324 B

	$		$
Sigma – statement balance	4,684	Payable ledger balance	3,034
Bank payment not yet recorded	(1,342)	Credit note not yet recorded by Parma Co	(276)
		Invoice not yet recorded by Parma Co	584
	3,342		3,342

325 C

	$		$
Omega – statement balance	1,783	Payable ledger balance	1,213
Contra not yet recorded	(421)	Credit note not yet recorded by Turin Co	(92)
		Invoice not yet recorded by Turin Co	241
	1,362		1,362

326 B

	$		$
Tau – original statement balance	5,432	Payable ledger balance	4,575
Invoice included in error	(875)	Credit note not yet recorded	(18)
	4,557		4,557

327 A

	$		$
Omicron – statement balance	8,314	Payable ledger balance	7,224
Automated payment	(2,546)	Invoice included in error	(1,456)
	5,768		5,768

328 B

The closing balance on the payables general ledger account will be a liability of $37,765.

329 C

	$		$
Phi – statement balance	8,866	Payable ledger balance .	6,727
Automated payment not on statement	(1,605)	Invoice not yet recorded by Trento Co	534
	_____		_____
	7,261		7,261
	_____		_____

PREPARING A TRIAL BALANCE

TRIAL BALANCE

330 C

All three items are limitations of a trial balance.

Figures in the trial balance are not necessarily the final figures to be reported in the financial statements; they are subject to year-end adjustments.

Errors of commission (where an entry has been posted to the wrong account) are not identified by the trial balance since an equal debit and credit entry are still posted.

Although a trial balance can identify if double entry has broken down, it does not indicate in which accounts wrong entries were made.

331

	True	False
The trial balance provides a check that no errors exist in the accounting records of a business.		✓
The trial balance is one of the financial statements prepared annually by an entity for its shareholders.		✓

When a trial balance agrees, this does not confirm that no errors have been made in the accounting records. Only those errors resulting from accounting entries without an equal debits and credits will be highlighted by the trial balance. An entity will prepare the statement of profit or loss and other comprehensive income, the statement of financial position, the statement of cash flows and the statement of changes in equity. The trial balance is not one of the financial statements prepared by an entity for its shareholders.

332 $4,500

	$	$
Property, plant and equipment	209,000	
Inventory	4,600	
Receivables and payables	5,900	6,300
Bank overdraft		790
Loan		50,000
Capital		100,000
Drawings	23,000	
Sales		330,000
Purchases	168,200	
Sales returns	7,000	
Sundry expenses	73,890	
Discounts received (β)		4,500
	491,590	491,590

333 B

	Increase	Decrease	
	$	$	$
Closing inventory	45,700		
Depreciation (20% × $470,800)		94,160	
Irrecoverable debt		230	
Deferred income		6,700	
	45,700	101,090	
Decrease in net assets			55,390

334 C

335 $23,690

	$	$
Sales		120,000
Opening inventory	2,600	
Purchases	78,900	
Closing inventory	(1,900)	(79,600)
Gross profit		40,400
Rental expense (3,400 – 200)	3,200	
Sundry expenses	13,900	
Bank interest	(270)	
Decrease in allowance	(120)	(16,710)
Operating profit		23,690

336 B

Depreciation charge	= Closing cost × percentage depreciation rate
	= **$5,000** (10% × $50,000)
Closing accumulated depreciation	= Accumulated depreciation b/f + charge for the year
	= $15,000 + $5,000 = $20,000
Carrying amount	= Closing cost less closing accumulated depreciation
Carrying amount	= $50,000 − $20,000 = **$30,000**

337 C

	Charge for the year					**Closing**
	$					$
Rent	24,000	Rent accrual				
		(12 × $2,000)	Due	24,000		
			Paid	22,000		
				———		2,000
Insurance	28,000	Insurance prepayment				
			Paid	30,000		
			Due	28,000		
				———		2,000

The rental charge in the statement of profit or loss will be $24,000 ($2,000 × 12 months). Only $22,000 has been paid, therefore an accrual of $2,000 will appear in the statement of financial position. The insurance charge will be according to the notes given after the trial balance totalling $28,000. The amount paid is $30,000, thus a prepayment of $2,000 will appear in the statement of financial position.

Note: In the trial balance the amount paid will be shown.

338 A

		$
Irrecoverable debts	1,600 + 3,000	4,600
Decrease in allowance for receivables (W1)		(440)
		———
Total irrecoverable debt expense		4,160
		———
Receivables	(29,600 – 3,000 irrecoverable debt)	26,600
Less: Closing allowance for receivables		(2,660)
		———
Net closing receivables		23,940
(W1) – movement in allowance for receivables		
Closing allowance for receivables		2,660
Opening allowance for receivables		3,100
		———
Decrease in allowance for receivables		440
		———

339 D

Depreciation charge = (Closing cost – accum dep'n b/f) × %age rate = ($50,000 – $21,875) × 25% = $7,031

Closing accumulated depreciation = Accum dep'n b/f + charge for the year = $21,875 + $7,031 = $28,906

Carrying amount = Closing cost less closing accum dep'n

Carrying amount = $50,000 – $28,906 = $21,094

340 $952,000

	Dr	Cr
	$	$
Premises and accumulated depreciation	500,000	120,000
Opening inventory	23,000	
Share capital		200,000
Retained earnings		105,000
Receivables	43,500	
Payables		35,900
Carriage in	1,500	
Allowance for receivables		3,400
Bank overdraft		1,010
Revenue		486,690
Purchases	359,700	
Sales returns	10,300	
Sundry expenses	14,000	
	———	———
	952,000	952,000

CORRECTION OF ERRORS

341 $93,000

Adjusted profit:

	$
Draft profit	78,500
Inventories write down to net realisable value ($112,000 – $120,000)	(8,000)
Capital expenditure (incorrectly expensed)	30,000
Depreciation charge ($30,000 × 25%)	(7,500)
	———
Adjusted profit	93,000
	———

342 A

The revised profit is calculated as:

	$
Draft profit	65,800
Sales invoice adjustment (2)	(1,000)
	————
Revised profit	64,800
	————

Error 1 does not affect profit as the correcting entries (Dr Bank and Cr Receivables) both affect the statement of financial position.

Error 3 does not affect profit as the correcting entries (Dr IT expense and Cr Depreciation expense) both affect the statement of profit or loss.

343 C

There is no change in the profit for the year. Profit is only affected when one (but not both) side of the correction journal is posted to the statement of profit or loss. Both entries in the journal to record cash drawings are to statement of financial position accounts. The expense of $420 has already been recorded when the allowance was made during the year.

To correct the misclassification, interest income will be reduced and rental income increased by the same amount. Accounting for the receipt from the credit customer does not affect the statement of profit or loss. Therefore, there is no effect on profit.

344 D

The error has been to debit the receivables account and credit the payables account, instead of debiting the supplier account and crediting the customer account. As a result, receivables are over-stated by 2 × $270 = $540, and payables are over-stated by $540. The error must be corrected, but sales and purchases are unaffected, so profit is unaffected. Total assets (receivables) and total liabilities (payables) are both $540 too high, so that net assets are unchanged.

345 C

	Current assets	Current liabilities
	$	$
1 – cash received and deferred income recognised	5,000	5,000
2 – reduction in bank balance to pay premium	(5,000)	
2 – insurance prepayment (3/6 × $5,000)	2,500	
3 – Loan cash received	12,000	
3 – interest accrual (5% × $12,000 × 6/12)		300
	————	————
Current assets and current liabilities	14,500	5,300
	————	————

Note that the liability to repay the loan is a non-current liability.

346 $72,200

$57,400 + $15,500 − (($15,500 − $1,500)/10 × 6/12) = $72,200

347 C

An error of principle breaks the 'rules' of an accounting principle or concept, for example incorrectly treating an expense as an item of asset expenditure. The purchase of a non-current asset should be debited to a non-current asset account, not to the purchases account.

348 B

The sales tax included within the purchase invoice is $750 × 20/120 = $125. The purchase cost needs to be reduced and input sales tax recorded with the following journal adjustment:

Dr Sales tax $125, and Cr Purchases $125

The gross amount of the invoice due to the supplier is unchanged.

349 D

The sales tax on this purchase is $3,300 × 20% = $660. The purchase cost needs to be reduced and input sales tax recorded with the following journal adjustment:

Dr Sales tax $660, and Cr Purchases $660

The gross amount of the invoice due to the supplier was correctly recorded and remains unchanged.

350 B

A gain arising on revaluation of a non-current asset should be accounted for in revaluation surplus, a component of equity. It should not be included in retained earnings. The accounting entries need only account for the gain arising i.e. $25,000, not the full revaluation amount.

351 B

352 C

Transaction recorded	Correct transaction	Error correction
Dr Payables $1,296 Cr Returns outwards $1,296	Dr Payables $1,296 Cr Returns outwards $1,200 Cr Sales tax $96	Dr Returns outwards $96 Cr Sales tax $96

353 D

354 A

355 D

356 C

Initial accounting entries to record sale were made correctly: Dr Receivables $700, Cr Sales $500 plus Cr Sales tax $200 (i.e. 40% of sale price).

Half of the goods were returned – i.e. gross value $350 (half of $700) = Sales $250 plus sales tax $100. Transaction recorded as: Dr Returns inwards $350, and Cr Receivables $350

Correction required by journal adjustment:

Dr Sales tax $100 and Cr Returns inwards $100.

SUSPENSE ACCOUNTS

357

	True	False
A separate suspense account should be opened for each error in the general ledger		Correct
A suspense account can be opened to complete the recording of a transaction in the general ledger whilst more information is obtained about it	Correct	

There is no need to open a separate suspense account for each error. Therefore, the first statement is false. A suspense account can be opened to complete the recording of a transaction in the general ledger whilst more information is obtained about it, so the second statement is true.

358 A

Suspense account

	$		$
Balance b/d	1,300	Irrecoverable debts expense	1,300
	———		———
	1,300		1,300
	———		———

The initial credit entry to the allowance for receivables account had been recorded correctly. Therefore, the debit entry must have been posted to suspense account. To clear this, a credit entry to suspense account is required, with a debit entry in the irrecoverable debts expense account.

359 A

Suspense account

	$		$
Balance b/d	5,850	Non-current assets – cost	5,850
	———		———
	5,850		5,850
	———		———

The initial credit entry to the bank ledger account had been recorded correctly. Therefore, the debit entry must have been posted to suspense account. To clear this, a credit entry to suspense account is required, with a debit entry in the non-current asset – cost account. This is not a repair as the machine has been enhanced and is now more productive.

360 A

Suspense account

	$		$
Share premium	20,000	Balance b/d	20,000
	———		———
	20,000		20,000
	———		———

The initial debit entry of $30,000 to the bank ledger account had been recorded correctly, as has the credit entry of $10,000 to the share capital account. The difference is that a $20,000 credit entry should be made to the share premium account. To clear this, a debit entry to the suspense account is required along with a credit entry in the share premium account.

361 C

Suspense account

	$		$
Irrecoverable debts	1,500	Balance b/d	1,500
	———		———
	1,500		1,500
	———		———

The initial debit entry of $1,500 to the bank ledger account had been recorded correctly, with the credit entry posted to the suspense account. As the debt had been written off as irrecoverable, the credit entry should be posted to the credit side of the irrecoverable debts account, thereby reducing the expense charged to the statement of profit or loss.

362 D

Suspense account

	$		$
Retained earnings	3,250	Balance b/d	3,250
	———		———
	3,250		3,250
	———		———

The initial debit entry of $3,250 to revaluation surplus account had been recorded correctly, with the credit entry posted to the suspense account. As this is regarded as a part-realisation of the revaluation surplus, it should be posted to retained earnings, not an income or profit account in the statement of profit or loss.

363

	True	False
A suspense account needs to be opened to correct a transaction account which was posted to the general ledger using the correct monetary amount but the wrong general ledger accounts		✓
A suspense account needs to be opened to record the removal of a duplicated transaction in the general ledger		✓

364 **C**

The debit entry in the payables' account was correctly recorded. The credit entry must have been made in the suspense account. To clear the suspense account requires the following:

Debit Suspense, and Credit Discount received

365 **C**

366 **D**

367 **A**

(1) is correct. The rent expense has incorrectly been credited to the rent account and the payment has been correctly recorded as a credit to cash. Therefore, two credit entries of $162 have been made so a debit to suspense of $324 would have arisen.

(2) is correct as an interest expense of $324 has not been transferred to the trial balance. When the interest was paid there would have been a credit to the bank and a debit to the interest expense account. This has not been recognised on the debit side of the trial balance and therefore, as this is missing, a suspense balance of $324 would arise on the debit side of the trial balance.

(3) is not correct as the cash sale has been correctly debited to cash but incorrectly debited to sales. Two debit entries have been posted; therefore, a credit of $324 will have been taken to suspense. (4) is not correct as recording an equal debit and credit entry means that no suspense account arises.

PREPARING BASIC FINANCIAL STATEMENTS

STATEMENT OF FINANCIAL POSITION AND STATEMENT OF PROFIT OR LOSS AND OTHER COMPREHENSIVE INCOME

368   A

Opening net assets + capital injections + profit – drawings = closing net assets

Opening net assets + $9,800 + $8,000 – $4,200 = $19,000

Opening net assets = Opening capital = $5,400

369

	Selection
It is the cheapest way for a company to raise finance through the issuing of shares	
It makes the shares in a company more marketable	✔
The total equity of the company will increase	
Share capital is brought more into line with assets employed in the company	✔

A bonus share issue does not raise finance, as the shares are issued for no consideration (i.e. for free). Each share becomes worth less (as there are more shares in issue but the value of the entity as a whole remains the same), and so more marketable.

Retained earnings or other components of equity (e.g. share premium) decrease when there is a bonus issue. The double entry is to debit retained earnings (or other components of equity) and credit the share capital. Share capital increases and so may seem more appropriate when compared to net assets.

370   B

	$	$
Sales (β)		25,600
Cost of sales		
Opening inventory	1,500	
Purchases	12,950	
Inventory drawings	(75)	
Closing inventory	(900)	
		(13,475)
Gross profit		12,125

371   B

The profit or loss charge would be $500 underprovision b/f plus the charge for the current year of $8,000 = $8,500. The liability outstanding would be $8,000.

372 D

Capital = net assets

If a supplier is paid by cheque, assets reduce as do liabilities, therefore there is no change to net assets.

If raw materials or non-current assets are purchased on credit, assets increase as do liabilities; again, there is no change to net assets.

If wages are paid in cash, assets decrease (the other effect is to reduce profits which in turn reduces capital).

373 D

The loan was included as a current liability but should be treated as a non-current liability. Correcting the error will reduce current liabilities, and this will increase net current assets (= current assets minus current liabilities).

374 B

Profit is the increase in net assets between the beginning and end of the period, plus drawings taken out of the business, minus new equity introduced in the period (which is not profit).

375 C

The separate business entity concept means that accounting information should only relate to the business, not the owner of the business. Therefore, goods taken by the owner must be treated as drawings and removed from the inventory of the business.

376 $70,000

Only the revaluation surplus arising in the year is included within other comprehensive income. The depreciation charge and the gain on disposal are accounted for in profit or loss.

377 D

Current assets	$	Current liabilities	$
Receivables	23,800	Overdraft	3,250
Allowances for receivables	(1,500)	Payables	31,050
Inventory	12,560	Rent accrual	1,200
Petty cash	150	Loan	25,000
	35,010		60,500

The bank statement shows a debit balance, indicating an overdraft (from the bank's perspective, they are owed money by Samim). The first instalment of the loan (25%) is due within 12 months and so shown as a current liability.

378 A

Assets	=	Liabilities	+	Capital
At start of week: 15,700	=	11,200	+	4,500(β)
1 May +300 +1,400		+ 300		+ 1,400
3 May −750				− 750
4 May −400				− 400
7 May +1,200 − 600				+ 1,200 − 600
At end of week: 16,850	=	11,500	+	5,350

379 **$18,000**

The development expenditure should be capitalised and should not, therefore be written off as an expense. The remaining items totalling $18,000 should be charged as an expense for the year.

380 **$900**

The original annual depreciation charge = $80,000/50 years = $1,600. The property has been depreciated for $16,000/$1,600 = 10 years, leaving a remaining estimated useful life of 40 years. The revised annual depreciation charge is ($100,000/40 years) = $2,500. The amount of the excess depreciation transfer is: $2,500 − $1,600 = $900.

381

	Selection
Statement of profit or loss and other comprehensive income	
Statement of financial position	
Statement of cash flows	✓
Statement of changes in equity	✓

Only dividend income is shown in the statement of profit or loss and other comprehensive income. Only dividends payable in respect of preference shares are shown in the statement of financial position. The statement of cash flows includes all dividends paid. The statement of changes in equity includes dividends paid and dividends payable.

382 D

Debit or Credit	Account	$
Debit	Non-current asset – property	40,000
Debit	Accumulated depreciation	40,000
Credit	Revaluation surplus	80,000

383 B

The first statement is false: the nominal value of the equity shares is $0.50 and therefore there are 200,000 in issue. The equity dividend paid is:

200,000 × $0.03 = $6,000

The second statement is true. A preference dividend is accounted for when it falls due and therefore the part of the dividend not yet paid must be accrued at the year end.

384 C

In accordance with IFRS 18 *Presentation and Disclosure in Financial Statements* income tax expense is presented in the statement of profit or loss and other comprehensive income. A revaluation gain is presented in the statement of profit or loss and other comprehensive income (as an item of other comprehensive income). The revaluation surplus is also presented as a component of equity in the statement of changes in equity and statement of financial position.

385 C

	Cost of sales	Selling expenses	General and administrative expense
	$	$	$
Opening inventory	12,500		
Closing inventory	(17,900)		
Purchases	199,000		
Selling expenses		35,600	
General and administrative expenses			78,800
Audit fee			15,200
Carriage in	3,500		
Carriage out		7,700	
Depreciation (70:30:0)	28,000		12,000
	225,100	43,300	106,000

386 C

Share premium			
	$		$
		Balance b/f	30,000
Bonus issue (W2)	12,500	Rights issue (W1)	90,000
Balance c/f	107,500		
	120,000		120,000

(W1)	**Rights issue**	Existing number of shares	400,000
		New shares	100,000

At $1.15 each   Dr Cash $115,000

	Cr Share capital	$25,000
	Cr Share premium	$90,000

(W2)	**Bonus issue**	Existing shares	500,000
		New shares	50,000
		Dr Share premium	$12,500
		Cr Share capital	$12,500

387 D

Dividends are not an expense in the statement of profit or loss and other comprehensive income but an appropriation of profit, which is presented in the statement of changes to equity. Unpaid dividends on equity share are only accrued at the year-end if they have been declared prior to the year end. This might be the case for an interim dividend, but not a final dividend (which would be based on profit for the year).

388

	True	False
An entity may make a rights issue if it wished to raise more equity capital.	✓	
A rights issue might increase the share premium account whereas a bonus issue is likely to reduce it.	✓	
A rights issue will always increase the number of shareholders in an entity whereas a bonus issue will not.		✓
A bonus issue will result in an increase in the market value of each share		✓

A rights issue involves the issue of new shares for cash and therefore more equity capital will be raised. The rights issue price will probably be above nominal value and therefore the share premium account will be increased by the amount of the premium. A bonus issue does not involve cash; when recording the transaction, the debit entry is normally made to the share premium account, therefore reducing it.

Both a rights and a bonus issue involve the potential issue of shares to existing shareholders. Therefore, neither will increase the number of shareholders in an entity. A bonus issue will result in more shares in issue without affecting the value of the entity. Therefore, each share will be worth less, not more.

389 C

An overprovision from a previous year (i.e. credit balance) reduces the income tax expense in the current year in the statement of profit or loss. Taxes payable is the full amount of the estimation of the expense for the year.

390

	Current	Non-current
A sale has been made on credit to a customer. They have agreed to terms stating that payment is due in 12 months' time.	✓	
A bank overdraft facility of $30,000 is available under an agreement with the bank which is available for the next three years.	✓	
Albatros Co purchases a small number of shares in another entity which it intends to trade.	✓	
A bank loan has been taken out with a repayment date 5 years hence.		✓

The credit sale is part of the entity's normal operating cycle and is therefore classified as a current asset. The bank overdraft is repayable on demand and therefore classified as a current liability. The shares have been purchased to sell and so are classified as a current asset investment.

391 D

	Share capital	Share premium	Revaluation surplus	Retained earnings	Total
	$	$	$	$	$
Share issue	2,000	3,000			5,000
Revaluation			230,000		230,000
Profit					
(178,000 – 45,000 – 5,600)				127,400	127,400
Dividends – equity				(12,000)	(12,000)
	─────	─────	─────	─────	─────
Total change	2,000	3,000	230,000	115,400	350,400
	─────	─────	─────	─────	─────

392 D

Preference shares do not generally carry voting rights. Preference dividends are fixed amounts, normally expressed as a percentage of their nominal value. Preference dividends are paid out in preference to equity dividends.

393 A

Accounting standards require that the commercial substance of a transaction is recorded rather than its legal form. Redeemable preference shares are repayable at a specified future date and therefore have the qualities of debt. They are therefore accounted for as liabilities.

394 B

A bonus issue is a capitalisation of retained earnings (or other component of equity). Therefore, retained earnings would decrease and share capital increase.

395 B

Loan notes can be issued at a discount to their nominal value (unlike shares). Interest is always paid based on the nominal value. Interest accrued $8,000 (12% × $400,000 × 2/12).

396 D

Transfers within equity (options A and B) have no effect on total equity; issuing shares at a premium increases equity; paying a dividend (normally out of retained earnings) will decrease equity.

397

	Choice: A, B or C
Excess depreciation on revaluation	C
Increase in carrying amount of the property	B
Depreciation charge	A

Tutorial note:

Excess depreciation is accounted for in the statement of changes in equity. It is not accounted for in the statement of profit or loss and other comprehensive income.

398 D

399 C

IFRS 15 *Revenue from Contracts with Customers* requires that revenue should recognised only when performance obligations have been complied with. As both transactions relate to the sale of goods, they would appear to be obligations satisfied at a point in time.

Eman has complied with the obligation to deliver the food processor on 28 August and transfers to control to Pitt on that date. Revenue can therefore be recognised on this transaction.

Similarly, it would appear the obligations to Damon were fulfilled on 26 August 20X7 when Damon collected the goods: control was transferred on that date. A receivable should be recognised for any amount due but not yet received on both transactions.

400 B

An expense in the statement of profit or loss will be less than the year-end liability after an adjustment for an overprovision in the prior year. If there had been an underprovision, the shortfall would be an expense in the current year, increasing the income tax expense in the statement of profit or loss.

401 $16,000

The revenue relating to the course fees relate to goods and services to be provided in 20X9. Therefore, revenue on the study materials and lectures should not be recognised in the financial statements for the year ended 20 December 20X8. Revenue can be recognised in 20X9 as and when the separate performance obligations are fulfilled.

The course materials sold to students is a completed transaction as at 31 December 20X8 and revenue can be recognised on this transaction at a total amount of $16,000 (40 × $400). There is no further obligation other than to deliver the study material, which was complied with prior to 31 December 20X8.

402 $0

Although customer orders have been received along with deposits, Vostok has not yet done anything to earn the revenue by 31 July 20X2. The deposits received should be accounted for as deferred income and treated as a current liability, rather than being recognised as revenue. It is only when the computer games have been despatched that Vostok will be able to regard the obligation as discharged and consequently recognise revenue.

403 $14,500

	$
Customers for a full year ((12 − 1) × $1,200)	13,200
Terminated contract to 31 August (5/12 × $1,200)	500
New contracts from 1 December (2 × 4/12 × $1,200)	800
	———
Revenue for the year ended 31 March 20X6	14,500
	———

Note that, for revenue recognition in this situation, it is irrelevant when the cash is received for the services provided. Revenue can be recognised only when it has been earned – in the case of service provision, this will occur when services are provided over a period of time.

404 C

	P & L	Liability	Asset
	$	$	$
Balance b/f 1 Jan 20X8		(2,350)	
Cash paid – March 20X8		2,050	
Credit overprovision to P/L	(300)	300	
Repayment due	(2,120)		2,120
	———	———	———
	(2,420)	0	**2,120**
	———	———	———

405 A

	P & L	Liability	Asset
	$	$	$
Balance b/f 1 July 20X5		(16,940)	
Cash paid		17,500	
Expense underprovision to P/L	560	(560)	
Repayment due	(4,500)		4,500
	─────	─────	─────
	(3,940)	0	**4,500**
	─────	─────	─────

406 D

The other options available include only part of the full definition and explanation of the meaning of aggregation when preparing the financial statements.

DISCLOSURE NOTES

407 C

Tutorial note:

IAS 38 requires that development costs should only be capitalised when the directors are satisfied that those costs will be recovered at some future date.

If the directors are not satisfied on this point, such costs cannot be capitalised, – they must be written off as incurred.

408 B

Statement A is inappropriate as there are strict criteria for application of the valuation model to be applied, rather than arbitrary judgement of the directors. Normally intangible assets should be accounted for using a consistent valuation model. In addition, there is no indication of the amortisation rate or useful lives of the intangible assets.

Statement C is inappropriate as any increases in carrying amount should be accounted for in other comprehensive income and other components of equity. In addition, the valuation model will only be relevant intangible assets are traded on an active market.

409 C

Statement A is inappropriate as it implies that land is also depreciated over 50 years. Land should not be depreciated as it does not have a finite useful life. Statement B is inappropriate as assets which have a finite useful life should be subject to depreciation to spread the cost over the estimated useful life to the business.

410 B

Statement A is inappropriate as compares the total cost of inventory with its total realisable value. This is likely to result in inventory being overvalued. Statement C would also result in an overvaluation of inventory.

411 B

The statement is false as, although non-adjusting events are not accounted for in the financial statements, if material, they must be disclosed in the notes to the financial statements.

412 D

413

	Disclosed	Not disclosed
Reconciliation of carrying amounts of non-current assets at the beginning and end of period.	✓	
Useful lives of assets or depreciation rates used.	✓	
Increases in asset values as a result of revaluations in the period.	✓	
Depreciation expense for the period.	✓	

Here is an example of a non-current asset disclosure note, which should demonstrate why items (1), (3) and (4) are all correct in this question as they would be disclosed within this note:

	Land and buildings	Plant and equipment
Asset	$	$
Balance b/f	X	X
Revaluation	X	X
Additions	X	X
Disposals	(X)	(X)
Balance c/f	X	X
Accumulated depreciation		
Balance b/f	X	X
Charge for year	X	X
Disposals	(X)	(X)
Balance c/f	X	X
Carrying amount at start of year (b/f)	X	X
Carrying amount at year end (c/f)	X	X

Don't forget that disclosures can be numerical and narrative. Hence Item (2) which is an example of a narrative note that would also be included, describing, in this example note, what the useful life or depreciation rates for land and buildings and plant and equipment would be.

414

	Selection
Revenue	✓
Closing inventory	
Interest expense	✓
Dividends paid	
Income tax expense	✓
Depreciation expense for the year	

Closing inventory is included in the statement of financial position. Dividends paid are included in the statement of changes in equity. When classifying expenses by function, depreciation expense is disclosed in the notes to the financial statements, rather than presented in the statement of profit or loss.

415 C

Disclosure requirements may be monetary (e.g. the depreciation charge for the year) or narrative (e.g. a statement of accounting policies).

416 FALSE

Disclosure is required of either the estimated useful lives or the depreciation rates used. In effect, disclosure of the depreciation rates used provides information regarding the estimated useful lives of the assets, and vice versa.

417 C

418 FALSE

In addition to stating the balance at the beginning and at the end of the year, the entity also needs to provide a reconciliation of the movement in the provision during the year.

419 D

There should be disclosure of depreciation and amortisation charges made during the year. In addition, in relation to revaluation of property, plant and equipment, the date of the valuation should be disclosed, together with a statement of whether or not the valuer was a person independent of the entity.

420 B

421 A

The double entry for the increase in provision is:

Dr Warranty expense $1,000

Cr Warranty provision $1,000

422 D

EVENTS AFTER THE REPORTING PERIOD

423   A

424

	Adjusting	Non-adjusting
A flood on 3 October 20X8 that destroyed a relatively small quantity of inventory which had cost $1,700.		✓
A credit customer with a balance outstanding at 30 September 20X8 was declared insolvent on 20 December 20X8.	✓	
Inventory valued at a cost of $800 at 30 September 20X8 was sold for $650 on 11 November 20X8.	✓	
A dividend on equity shares of 4 cents per share was declared on 1 December 20X8.		✓

The flood on 3 October does not provide additional information of conditions that existed at the year end and therefore is non-adjusting. The credit customer's insolvency is confirmed before the financial statements were approved and provides evidence of irrecoverability of the amount outstanding at 30 September and is therefore an adjusting event. The sale of inventory in November provides evidence of its net realisable value for the inventory valuation at 30 September 20X8 and is therefore an adjusting event. The declaration of the equity dividend is a non-adjusting event.

425   D

Details of adjusting events are not disclosed in the notes; instead, if material, the event is accounted for in the financial statements. The sale of inventory after the reporting date at a price lower than that at which it is valued in the statement of financial position is an adjusting event. A fall in the market value of property, plant and equipment after the reporting date is a non-adjusting event. It should therefore be disclosed if material. Statement (4) is a definition of an event after the reporting date.

426   B

Events 2 and 4 occur between the reporting date and date of approval of the financial statements and each provides additional information of the situation as at the reporting date. Each of these is an adjusting event. Event 1 is a non-adjusting event as it occurred after the reporting date and does not provide additional information of the situation at that date. However, as the going concern basis is no longer appropriate, the basis of accounting must be changed and hence amounts in the financial statements will be adjusted.

Event 3 is specifically identified in IAS 10 as non-adjusting.

427 B

Tutorial note:

IAS 10 specifically precludes adjusting for a dividend that was proposed before the year end and paid after the year end.

428 D

Per IAS 10, events after the reporting period are classified as either adjusting or non-adjusting. Adjusting events are those that provide evidence of conditions that existed at the end of the reporting period and non-adjusting events relate to conditions that arose after the reporting period.

In (1), the legal action begins in December 20X8. This is after the reporting period end and therefore a non-adjusting event. Non-adjusting events are to be disclosed if they are material, which is stated in the scenario.

In (2), the unfair dismissal took place during the current accounting year (i.e. conditions existed at the reporting date) and should be provided for.

REVENUE FROM CONTRACTS WITH CUSTOMERS

429 C

IFRS 15 *Revenue from Contracts with Customers* requires revenue to be recognised when a performance obligation is satisfied.

In C, Rajesh entered into a contract to supply goods to another business and the goods have been delivered. Therefore, the performance obligation has been satisfied and the revenue can be recognised.

A is incorrect as the sale does not meet the IFRS 15 definition of revenue (i.e. 'income arising in the course of an entity's ordinary activities'). Rajesh sells computers and therefore the sale of the van should be treated as the disposal of property, plant and equipment.

The receipt of the $100 deposit in B cannot be recognised as revenue as the performance obligation (to provide the customer with a computer) has not been satisfied.

D is incorrect. The obligation was satisfied two weeks ago when the delivery of the computers took place. This is a simple receipt from a credit customer.

430 $8,000

Rep Co has the obligation to arrange the sale and to collect the cash from the customer. Its obligations are therefore discharged on 28 September. Revenue of $8,000 (10% × $80,000) can be recognised in the year ended and 30 September 20X4. Note that as $80,000 was received from the customer, the balance of $72,000 ($80,000 – $8,000 commission earned) should be accounted for as a liability until it is paid to Zip Co.

431 $880

Loc Co should only recognise revenue when a performance obligation has been satisfied. The obligations to deliver and install the machine are satisfied at a point in time and were completed on 1 October 20X5, so revenue of $850 ($750 + $100) can be recognised. Revenue relating to the supply of the service support agreement is recognised over a period of time and, at the reporting date, three months of support service has been provided to the customer, so $30 ($120 × 3/12) can also be recognised as revenue in the year ended 31 December 20X5. Total revenue recognised on this transaction in the year is therefore $880.

432 C

Revenue on the contract with Far Co has been recognised appropriately. Revenue on the contract with Res Co should be only for commission earned, not the full contract price. Revenue on the contract with Cap Co should be spread evenly over the time period for the supply of the service, and only nine months of service has been provided, not a full year. Revenue on the contract with Ber Co should be $50,000, the cost of sales and gross profit would both be $25,000.

433 B

Contracts do not need to be in writing, although many business entities may prefer to have written contracts so that there is certainty as to what has been agreed with customers.

434

	True	False
On any reasonable basis		✓
At a point in time	✓	
Annually		✓
Over a period of time	✓	

Revenue should be recognised when an obligation has been discharged, either at a point in time (usually for the sale of goods) or over a period of time (usually for provision of a service).

435 C

Revenue is recorded at the amount the business expects to receive in exchange of the supply of goods and/or services. Trade discount is always deducted from the value of the goods before recording the transaction. Early settlement discount is only deducted when initially recording the transaction if the customer is expected to take advantage of the discount terms offered; this is not the case in this situation. The issue of a free sample is not expected to generate any revenue; therefore, it should not have a sale value included in the accounting records and financial statements.

STATEMENTS OF CASH FLOWS

436 D

	Share cap	Share prem
	$	$
Brought fwd	120,000	100,000
Bonus issue 1/12 of 120,000	10,000	(10,000)
	130,000	90,000
Issue for cash (bal fig)	170,000	170,000
	300,000	260,000

Total proceed of shares issued for cash = $340,000 plus $300,000 proceeds of loan note = $640,000 cash inflow from financing activities, less interest paid of $12,000 = $628,000 net cash inflow relating to finance activities.

437 $13,000 INFLOW

Interest received = $13,000. All the other cash flows are classified as financing activities.

438 C

Bonus (capitalisation) issues do not involve the transfer of cash, whereas rights issues result in a cash inflow. The revaluation of non-current assets does not involve the movement of cash.

439

	Selection
Depreciation should be deducted, not added	
Increase in inventories should be added, not deducted	
Decrease in receivables should be added, not deducted	✓
Increase in payables should be added, not deducted	✓

Depreciation is a non-cash expense and should therefore be added back to operating profit. An increase in assets (inventory and receivables) means that less cash is available (as it has been used to fund assets), hence an increase in assets is shown as a deduction in the cash flow statement. An increase in liabilities (payables) means that more cash is available (i.e. it has not been used to pay liabilities), hence an increase in liabilities is shown as an addition in the cash flow statement.

440 D

The carrying amount of non-current assets is shown in the statement of financial position. Depreciation on non-current assets and any profit or loss on disposal is shown in the statement of profit or loss and other comprehensive income. Proceeds from the disposal of non-current assets are presented in the statement of cash flows as cash inflows from investing activities.

441 A

	$000
Operating profit (β)	**1,175**
Adjustments for:	
Depreciation	100
Increase in receivables & inventory	(575)
Cash from operating activities before income taxes	700
Income taxes paid	(100)
Purchase of property, plant and equipment (investing activity)	(200)
Cash from issue of shares (financing activity)	1,100
Repayment of debentures (financing activity)	(750)
Increase in cash	750

442 D

	$	$
Net cash from operating activities (β)		419,254
Cash flows from investing activities		
Purchase of property, plant and equipment	(47,999)	
Proceeds from sale of property, plant and equipment	13,100	
Net cash from investing activities		(34,899)
Cash flows from financing activities		
Redemption of loans	(300,000)	
Interest and dividends paid	(87,566)	
Net cash used in financing activities		(387,566)
Decrease in cash and cash equivalents		(3,211)

Note that not all information provided in the question was necessary to arrive at the answer. It is not possible to calculate net cash from operating activities because operating profit was not given. Therefore, it is necessary to work 'backwards' from the movement in cash and cash equivalents.

443 B

Non-current assets at carrying amount

	$		$
Balance b/f	50,000	Disposals (4,000 – 1,500)	2,500
Additions (β)	7,500	Depreciation	9,000
		Balance c/f	46,000
	_____		_____
	57,500		57,500
	_____		_____

444

	True	False
A statement of cash flows prepared using the 'direct method' produces a different figure for investing activities in comparison with that produced if the indirect method is used.		✓
A bonus issue of shares does not feature in a statement of cash flows.	✓	
The amortisation charge for the year on intangible assets will appear as an item under 'Cash flows from operating activities' in a statement of cash flows.		✓
Loss on the sale of a non-current asset will appear as an item under 'Cash flows from investing activities' in a statement of cash flows.		✓

445 D

	$
Operating profit for the year	20,750
Depreciation	1,250
Income taxes paid	(2,000)
Non-current asset purchases	(8,000)
Decrease in inventories	1,800
Increase in receivables	(1,000)
Increase in payables	350
	_____
Increase in cash and cash equivalents	13,150
	_____

446 D

Items added include the depreciation charge for the period, any losses on disposals of non-current assets, reductions in inventories and receivables (including prepayments) and any increase in trade payables (including accruals).

447

	True	False
The direct method of calculating net cash from operating activities leads to a different figure from that produced by the indirect method, but this is balanced elsewhere in the statement of cash flows.		✓
An entity making high profits must necessarily have a net cash inflow from operating activities.		✓
Profits and losses on disposals of non-current assets are classified as investing activities in the statement of cash flows.		✓

The first statement is incorrect: net cash flow from operating activities is the same, whichever method of presentation is used. The second statement is incorrect. Companies with high profits can be cash-negative, due to high spending on new non-current assets and/or a large build-up of working capital. The last statement is incorrect. Profits and losses on non-current asset disposals are shown as an adjustment to operating profit in the calculation of net cash from operating activities (indirect method only).

448 D

Purchases are given as additions of $2,000. The assets disposed of had a cost of $3,000 and accumulated depreciation at the time of disposal of $1,500. Their carrying amount at disposal was therefore $1,500. The profit on disposal was $500, so the cash received from the disposal was $2,000.

449 A

The statement of cash flows itself does not aim to highlight the effect of non-cash transactions. Its primary purpose is to show the cash inflows and outflows from operating, investing and financing activities. While non-cash items are shown when using the indirect method, they are not the focus of the statement but an adjustment to reconcile operating profit to cash from operating activities.

450 D

	$
Cash sales	212,500
Less:	
Cash purchases	(4,600)
Cash expenses	(11,200)
Cash paid to credit suppliers (W1)	(121,780)
Cash paid as wages and salaries (W2)	(33,800)
	————
Cash generated from operations	41,120
	————

Workings:

(W1)

Payables

	$		$
		Balance b/f	12,300
Cash paid **(β)**	121,780	Purchases	123,780
Balance c/f	14,300		
	———		———
	136,080		136,080
	———		———

(W2)

Wages and salaries

	$		$
		Balance b/f	1,500
Cash paid **(β)**	33,800	Expense (P/L)	34,600
Balance c/f	2,300		
	———		———
	36,100		36,100
	———		———

451 C

	$000
Retained earnings for the year ($82,000 – $72,000)	10,000
Add back:	
Dividends payable (current year's)	1,600
Income taxes payable (current year's estimate)	15,000
Interest expense (10% × $40,000)	4,000
	———
Operating profit	30,600
	———

The additional $10,000 loan notes were issued at the beginning of the year. Therefore, the total loan notes at the start of the year will be $40,000. The interest expense for the year will be $4,000 (i.e. 10% × $40,000).

452 $75,000 Outflow

	$
Cash purchase of non-current assets	(140,000)
Disposal proceeds of non-current assets ($50,000 – $3,000)	47,000
Disposal proceeds of investments	18,000
	———
Net cash outflow from investing activities	(75,000)
	———

453 $10,000 Inflow

	$
Proceeds of issue of share capital	60,000
Repayment of bank loan ($150 – $100)	(50,000)
Net cash inflow from financing activities	10,000

454 $1,395 Outflow

	$000
Balance b/f	2,500
Revaluation in year ($1,700 – $1,200)	500
Depreciation charge for the year	(75)
Disposal removed at carrying amount	(120)
Cash paid for additions (β)	**1,395**
Balance c/f	4,200

455

	Selection
Payments to suppliers	✓
Increase or decrease in receivables	
Receipts from customers	✓
Increase or decrease in inventories	
Increase or decrease in payables	
Payments to employees	✓

The other items are relevant only under the indirect method of preparation of the statement of cash flows.

456 TRUE

Using the direct or indirect method to prepare a statement of cash flows, there are no differences in the presentation of 'cash flows from investing activities' and 'cash flows from financing activities'. Only the presentation of 'cash flows from operating activities' will differ.

457 FALSE

The depreciation charge for the year is disclosed as an adjustment to reported profit for the year within 'cash flows from operating activities' using the **indirect** method, not the direct method.

INCOMPLETE RECORDS

458 D

	$	$	%
Sales (100/70 × $756,000)		**1,080,000**	100
Cost of sales			
Opening inventory	77,000		
Purchases	763,000		
Closing inventory	(84,000)		
	———	(756,000)	70
		324,000	30

459 A

	$	$	%
Sales		650,000	100
Cost of sales			
Opening inventory	380,000		
Purchases	480,000		
Lost inventory (β)	**(185,000)**		
Closing inventory	(220,000)		
	———	(455,000)	70
Gross profit		195,000	30

460 $8,774

	$	$	%
Sales (174,825 – 1,146)		173,679	125%
Cost of goods sold			
Opening inventory	12,274		
Purchases (136,527 – 1,084)	135,443		
Closing inventory (β)	**(8,774)**		
	———		
$173,679 × 100/125		(138,943)	100%
Gross profit		34,736	25%

461 D

	$	$	%
Sales		630,000	140
Cost of sales			
Opening Inventory	24,300		
Purchases (β)	458,450		
Closing Inventory	(32,750)		
100/140 × $630,000		(450,000)	100
		180,000	40

Purchases – cash and credit

	$		$
		Balance b/f	29,780
Cash paid to suppliers (β)	**453,630**	Purchases (cash and credit)	458,450
Balance c/f	34,600		
	488,230		488,230

462 C

	$
Inventory at 6 January 20X6	32,780
Sales at cost (β)	6,020
Purchases	(4,200)
Inventory at 31 December 20X5	34,600

Profit on sales: $8,600 – $6,020 = $2,580

Gross margin: $\dfrac{2,580}{8,600} = 30\%$

463 D

Cash and bank

	$		$
Balance b/f	620		
Receipts from customers (β)	16,660	Payments	16,780
		Balance c/f	500
	17,280		17,280

Receivables

	$		$
Balance b/f	6,340		
Sales (β)	15,520	Cash receipts	16,660
		Balance c/f	5,200
	———		———
	21,860		21,860
	———		———

Gross profit: 25/125 × $15,520 = $3,104

464   B

	$	$
Sales		148,000
Opening inventory	34,000	
Purchases	100,000	
	———	
	134,000	
Closing inventory (β)	**(26,000)**	
	———	
Cost of sales (148,000 – 40,000)		108,000
		———
Gross profit		40,000
		———

465   C

You might need to answer this by testing each answer in turn.

$$\frac{\text{Gross profit}}{\text{Cost of sales}} \qquad \frac{28,800}{72,000} = 40\%$$

	$
Sales	100,800
Cost of sales	(72,000)
	———
Gross profit	28,800
	———

466   C

	$	$	%
Sales		480,000	150
Cost of sales			
Opening inventory	36,420		
Purchases (β)	324,260		
Closing inventory	(40,680)		
100/150 × $480,000		(320,000)	100
		160,000	50

Payables

	$		$
		Balance b/f	29,590
Cash paid (β)	**319,975**	Purchases	324,260
Balance c/f	33,875		
	353,850		353,850

467   B

Closing net assets	=	Opening net assets	+	Capital injections	–	Loss for the period	–	Drawings
($56,000 – $18,750)		($40,000 – $14,600)						($6,800 + $250)
$37,250	=	$25,400	+	$20,000	–	(β) **$1,100**	–	$7,050

468   D

As the inventory is insured, its cost (not selling price) is recoverable from the insurer. Therefore, this amount is shown as a current asset.

The cost should also be taken out of cost of sales as these goods have not been sold.

469 **$85,100**

	$	Notes:
Trade receivables at 31 December 20X5	65,800	
Cash received from credit customers	(76,100)	Dr Bank, Cr Receivables
Contra	(3,400)	Dr Payables, Cr Receivables
Discounts allowed not expected to be paid	(5,200)	Record sale at gross amount (IFRS 15)
Interest charged on overdue accounts	3,200	Dr Receivables, Cr Interest income
	(15,700)	
Credit sales revenue	**85,100**	
Trade receivables at 22 March 20X6	69,400	

PREPARING SIMPLE CONSOLIDATED FINANCIAL STATEMENTS

470 **A**

	$
Cost of investment	1,400,000
FV of NCI @ acquisition	300,000
Less fair value of net assets at acquisition –	
$(600,000 \times 0.50) + \$800,000$	(1,100,000)
	600,000

471 **C**

	$
Other components of equity (OCE) of Tom	400,000
Post-acquisition OCE of Jerry:	
$(\$20,000 \times 80\%)$	16,000
	416,000

472   C

	$
Cost of investment	65,000
FV of NCI @ acquisition	20,000
Less fair value of net assets at acquisition –	
$20,000 + $40,000	(60,000)
Goodwill	25,000

473   B

	$
FV of NCI @ acquisition	25,000
Post-acquisition other components of equity of Barlow	2,000
(15,000 – 10,000) × 40%	
	27,000

474   A

	$
FV of NCI @ acquisition	50,000
Post-acquisition other components of equity of Barlow	5,250
(75,000 – 60,000) × 35%	
	55,250

475   B

	$	
Sales value	1,500	120%
Cost	1,250	100%
Profit	250	20%

Workings:

Mark-up means profit is based on cost, therefore cost represents 100%. If profit is 20%, the sales value must be 120% of cost.

Total profit is $250 and 60% is still unsold by Pepper = $150

476   A

Receivables = 540 + 160 – 40 =	$660,000
Payables = 320 + 180 – 40 =	$460,000

477 $4,400,000

Non-current assets = $1,800,000 + $2,200,000 + fair value adjustment 400,000 = $4,400,000

478 C

	$m	
Sales value	24	100%
Cost value	18	75%
	——	——
Total profit	6	25%
	——	——

Workings:

Profit is $6m and half of the amount is still in inventory i.e. $3m

479 A

Profit attributable to non-controlling interest should be $6,000,000 × 20% = $1,200,000

The PURP adjustment does not affect the NCI as the parent is selling to the subsidiary.

480 D

Sales = 120 + 48 – 24 (intra-group) = $144m

Cost of sales = 84 + 40 – 24 + 3 (PURP) = $103m

481 $3,878,000

Property, plant and equipment = $1,918,000 + $1,960,000 = $3,878,000

482 B

	$	
Other components of equity (OCE) of Really	2,464,000	
Post-acquisition OCE – ($112,000 + 1,204,000) × 75%	987,000	i.e. from retained loss to retained earnings
	—————	
	3,451,000	
	—————	

Note that the interest in the Work was obtained on the reporting date, so the Really Group is not entitled to any of Works' retained earnings.

483 C

Ownership of more than 50% of the equity shares of another entity indicates a control relationship – such investments should be accounted for as a subsidiary. Ownership of less than 20% of the equity shares of another entity is not normally enough to indicate either significant influence or control relationships: such a shareholding should be accounted for as a trade investment.

484 D

The ability to exercise significant influence relates to an investment classified as an associate.

485 B

The ability of one entity to exercise significant influence over another is normally indicated by the ability to appoint at least one director to the board of that entity. If an entity was able to appoint a majority of the board of directors that would normally be regarded as having control of that other entity.

486 C

The ability of one entity to exercise control over another is normally indicated by the ability to appoint a majority of the board of directors of that other entity. Significant influence over another is normally indicated by the ability to appoint at least one director to the board of that entity.

487 A

The ability of one entity to exercise control over another is normally indicated by ownership of a majority of equity shares in that other entity.

488 D

The ability of one entity to exercise significant influence over another is normally indicated by ownership of between 20% and 50% of the equity shares of that other entity.

489 D

	$000
100,000 × 60% × 3/2 × $3.50	315

490 $1,020,000

	$000
250,000 × 80% × $3.00 cash	600
250,000 × 80% × 3/5 × $3.50	420
	1,020

491 A

	$000
S2m + ($1.5m × 3/12) – $0.1m	2,275

492 A

	$000
S5m + ($3m × 9/12) – $0.5m	6,750

493 C

	$000
10m + (9/12 × 4m)	13,000
Less: post-acq'n intra-group sales	(1,600)
Add: PURP re closing inventory	80
(1.6m × 25/125 × 1/4)	
	11,480

494 $10,300

	$000
10m + (4/12 × 6m)	12,000
Less: post-acq'n intra-group sales	(1,800)
Add: PURP re closing inventory	100
(1.8m × 20/120 × 1/3)	
	10,300

495 $7,000

	$000	$000
Consideration paid		20,000
FV of NCI at acquisition		6,000
FV of net assets acquired:		
Equity share capital	8,000	
Retained earnings to I Jan X4	10,000	
Retained earnings to acquisition		
(6/12 × 2,000,000)	1,000	
		(19,000)
Goodwill on acquisition		7,000

496 B

	$000	$000
Consideration paid		43,000
FV of NCI at acquisition		10,000
FV of net assets acquired:		
Share capital	25,000	
Retained earnings at I July X7	15,000	
Retained earnings to acquisition		
(8/12 × 6,000,000)	4,000	
Fair value adjustment	1,000	
		(45,000)
Goodwill on acquisition		8,000

497 $16,000

		$000
Cash paid (10m × 60% × $3)		18,000
Shares (10m × 60% × 2/1 × $4.50)		54,000
FV of NCI at acquisition		14,000
FV of net assets acquired:		
Equity share capital	10,000	
Share premium	10,000	
Retained earnings	50,000	
	———	(70,000)
Goodwill on acquisition		16,000

498 A

		$000
Cash paid (15m × 75% × $4.50)		50,625
Shares (15m × 75% × 1 × $5.00)		56,250
FV of NCI at acquisition		27,000
FV of net assets acquired:		
Equity share capital	15,000	
Share premium	5,000	
Retained earnings	76,875	
FV adjustment	2,000	
	———	(98,875)
Goodwill on acquisition		35,000

499 $65,000

		$000
Cash paid (200 × 90% × $3)		540
Shares issued (200 × 90% × 1 × $2)		360
FV of NCI at acquisition		75
FV of net assets acquired:		
Equity share capital	200	
Share premium	100	
Retained earnings	590	
FV adjustment ($90 – $70)	20	
	———	(910)
Goodwill on acquisition		65

500 B

	$000
NCI share of group profit	
(400 × 6/12 × 40%)	80

Note: Huyton made the intra-group sales and therefore bears all of the PURP adjustment. Only the post-acquisition element of Speke's profit is taken into account.

501 D

	$
Equity share capital	1,000
Retained earnings	585
($710 − (6/12 × $250)	1,585

	$
Goodwill is calculated as:	
Consideration transferred (75% × 1000) × $2 = $1,500	1,500
FV of NCI	300
	1,800
Less FV of NA at acquisition	(1,585)
Goodwill	215

The financial statement extracts are given at the year-end date of 30 September 20X3. Therefore, the net assets at the acquisition date (1 April 20X3) must be calculated by deducting the amount of retained earnings that was earned in the 6 months since the acquisition.

502 $114,667

The interest in Seal Co was acquired on 31 August 2012, which means that during the year ended 31 December 2012, Seal Co had only been a subsidiary for 4 months of the year, therefore only the post-acquisition results of the subsidiary should be consolidated.

Intra-group sales should also be eliminated, and as all these were made in October, they are all in the post-acquisition period and need to be cancelled. This means the consolidated revenue for Panther Group would be calculated as:

$100,000 + (4/12 × $62,000) − $6,000 = $114,667.

503 $22,900

The 70% holding was acquired on 1 March 20X2, which means that during the year ended 31 August 2012, Daffodil Co had only been a subsidiary for 6 months of the year. Only post-acquisition results of the subsidiary should be consolidated. This means the consolidated gross profit would be reported as:

Tulip $18,300 + Daffodil ($9,200 × 6/12) $4,600 = $22,900.

504 **$147,750**

	$
Fair value of consideration transferred:	
Cash paid 75% × 100,000 = 75,000 acquired × $2	150,000
Shares issued in Venus 75% × 100,000 = 75,000 × 1/1 × $1.75	131,250
	———
	281,250
Plus: Fair value of the non-controlling interest at acquisition	82,000
	———
	363,250
Less: Fair value of net assets at acquisition	(215,500)
	———
Goodwill	147,750

505 **B**

An associate is often identified when between 20% and 50% of the equity shares of another entity are held as this is presumed to give significant influence over that entity. However, for an associate to exist, it is not a case of just a matter of the percentage of equity shares held, it also depends on whether the investing entity can exercise significant influence, which can be evidenced through the number of directors who can be appointed on the board and who participate in decision making. The investment in statement 3 is not equity accounted as the entity has appointed the majority of the board of directors, giving it control.

506

	True	False
Equity accounting will always be used when an investing entity holds between 20% – 50% of the equity shares in another entity.		✓
Dividends received from an investment in associate will be presented as investment income in the consolidated financial statements.		✓

The first statement is incorrect. Firstly, if an investing entity holds 30% in another entity and has no other investments, consolidated accounts would not be produced and therefore equity accounting would not be used. Secondly, despite an investing entity having a 20% holding in another entity, significant influence may not exist. i.e. another entity may hold the remaining 80% of the shares and hence equity accounting would not be used in the investing entity books.

The second statement is also incorrect. In the consolidated accounts, the basic principle of equity accounting is that the group's share of the associate's profit is included, not the dividend income which would be shown in the investing entity's own statement of profit or loss.

507

		True	False
1	Goodwill in associates is presented separately on the consolidated statement of financial position		✓
2	Associates are accounted for using equity accounting	✓	
3	An associate's total profit for the year is presented in the consolidated statement of profit or loss		✓
4	The group share of an associate's assets and liabilities are consolidated on a line-by-line basis		✓

(1) is false. Unlike subsidiaries, goodwill for an associate is not presented separately. It is, effectively, included in the 'Investment in associate' balance.

(3) is false. Under equity accounting, it is the **share** of the associate's profit that is presented in the statement of profit of loss.

(4) is false. Adding the group share of an associate's assets and liabilities on a line-by-line basis ('proportional consolidation') is prohibited. In the consolidated statement of financial position, 'Investments in associates' is a single line item within non-current assets.

INTERPRETATION OF FINANCIAL STATEMENTS

508 27.30% and 48.00%

ROCE: PBFIT/Capital employed × 100, where capital employed is defined as equity plus long-term loans.

Where PBFIT = Profit before financing and income taxes.

Note: remember that, for ACCA FA, profit before financing and income taxes is likely to be identical to operating profit.

20X4: 179,545/(596,165 + 61,600) × 100 = 27.30%

20X3: 235,450/(407,420 + 83,100) × 100 = 48.00%

509 24.5% and 35.04%

Gross profit margin: Gross profit/Revenue × 100

20X4: 340,995/1,391,820 × 100 = 24.50%

20X3: 406,400/1,159,850 × 100 = 35.04%

510 12.9% and 20.30%

Operating profit margin: Operating profit/Revenue × 100).

20X4: 179,545/1,391,820 × 100 = 12.90%

20X3: 235,450/1,159,850 × 100 = 20.30%

511   2.12 and 2.36

Asset turnover: Revenue/Capital employed

20X4: 1,391,820/(596,165 + 61,600) = 2.12

20X3: 1,159,850/(407,420 + 83,100) = 2.36

512   1.23 and 1.62

Current ratio: Current assets/Current liabilities

20X4: 528,855/430,680 = 1.23

20X3: 390,710/241,590 = 1.62

513   0.97 and 1.25

Quick 'acid test' ratio: (Current assets – inventory)/Current liabilities

20X4: (528,855 – 109,400)/430,680 = 0.97

20X3: (390,710 – 88,760)/241,590 = 1.25

514   38 days and 43 days

Inventory holding period: Inventories/Cost of sales × 365

20X4: 109,400/1,050,825 × 365 = 38 days

20X3: 88,760/753,450 × 365 = 43 days

515   110 days and 65 days

Receivables collection period: Receivables/Credit sales × 365, where in the absence of information to the contrary, all sales are assumed to be on credit terms.

20X4: 419,455/1,391,820 × 365 = 110 days

20X3: 206,550/1,159,850 × 365 = 65 days

516   120 days and 87 days

Payables payment period: Payables/Cost of sales × 365

20X4: 345.480/1,050,825 × 365 = 120 days

20X3: 179,590/753,450 × 365 = 87 days

517   10.33% and 20.40%

Debt-equity ratio: Long-term loans/Equity × 100

20X4: 61,600/596,165 × 100 = 10.33%

20X3: 83,100/407,420 × 100 = 20.40%

518   9.37% and 16.94%

Gearing ratio: Long-term loans/(Equity + long-term loans) × 100

20X4: 61,600/(596,165 + 61,600) × 100 = 9.37%

20X3: 83,100/(407,420 + 83,100) × 100 = 16.94%

519   17.95 times and 16.82 times

Interest cover: PBFIT/Interest payable × 100

20X4: 179,545/10,000 × 100 = 17.95 times

20X3: 235,450/14,000 × 100 = 16.82 times

520   D

4,600/20,000 × 100 = 23%

521   A

20X5: 2,140/20,000 × 100 = 10.7%

20X6: 2,180/26,000 × 100 = 8.38%

522   A

20X5: 4,400/20,000 × 365 = 80 days

20X6: 6,740/26,000 × 365 = 95 days

523   A

12,715/5,000 = 2.54 times

524   C

		$
Selling price (SP)	140	700
Cost of sales (COS)	100	???
Gross profit	40	???

Cost of sales × 140/100 = 700 Cost of sales = 700/1.4 = $500

525   D

Inventory turnover is found by dividing cost of goods sold by average inventory.

Average inventory is

$$\left(\frac{24,000 \ + \ 20,000}{2}\right) = \$22,000$$

$$\text{Inventory turnover} \ = \frac{\text{Cost of sales}}{\text{Average inventory}}$$

	$
Opening inventory	24,000
Purchases	160,000
	184,000
Less: Closing inventory	(20,000)
Cost of goods sold	164,000

Inventory holding period is therefore 22,000/164,000 × 365 = 49 days.

526   D

You need only know the correct formula here.

527   C

The current ratio is current assets divided by current liabilities: 5,800/2,200 = 2.64:1.

528   A

The gearing ratio is the proportion of long-term loans ('debt') to equity, thus it follows that if a decrease in long-term loans is less than a decrease in the equity, the gearing ratio will rise. If interest rates rise, this may not affect profit (and therefore equity) if an entity has fixed-rate borrowings. Also, if an increase in interest rates results in reduced profit for the year (and therefore equity), the impact is likely to be negligible.

529   B

The quick ratio is: current assets less inventory divided by current liabilities that is 2,000:2,200 = 0.9:1.

530   A

The formula to calculate interest cover is: Profit before financing and income taxes/Interest expense. The complication in this question is that this profit line is not given and so must be calculated. PBFIT = (133 – 59)/26 = 2.85

531   **29 days and 40 days**

20X6: 4,400/55,000 × 365 = 29 days   20X5: 5,300/48,000 × 365 = 40 days

532 False

An issue of equity shares will reduce the gearing ratio.

533 True

The gross profit margin will increase if unit purchase or production costs fall whilst unit selling price remains unchanged.

534 1.86 and 1.95

20X3: 38,595/20,750 = 1.86   20X2: 37,050/19,000 = 1.95

535 False

Return on capital employed (ROCE) = Profit before financing and income taxes/Capital employed. An increase in long-term loans would increase capital employed which, in turn, would reduce ROCE.

536 5.0% and 7.0%

20X8: 4,500/90,000 = 5.0%   20X7: 5,600/80,000 = 7.0%

Note that this ratio excludes current liabilities.

537 C

If a significant discount is offered to credit customers, they are likely to take advantage of this, which will reduce the trade receivables collection period. Similarly, application of effective credit controls is likely to reduce the trade receivables collection period. The period taken to pay trade payables will not affect the trade receivables collection period. As an isolated factor, an increase in the volume of credit sales will not affect the trade receivables collection period.

538 B

Taking advantage of settlement discounts offered by suppliers will reduce the trade payables payment period. Buying proportionately more, or proportionately fewer, goods on credit will not affect calculation of the trade payables payment period. Offering a discount to credit customers will not affect the trade payables payment period.

539 A

Option A would result in increased inventory levels, and therefore increase the inventory holding period. All other answers are likely to lead to a reduction in the inventory holding period.

540 43 days

365/8.49 = 43 days

541 C

The effect of a bonus issue of shares would be to increase equity share capital and reduce either share premium or retained earnings. There would be no change to either equity or to long-term loans – the gearing ratio would remain unchanged.

542 D

An issue of shares would increase capital employed and would therefore lead to a reduction in the return on capital employed ratio. A reduction in long-term borrowings would reduce capital employed, and consequently increase the return on capital employed ratio. Similarly, an improved profit margin would increase profit, and therefore lead to an increase in the ratio.

543 C

A rights issue of shares will result in B Co receiving cash in exchange for the issue of shares, which will either reduce an overdraft or increase cash and bank balances. This will increase equity, and the gearing ratio will decrease.

544 C

If credit customers take advantage of extended credit periods, this will increase trade receivables. If all other factors remain unchanged, there will be an increase in current assets and, consequently, in the current ratio.

545 C

An issue of equity shares will increase equity, and the repayment of a non-current liability loan will decrease liabilities. These two factors will combine to reduce the debt/equity ratio.

546 A

There is an increase in the payables payment period from 35 days in 20X8 to 45 days in 20X9.

547 A

Trade receivables collection period is calculated as:

	20X6	20X5
Trade receivables/Revenue × 365		
45,900/500,000 × 365	34 days	
51,300/450,000 × 365		42 days

In 20X6, customers are paying their date, on average, nine days quicker; therefore, (1) is correct.

Customers paying earlier means that the credit control department has been more efficient at collecting outstanding debts from its credit customers. Therefore, (4) is correct.

(2) is incorrect as an increase in revenue will not necessarily result in an increase in profitability. (3) is incorrect as lower receivables days in 20X6 is an improvement, not a deterioration.

548

	Selection
Ratios help the user of financial information to focus attention on significant issues	✓
Ratios are only useful when comparing a business' results from one year to the next	
Ratios provide all the information needed for interpreting company accounts	
Ratios can provide information about the profitability, liquidity, efficiency and position of the company	✓

Option (2) is incorrect. Whilst a comparison year-on-year is useful when assessing the performance of an entity, it may also be useful to compare to other data such as competitor or industry ratios.

Option (3) is incorrect. Other information will be required when interpreting company accounts such as disclosure notes or debt covenants.

549

	Selection
Ratios can be affected by a business' choice of accounting policies	✓
If there is an increase in any calculated accounting ratio, it is seen as favourable	
Gearing may indicate how risky a business is	✓
Interest cover will give an investor information about whether a dividend will be paid	

Option (2) is incorrect. An increase in an accounting ratio is not always considered favourable (e.g. an increase in gearing may be unfavourable).

Option (4) is incorrect. Interest cover provides information about the ability to cover interest with profit but does not give any indication of whether a company is likely to pay a dividend or not.

550 C

The revaluation of land and buildings does not affect current assets or current liabilities. Consequently, the current ratio would remain unchanged. The revaluation will increase other components of equity in the statement of changes in equity, without any increase in long-term liabilities. Consequently, this would reduce the gearing ratio.

Section 4

ANSWERS TO MULTI-TASK QUESTIONS – SECTION B

1 ICE CO

Key answer tips

This question tests your knowledge of accounts preparation for a corporate entity.

It examines several different syllabus areas, and you therefore need to have a sound understanding of the syllabus as a whole. As each of the tasks is independent, you can attempt them in any order. Apply good exam technique to deal first with the topics you feel most confident about.

The question includes classification of expenses, deciding whether a provision or disclosure is required and whether to classify several items of expenditure as asset expenditure.

Task 1

(a) **How should the following items be classified in the statement of profit or loss?**

(1 mark)

	Cost of sales	Selling expenses	General and administrative expenses
Carriage inwards	Correct		
Carriage outwards		Correct	

Tutorial note

The cost of inventory includes all costs incurred in bringing it to its location and condition. This will include carriage inwards costs, and they should be included as part of cost of sales. Carriage outwards relate to the delivery of finished goods to customers and are not, therefore, part of cost of sales.

(b) **Using the information available, what was Ice Co's gross profit for the year ended 31 December 20X1?** **(2 marks)**

$363,500

Workings:		$
Revenue ($600,000 – $500 returns inwards)		599,500
Less: Cost of sales:		
Opening inventory	24,000	
Purchases	240,000	
Carriage inwards	2,000	
Less: Closing inventory	30,000	
	————	236,000
		————
Gross profit		363,500
		————

Tutorial note

Remember that 'returns inwards' relates to returns made by customers of goods previously sold to them by the business. Consequently, the value of any returns inwards must be deducted from revenue in the statement of profit or loss. Returns inwards are not an expense item.

(c) **Using the information available, identify the adjustments required to gross profit to calculate Ice Co's draft profit before income taxes.** **(2 marks)**

		Selected answer
(i)	Gross profit – $30,000 – $180,000 – $75,000	
(ii)	Gross profit – $500 – $2,000 – $180,000 – $75,000	
(iii)	Gross profit – $3,000 – $180,000 – $75,000	Correct

Task 2

(a) **What interest expense should be included in Ice Co's statement of profit or loss in relation to the loan?** **(1 mark)**

$4,500 $100,000 × 6% × 9/12

(b) **How should the loan be classified in the statement of financial position at 31 December 20X1?** **(1 mark)**

		Selected answer
(i)	An equity component	
(ii)	A non-current liability	Correct
(iii)	A current liability	

Task 3

How should this matter be reflected in Ice Co's financial statements for the year ended 31 December 20X1? **(2 marks)**

		Selected answer
(i)	It should not be recognised or disclosed in the financial statements for the year ended 31 December 20X1	
(ii)	It should be disclosed only in the financial statements for the year ended 31 December 20X1	
(iii)	It should be recognised as a liability in the financial statements for the year ended 31 December 20X1	Correct

Task 4

(a) **State whether each of the following costs should be classified as asset expenditure or treated as an expense.** **(4 marks)**

		Asset/Expense
(i)	Work to install additional, high-specification, electrical power cabling and circuits so that additional plant and equipment can become operational	Asset
(ii)	Replacement of some loose and damaged roof tiles following a recent storm	Expense
(iii)	Repainting the factory administration office	Expense
(iv)	Modifications to the factory entrance to enable a large item of plant and equipment to be installed	Asset

(b) **Calculate the depreciation charge for the year that should be included as an expense within cost of sales.** **(2 marks)**

Building	$1,000	$50,000 × 2%
Plant and equipment	$15,750	($120,000 − $15,000) × 15%

(Total: 15 marks)

Marking scheme	
	Marks
Task 1 – Profit of loss account preparation	5
Task 2 – Accounting for loan liability and finance	2
Task 3 – Accounting treatment of injury claim	2
Task 4 – Property, plant and equipment	6
	——
Total	**15**
	——

2   WILLOW CO

Key answer tips

This question tests your knowledge of accounts preparation for a corporate entity. It examines your knowledge of double-entry bookkeeping, along with technical knowledge of accounting for inventories and intangible assets. Ensure that you are able to state definitions and apply those definitions when performing relevant calculations.

Each of the tasks is independent and can be attempted in any order. If you do attempt questions out of order, ensure that you remember to check that you have answered all questions required. Apply good exam technique to deal first with the topics about which you feel most confident.

Task 1

(a)   Complete the following table to state the accounting entries required to record the invoices in the general ledger.   **(2 marks)**

	$	Credit/Debit
Bank and cash		
Payables	2,300	Credit
Purchases ($2.300 × 100/115)	2,000	Debit
Sales tax ($2.300 × 15/115)	300	Debit
Suspense account		

(b)   Complete the following statement relating to the omitted purchases invoices.
    (1 mark)

This accounting error **will not** result in the totals of the trial balance failing to agree.

Note: as the invoices have been omitted completely from the general ledger, the trial balance will still agree.

Task 2

Complete the following table to identify the accounting entries required to record the bonus issue.   **(4 marks)**

	$000	Credit/Debit
Bank and cash		
Equity shares ($72,000 × 1/6)	12,000	Credit
Retained earnings		
Share premium	12,000	Debit

Tutorial note

The trial balance is dated at the year-end – i.e. after the share issue has been made. Therefore, the total of 72,000 needs to be reduced by 12,000 (1/6 × 72,000) = 60,000. Consequently, when the '1 for 5' bonus issue is made, 12,000 shares will be issued. As no cash is raised from the share issue, the debit entry can be made to the share premium account (it is a non-distributable reserve). If there was no share premium account, the debit entry could be made against retained earnings.

Task 3

(a) **Calculate the correct total value of each product that should be included in the inventory valuation at 30 June 20X1 in accordance with IAS 2 *Inventories*. (3 marks)**

Standard	$70,000	70 × $1,000 i.e. cost
Super	$72,500	50 × ($1,800 – $350) i.e. NRV
Elite	$74,000	40 × ($2,500 – $650) i.e. NRV

Inventory is measured at the lower of cost and net realisable value for each separate product or item.

(b) **What adjustment should be made to the inventory valuation stated at cost of $9,420,000 to ensure that it complies with the requirements of IAS 2 *Inventories*?**

(2 marks)

$8,500	Decrease	($75,000 – $72,500) + ($80,000 – $74,000)

Reduce the Super and Elite products to net realisable value as this is lower than cost.

Task 4

(a) **A licence is an example of which type of asset? (1 mark)**

Intangible

(b) **Calculate the amortisation charge for the year ended 30 June 20X1 and the carrying amount of the licence at that date. (2 marks**

Amortisation charge	$400,000	$2,000,000/5 years
Carrying amount	$1,600,000	$2,000,000 – $400,000

(Total: 15 marks)

Marking scheme	
	Marks
Task 1 – Purchase invoices and trial balance	3
Task 2 – Bonus issue	4
Task 3 – Inventory valuation	5
Task 4 – Intangible asset	3
	___
Total	**15**
	___

3   CLER CO

Key answer tips

This question tests your knowledge of accounts preparation for a corporate entity. It tests your knowledge of double-entry bookkeeping, including performing a bank reconciliation. Part of this question relates to accounting for inventories and you need to ensure that you have a sound understanding of accounting and disclosure requirements relating to inventories. Apply good exam technique to ensure that you answer all parts of the multi-task question.

Task 1

(a)   **State the accounting entries required to write-off this amount in the general ledger.**

(1 mark)

	$	Credit/Debit
Allowance for receivables		
Irrecoverable debts	3,500	Debit
Trade payables		
Trade receivables	3,500	Credit

(b)   **Complete the following statement**   (2 marks)

For Cler Co to record the contra entries in its general ledger, it must **debit** the trade payables' account and **credit** the trade receivables' account.

(c)   **State the accounting entries required to record this transaction in the general ledger.**

(2 marks)

	$	Credit/Debit
Discount received		
Revenue	1,710	Credit
Trade payables		
Trade receivables	1,710	Debit

Workings:

		$
		$
List price of goods less 10% trade discount	$2,000 × 90%	1,800
Less: early settlement discount	5% × $1,800	(90)
Net invoice price		1,710

Tutorial note

Trade discount is always deducted in arriving at the invoice price. Early settlement discount is also deducted if the customer is expected to take advantage of the early settlement discount terms offered.

Task 2

Using the information available to you, complete the bank reconciliation as at 31 December 20X7: (4 marks)

	$	
Debit balance per bank statement	1,500	
Payments not yet presented	2,400	
	———	
Sub-total	3,900	
Lodgments not yet cleared	3,400	
	———	
Balance per bank ledger account	500	**Credit**
Automated payment returned unpaid by customer's bank	1,000	
	———	
Updated balance per bank ledger account	1,500	**Credit**
	———	

Tutorial note

Remember that a debit balance on the bank statement indicates that the customer owes money to the bank i.e. the bank balance is overdrawn. Consequently, the bank account balance in Cler Co's general ledger reflecting the same information would be a credit balance i.e. a liability.

Task 3

(a) **At what valuation should inventory be stated in the financial statements at 31 December 20X7?** (1 mark)

$190,871

Inventory is valued at the lower of cost of $4,000 and net realisable value of $4,500 ($6,000 – 1,500). This product will continue to be valued at cost of $4,000, so no change in required to the inventory valuation.

(b) **Complete the accounting policy disclosure note for inventory for inclusion in the financial statements for the year ended 31 December 20X7.** (2 marks)

Inventory is stated at the **lower** of cost and **net realisable value** for each separate item or product.

(c)   Complete the following table to state whether each of the following items should be included as part of the cost of inventory.   (3 marks)

		Included/excluded
(i)	Selling expenses	Excluded
(ii)	Transport costs from supplier to Cler Co premises	Included
(iii)	Storage costs	Excluded

Tutorial note:

Only those costs incurred in bringing inventory to its location and condition can be classified as part of the cost of inventory. Any post-production costs or storage costs cannot be regarded as part of cost of inventory.

(Total: 15 marks)

Marking scheme	
	Marks
Task 1 – Trade receivables and trade payables	5
Task 2 – Bank reconciliation	4
Task 3 – Accounting for inventory	6
	―
Total	**15**
	―

4   CARBON CO

Key answer tips

This question tests your knowledge of accounts preparation for a corporate entity.

In particular, you need to be able to apply the accounting requirements relating to revaluation of property, plant and equipment. Additionally, your knowledge of accounting for income taxes and a rights issue is tested. Ensure that you understand the difference between a rights issue and a bonus issue of shares. This question also tests your knowledge of preparing financial statements for a single entity by requiring you to identify relevant items for inclusion in the statement of changes in equity. Finally, there is a small task requirement dealing with interpretation of financial statements.

Task 1

(a) **State whether each of the following statements relating to accounting for property, plant and equipment is true or false:** **(3 marks)**

		True/False
(i)	When an entity does revalue its land and buildings, it is compulsory to make an annual transfer of 'excess depreciation' from revaluation surplus to retained earnings	False
(ii)	Any gain on revaluation of property, plant and equipment is presented as operating income in the statement of profit or loss	False
(iii)	The revaluation surplus is accounted for as an adjustment to cash inflows from operating activities	False

There is a choice of accounting policy to either make the annual transfer of 'excess depreciation', or not to make the annual transfer. Whichever policy is adopted, it should be applied consistently from year to year.

A revaluation gain is presented as an item of 'other comprehensive income, and not in the statement of profit or loss.

Tutorial note

The revaluation surplus is not a relevant item for inclusion in the statement of cash flows. It does not affect the reconciliation of operating profit, and it is not a cash flow.

(b) **State the accounting entries required to account for the revaluation at 31 December 20X5.** **(3 marks)**

	$000	Credit/Debit
Land and buildings	2,000	Debit
Depreciation charge for the year		
Accumulated depreciation provision	120	Debit
Revaluation surplus	2,120	Credit

Revaluation surplus – Land: $4m – $2.5m = $1.5m

Revaluation surplus – Buildings: $2m – (1.5m × 46/50) = ($2m – $1.38m) = $0.62m

Note that depreciation for four years is deducted to arrive at the carrying amount of the buildings immediately before accounting for the revaluation. This is because the revaluation was performed at 31 December 20X5.

Task 2

What was the income tax expense included in the statement of profit or loss for the year ended 31 December 20X5? **(1 mark)**

$2,450,000

$2,400,000 + $50,000 under-provision relating to the previous year

Task 3

(a) **How many shares were issued as a result of making the rights issue?** **(1 mark)**

| 2,000,000 | $10,000,000 \times 1/5 = 2,000,000$ |

Tutorial note

Note that the trial balance is dated 31 December 20X5, i.e. after the rights issue has been made. For every four shares that were in issue, following the rights issue, there will now be five shares. Therefore, you need to reduce the number of shares by 4/5 to calculate the number of shares that were in issue prior to the rights issue. You can then apply the rights fraction of 1/4 to calculate the number of shares issued.

(b) **What were the total proceeds raised as a result of making the rights issue? (1 mark)**

| $5,000,000 | $2,000,000 \times \$2.50 = \$5,000,000$ |

(c) **What was the balance on the share premium account as a result of making the rights issue?** **(1 mark)**

| $3,000,000 | $2,000,000 \times (\$2.50 - \$1.00) = \$3,000,000$ |

Task 4

Identify whether or not each of the following items would be presented in the statement of changes in equity. **(3 marks)**

	Included/Excluded
Depreciation charge for the year	Excluded
Share issue made in the year	Included
Proposed dividend due to be paid on 26 February 20X6	Excluded
Dividend paid on 28 October 20X5	Included

Task 5

Which one of the following statements could be a plausible reason for the increase in the gross profit margin during 20X5? **(2 marks)**

		Selected answer
(i)	Selling expenses reduced during 20X5	
(ii)	Carbon Co sold more goods during 20X5 due to a successful marketing campaign early in the year	
(iii)	There was a change in the sales mix during 20X5, with Carbon Co selling proportionately fewer of its low-margin goods	Correct

Tutorial note

Selling expenses do not affect the calculation of gross profit. Selling a greater quantity of goods may increase the gross profit, but not necessarily the margin made on those sales. A reduction in the proportion of goods sold at lower margins will improve the gross profit margin.

(Total: 15 marks)

Marking scheme	
	Marks
Task 1 – Property, plant and equipment	6
Task 2 – Accounting for income taxes	1
Task 3 – Rights issue	3
Task 4 – SOCIE	3
Task 5 – Interpretation of information	2
	——
Total	**15**
	——

5 HARUMI

Key answer tips

This question tests your knowledge of accounts preparation for a sole trader.

When dealing with accounts preparation for a sole trader, ensure that you understand the composition of the capital account, along with how withdrawals of cash and/or goods for personal use should be accounted for. Knowledge of bookkeeping is tested with the requirement to account for a return of goods to a supplier – have a clear understanding of the difference between returns inwards and returns outwards. Knowledge of accounting for discounts is also tested in this question. Therefore, ensure that you understand the difference between a trade discount and an early settlement discount. Finally, ensure that you understand how to account for early settlement discount offered to credit customers, depending on whether the customer is expected to take advantage of the discount terms offered.

Task 1

State the accounting entries required to record the return of goods to the supplier.

(2 marks)

	$000	Credit/Debit
Revenue		
Returns inwards		
Returns outwards (100/120 × $300)	250	Credit
Sales tax (20/120 × $300)	50	Credit
Trade payables	300	Debit
Trade receivables		

Task 2

State the accounting entries required to record withdrawal of goods from the business by Harumi for personal use. **(3 marks)**

	$000	Credit/Debit
Drawings	15	Debit
Trade payables		
Purchases	15	Credit
Revenue		

Task 3

State whether each of the following statements is true or false. **(3 marks)**

		True/False
(i)	Trade discount allowed to customers should be included as an expense in the statement of profit or loss	False
(ii)	Early settlement discount allowed to credit customers should be deducted from the invoice value at the point of sale when the customer is not expected to take advantage of the early settlement discount terms offered	False
(iii)	Early settlement discount earned from suppliers should be included in the statement of profit or loss	True

Tutorial note

Trade discount is never recognised in the financial statements. It is always deducted by the seller at the point of sale when preparing the invoice. Early settlement discount offered to a credit customer is only deducted from the invoice price at the point of sale when the customer is expected to take account of the early settlement discount terms offered.

Task 4

Complete each of the following three statements in relation to the information contained in this Task. **(3 marks)**

Accounting for the insurance **prepayment** will **increase** the profit for the year ended 30 April 20X5.

Accounting for the legal fees **accrual** will **reduce** the profit for the year ended 30 April 20X5.

The net effect on the profit for the year ended 30 April 20X5 as a result of accounting for the accrual and/or prepayment required for insurances and legal fees will be to **increase** profit for the year by **$6,000**.

Insurance prepayment = 8/12 × $18,000 = $12,000 = increase profit for the year.

Legal fees accrual = $6,000 = reduction in profit.

Task 5

Identify whether each of the following items is relevant or not to reconcile and clear the suspense account (4 marks)

		Relevant/ Not relevant
(i)	The cost of a machine was recorded in the appropriate general ledger accounts but at a cost of $4,280, rather than the correct amount of $8,240	Not relevant
(ii)	Discounts received were credited to the discounts received account and debited to the suspense account	Relevant
(iii)	The total of purchases for March was debited to the trade payables account and credited to the purchases account	Not relevant
(iv)	A contra had been debited to the payables account and credited to the receivables account	Not relevant

(i)   An equal value of debits and credits were posted to the general ledger, so a suspense account entry would not be relevant.

(ii)   This would be relevant at one part of the transaction would have been posted to the suspense account pending further review and correction.

(iii)   This transaction has been correctly accounted for, so a suspense account entry is not required.

(iv)   This transaction has been correctly accounted for, so a suspense account entry is not required.

(Total: 15 marks)

Marking scheme	
	Marks
Task 1 – Accounting for return of goods	2
Task 2 – Accounting for drawings	3
Task 3 – True or false statements = 1 mark for each correct statement	3
Task 4 – Accruals and prepayments – 1 mark for correctly completed statement	3
Task 5 – Suspense account statements – 1 mark per correct answer	4
	___
Total	15
	___

6   FIREWORK CO

Key answer tips

Ensure that you are familiar with the pro-forma of a statement of cash flows – it will help you to complete relevant extracts in an examination question. Ensure that you understand the cash flows that may be included within each of the three classifications: operating, investing and financing. Note that the question tests your knowledge of the starting point for reporting cash flows from operating activities under the indirect method.

Firework Co – Statement of cash flows for the year ended 30 June 20X5

	$000		Marks
Cash flows from operating activities			
Operating profit	31,750		0.5
Adjustments for:			
Depreciation	15,000	Add	0.5
Loss on sale of plant and equipment	2,000	Add	0.5
Increase in inventories ($36,000 – $30,000)	6,000	Subtract	1.0
Increase in trade receivables ($40,000 – $35,000)	5,000	Subtract	1.0
Increase in trade payables ($36,500 – $30,000)	6,500	Add	1.0
	———		
Cash from operating activities before income taxes	44,250*		
Income taxes paid (W3)	9,500	Subtract	1.5
	———		
Net cash from operating activities	34,750*		
Cash flows from investing activities			
Cash purchase of property, plant and equipment (W1)	40,000	Subtract	1.0
Disposal proceeds of plant and equipment (W2)	8,000	Add	1.0
	———		
Net cash used in investing activities	(32,000)*		
Cash flows from financing activities			
Repayment of bank loan (W4)	10,000	Subtract	1.0
Proceeds of share issue ($5,000 + $5,000) (W5)	10,000	Add	2.0
Finance costs paid	750	Subtract	0.5
Dividend paid (W6)	14,000	Subtract	1.5
	———		
Net cash used in financing activities	(14,750)*		
Net **decrease** in cash and cash equivalents ($10,000 + $2,000)	12,000		1.0
Cash and cash equivalents at start of year	10,000	Add	0.5
	———		
Cash and cash equivalents at end of year	2,000	Net overdraft	0.5
	———		———
			15.0

Note: The subtotals (*) are included for completeness and to show the movement in cash and cash equivalents: ($44,250 – $34,750 – $14,750) = $12,000 decrease.

Workings:

(W1) PPE additions in the year

	$000	
PPE Carrying amount b/f	93,000	Add
Carrying amount of disposals ($8,000 + $2,000 loss)	10,000	Subtract
Depreciation charge	15,000	Subtract
Revaluation in year	2,000	Add
Cash paid for PPE additions (β)	40,000	Add
PPE Carrying amount c/f	110,000	

Tutorial note

When preparing the reconciliation of property, plant and equipment movements in the year, don't forget to include any revaluation surplus recognised in the year. You will find the relevant information either in the notes to the question or, as in this case, by identifying the gain on revaluation presented in 'other comprehensive income'.

(W2) Loss on disposal of plant and equipment

	$000	
Carrying amount of disposals ($8,000 + $2,000) (β)	10,000	Add
Loss on disposal in cost of sales	2000	Subtract
Disposal proceeds received	8,000	

(W3) Income taxes paid

	$000	
Income tax liability b/f	10,000	Add
Income tax expense for the year per P/L	6,000	Add
Cash paid in year	9,500	Subtract
Income tax liability c/f	6,500	

(W4) Bank loan – amount repaid

	$000	
Bank loan b/f	17,000	Add
Cash paid	10,000	Subtract
Bank loan c/f	7,000	

(W5) Issue of shares in the year

	Share capital $000	Share premium $000
Balance b/f	15,000	3,000
Proceeds of share issue in year	5,000	5,000
	———	———
Balance c/f	20,000	8,000
	———	———

(W6) Dividend paid

	$000	
Retained earnings b/f	85,000	Add
Profit for the year	25,000	Add
Cash paid	14,000	Subtract
	———	
Retained earnings c/f	96,000	
	———	

Marking scheme	
	Marks
Statement of cash flows (per answer)	15
	——
Total	**15**
	——

7 CRACKER CO

Key answer tips

Ensure that you understand which items are classified under each of the headings in a statement of cash flows. It will help you to complete relevant parts of a question efficiently. Begin with cash flows from operating activities, with the first item as 'operating profit' from the statement of profit or loss. Use standard workings to calculate the required values for inclusion in the statement of cash flows.

Cracker Co – Statement of cash flows for the year ended 31 March 20X1

	$000		Marks
Cash flows from operating activities			
Operating profit	13,480		0.5
Adjustments for:			
Depreciation	500	Add	0.5
Gain on disposal of plant and equipment	300	Subtract	1.0
Increase in inventories ($27,500 – $25,500)	2,000	Subtract	1.0
Increase in trade receivables ($37,500 – $33,000)	4,500	Subtract	1.0
Decrease in trade payables ($31,900 – $29,450)	2,450	Subtract	1.0
	_____		
Cash from operating activities before income taxes	4,730*		
Income taxes paid (W3)	2,310	Subtract	1.0
	_____		
Net cash from operating activities	_2,420*_		
Cash flows from investing activities			
Interest income received	320	Add	0.5
Cash purchase of property, plant and equipment (W1)	3,800	Subtract	1.0
Disposal proceeds of plant and equipment (W2) (Item 1)	1,100	Add	1.0
	_____		
Net cash used in investing activities	_(2,380)*_		
Cash flows from financing activities			
Proceeds of loan raised (W4)	3,500	Add	1.0
Proceeds of share issue ($1,000 + $610)(W5) (Item 2)	1,610	Add	2.0
Finance costs paid	2,150	Subtract	0.5
	_____		
Net cash from in financing activities	_2,960*_		
Net **increase** in cash and cash equivalents for the year	3,000	Increase	1.0
Cash and cash equivalents at start of the year	1,250	Add	1.0
	_____		
Cash and cash equivalents at end of the year	4,250		1.0
	_____		_____
			15.0

Note: The subtotals (*) are included for completeness and show the movement in cash and cash equivalents: ($2,420 – $2,380 + $2,960) = $3,000 increase.

Item 1: Disposal proceeds of plant and equipment (all figures in $000):

		Selected answer
(i)	$800 – $300	
(ii)	$800 + $300	Correct
(iii)	$800	

Item 2: Proceeds of the share issue (all figures in $000):

		Selected answer
(i)	$11,000 – $10,000	
(ii)	$11,000 – $10,000 + $610	Correct
(iii)	$11,000 – $10,000 – $610	

Workings

(W1) PPE additions in the year

	$000	
Carrying amount b/f	70,500	Add
Carrying amount of disposals	800	Subtract
Depreciation charge	500	Subtract
Cash paid for PPE additions	3,800	Add
	———	
Carrying amount c/f	73,000	
	———	

(W2) Gain on disposal of plant and equipment

	$000	
Carrying amount of disposals	800	Add
Profit on disposal per P/L	300	Add
	———	
Disposal proceeds received	1,100	
	———	

Tutorial note

The statement of profit or loss includes the profit on disposal of plant and equipment, and the notes to the question specify the carrying amount of the items disposed of. From this, you can identify the disposal proceeds received. Also, don't forget to remove the carrying amount of the items disposed of within the property, plant and equipment reconciliation.

(W3) Income taxes paid

	$000	
Income tax liability b/f	2,310	Add
Income tax expense for the year per P/L	2,900	Add
Cash paid in year	2,310	Subtract
	———	
Income tax liability c/f	2,900	
	———	

(W4) Loan finance – additional loan finance raised

	$000	
10% debenture Loan liability b/f	20,000	Add
Cash received – additional loan finance	3,500	Add
	———	
10% debenture Loan liability c/f	23,500	
	———	

(W5) Issue of shares in the year

	Share capital	Share premium
	$000	$000
Balance b/f	10,000	Nil
Proceeds of share issue in year	1,000	610
Balance c/f	11,000	610

Marking scheme	
	Marks
Statement of cash flows (per answer)	15
	——
Total	**15**
	——

8   SPARKLER CO

Key answer tips

IAS 7 *Statement of Cash Flows* permits inclusion of items under the classifications of investing activities and financing activities respectively in any order. The key point is that they are included within the correct classification. Similarly, many of the items within operating activities can also be included in any order, although it must begin with 'operating profit' and end with 'tax paid'. However, in a computer-based examination, the sequence in which items are included within each heading is likely to be pre-determined.

Sparkler Co – Statement of cash flows for the year ended 30 September 20X9

	$000		*Marks*
Cash flows from operating activities			
Operating profit	20,700		*0.5*
Adjustments for:			
Depreciation (W1)	12,500	Add	*0.5*
Profit on sale of plant and equipment	500	Subtract	*0.5*
Decrease in inventories ($36,000 – $30,750)	5,250	Add	*1.0*
Decrease in trade receivables ($45,000 – $39,250)	5,750	Add	*1.0*
Decrease in trade payables ($38,500 – $35,000)	3,500	Subtract	*1.0*
	———		
Cash from operating activities before income taxes	40,200		
Income taxes paid (W3)	4,000	Subtract	*1.0*
	———		
Net cash from operating activities	*36,200**		

Cash flows from investing activities

Cash purchase of property, plant and equipment (W1)	21,000	Subtract	*1.5*
Disposal proceeds of plant and equipment (W2)	2,000	Add	*1.0*
	———		
Net cash used in investing activities	*(19,000)**		
Cash flows from financing activities			
Proceeds of loan raised (W4)	5,000	Add	*1.0*
Proceeds of share issue ($6,000 + $2,000) (W5)	8,000	Add	*2.0*
Finance costs paid (W6) (Item 1)	2,575	Subtract	*1.0*
Dividend paid (W7) (Item 2)	20,125	Subtract	*1.0*
	———		
Net cash used in financing activities	*(9,700)**		
Net change in cash and cash equivalents ($4,500 + $3,000)	7,500	Increase	*1.0*
Cash and cash equivalents b/f	4,500	Subtract	*0.5*
	———		
Cash and cash equivalents c/f	3,000		*0.5*
	———		——
			15.0

Note: The subtotals (*) are included for completeness and show the movement in cash and cash equivalents: ($36,200 − $19,000 − $9,700) = $7,500 increase.

Item 1: Finance costs paid: Select the correct calculation of finance costs paid (all figures in $000):

		Selected answer
(i)	$2,700 − $625 − $500	
(ii)	$2,700 + $500 + $625	
(iii)	$2,700 + $500 − $625	Correct

Item 2: Dividend paid: Select the correct calculation of dividend paid in the year:

		Selected answer
(i)	Retained earnings b/f + Profit − Retained earnings c/f	Correct
(ii)	Retained earnings b/f + Total comprehensive income − Retained earnings carried forward	
(iii)	Retained earnings b/f − Profit + Retained earnings c/f	

Workings:

(W1) PPE additions in the year

	$000	
Carrying amount b/f	85,000	Add
Less: Carrying amount of disposals	1,500	Subtract
Revaluation in year	3,000	Add
Less: Depreciation charge	12,500	Subtract
Cash paid for PPE additions	21,000	Add
	———	
Carrying amount c/f	95,000	
	———	

(W2) Gain on disposal of plant and equipment

	$000	
Carrying amount of disposals	1,500	Add
Profit on disposal per P/L	500	Add
Disposal proceeds received	2,000	

(W3) Income taxes paid

	$000	
Income tax liability b/f	4,000	Add
Income tax expense for the year per P/L	3,500	Add
Cash paid in year	4,000	Subtract
Income tax liability c/f	3,500	

(W4) Loan finance – additional loan finance raised

	$000	
10% debenture Loan liability b/f	20,000	Add
Cash received – additional loan finance	5,000	Add
10% debenture Loan liability c/f	25,000	

(W5) Issue of shares in the year

	Share capital	Share premium
	$000	$000
Balance b/f	24,000	8,000
Proceeds of share issue in year	6,000	2,000
Balance c/f	30,000	10,000

(W6) Finance costs paid in the year

	$000
Interest payable b/f	500
Profit or loss expense for the year	2,700
Finance costs paid in the year	(2,575)
Interest payable c/f	625

(W7) Dividend paid in the year

	$000	
Retained earnings b/f	66,500	Add
Profit for the year	14,500	Add
Dividend paid in the year	20,125	Subtract
	———	
Retained earnings c/f	60,875	
	———	

Tutorial note

The dividend paid in the year can be calculated by reconciling the movement in retained earnings from the start of the year to the end of the year. Remember to include the profit from the statement of profit or loss as part of your calculations. Note – do not include any revaluation surplus arising in the year (as included as an item of 'other comprehensive income' as this is not part of retained earnings.

Marking scheme	
	Marks
Statement of cash flows per answer	15
	—
Total	**15**
	—

9 OUTFLOW CO

Key answer tips

IAS 7 *Statement of Cash Flows* permits you to include items under the classification of investing activities and financing activities respectively in any order, provided that they are within the appropriate classification – there is not a defined sequential order. Note that this question includes an operating loss in the statement of profit or loss. There is also a revaluation of property, plant and equipment, so ensure that you understand how this affects the statement of cash flows. The revaluation gain for the year does not affect operating profit (or loss), so should be excluded from the statement. Other items, such as annual depreciation and the gain or loss on disposal should be adjustment for, as usual.

Outflow Co – Statement of cash flows for the year ended 30 April 20X2

	$000		Marks
Cash flows from operating activities			
Operating loss	(3,300)		1.0
Adjustments for:			
Depreciation (W2)	11,000	Add	0.5
Loss on scrapped assets (W1)	1,000	Add	0.5
Decrease in inventories ($33,000 – $30,000)	3,000	Add	1.0
Decrease in receivables ($52,000 – $48,750)	3,250	Add	1.0
Decrease in payables ($27,500 – $26,300)	1,200	Subtract	1.0
	———		
Cash from operating activities before income taxes	13,750*		
Income taxes paid (W3)	5,000	Subtract	1.0
	———		
Net cash from operating activities	8,750*		
Cash flows from investing activities			
Cash purchase of PPE (W2) (Item 1)	20,000	Subtract	1.5
	———		
Net cash used in investing activities	(20,000)*		
Cash flows from financing activities			
Proceeds of loan raised (W4)	7,500	Add	1.0
Proceeds of share issue ($4,000 + $1,000)(W5) (Item 2)	5,000	Add	2.0
Finance costs paid	1,000	Subtract	1.0
Dividend paid (W6)	1,000	Subtract	1.0
	———		
Net cash from financing activities	10,500*		
Net change in cash and equivalents in the year	750	Decrease	1.0
Cash and cash equivalents b/f	3,250	Net overdraft	0.5
	———		
Cash and cash equivalents c/f	4,000	Net overdraft	0.5
	———		——
			15.0

Note: The subtotals (*) are included for completeness and show the movement in cash and cash equivalents: ($8,750 – $20,000 + $10,500) = $750 decrease.

Item 1: Additions to property, plant and equipment in the year (all figures in $000)

		Selected answer
(i)	$110,000 + $2,000 – $100,000 + $11,000 + $1,000	
(ii)	$110,000 – $100,000 + $11,000	
(iii)	$110,000 – $2,000 – $100,000 + $1,000 + $11,000	Correct

Item 2: Proceeds of the share issue (all figures in $000):

		Selected answer
(i)	$40,000 + 4,000 – $44,000	
(ii)	$44,000 + $5,000 – $40,000 – $4,000	Correct
(iii)	$44,000 – $40,000	

Workings:

(W1) Loss on disposal of scrapped assets

	$000	
Disposal proceeds received	Nil	Add
Carrying amount of scrapped items	1000	Subtract
	———	
Loss on disposal	1000	
	———	

(W2) PPE additions in the year

	$000	
Carrying amount b/f	100,000	Add
Additions in year (β)	20,000	Add
Depreciation charge	11,000	Subtract
Disposals in year	1,000	Subtract
Revaluation in year	2,000	Add
	———	
Carrying amount c/f	110,000	
	———	

(W3) Income taxes

	$000	
Income tax liability b/f	5,000	Add
Income tax income per P/L	500	Subtract
Cash paid in year (β)	5,000	Subtract
	———	
Income tax receivable (asset) c/f	500	
	———	

(W4) Bank loan – additional loan finance raised

	$000	
Bank loan liability b/f	8,000	Add
Cash received – additional loan finance (β)	7,500	Add
	———	
Bank loan liability c/f	15,500	
	———	

(W5) Issue of shares in the year

	Share capital	Share premium
	$000	$000
Balance b/f	40,000	4,000
Proceeds of share issue in year (β)	4,000	1,000
Balance c/f	44,000	5,000

Tutorial note

Calculate the total cash proceeds received from the share issue by identifying movements in both the share capital and share premium accounts.

(W6) Dividend paid in the year

	$000	
Retained earnings b/f	77,250	Add
Loss after tax for the year	3,800	Subtract
Dividend paid in the year (β)	1,000	Subtract
Retained earnings c/f	72,450	

Marking scheme	
	Marks
Statement of cash flows (per answer)	15
Total	**15**

10 PATTY AND SELMA

Key answer tips

This question deals with the mid-year acquisition of a subsidiary. Ensure that you pro-rate the calculation of each item of income and expense in the subsidiary's statement of profit or loss to identify the post-acquisition element as part of your consolidation workings.

Look for any intra-group trading to remove it from the consolidated statement, ensuring that you have also identified and adjusted properly for any unrealised profit on closing inventory. Remember that intra-group trading will always be post-acquisition.

Task 1

Complete the following consolidated statement of profit or loss for the year ended 31 December 20X1. **(8 marks)**

	$000	Marks
Revenue ($987 + ($567 × 8/12) – $120 (W1))	1,245	1.5
Less: Cost of sales ($564 + ($336 × 8/12) – $120 (W1) + $5 (W1)) (Item 1)	673	1.5
	———	
Gross profit	572	
Less: General and administrative expenses ($223 + ($123 × 8/12))	305	1.0
	———	
Operating profit/Profit before financing and income taxes	267	
Less: Interest expense ($50 + ($30 × 8/12)) (Item 2)	70	1.0
	———	
Profit before income taxes	197	
Less: Income tax expense ($40 + ($24 × 8/12))	56	1.0
	———	
Profit for the year	141	
	———	
Profit attributable to:		
Owners of Patty (β)	130.2	
Non-controlling interest (W2) (Item 3)	10.8	2.0
	———	———
	141.0	8.0
	———	———

Item 1: Select the correct calculation for cost of sales

	All figures are in $000	Selected answer
(i)	$564 + ($336 × 8/12) – $120 – $5	
(ii)	$564 + ($336 × 8/12) + $120 – $5	
(iii)	$564 + ($336 × 8/12) – $120 + $5	Correct

Item 2: Select the correct calculation for interest expense

	All figures are in $000	Selected answer
(i)	$50 – ($30 × 8/12)	
(ii)	$50 + ($30 × 8/12)	Correct
(iii)	$50 + $30	

Item 3: Select the correct formula to calculate the non-controlling interest share of the consolidated profit for the year

		Selected answer
(i)	(NCI% × Subsidiary's profit before income taxes × 8/12) + NCI's share of unrealised profit on inventory	
(ii)	(NCI% × Subsidiary's profit × 8/12) – NCI's share of unrealised profit on inventory	
(iii)	NCI% × Subsidiary's profit × 8/12	Correct

Workings:

(W1) **Intra-group transactions and PURP**

Remember to remove intra-group sales and purchases of $120k in the calculations. Note that these transactions do not need to be pro-rated as the question states that they are all post-acquisition.

Profit on intra-group sales = $120k × (20/120) = $20k

The proportion of this profit remaining in inventory must be eliminated:

$20k × 25% = $5k. The double entry to adjust for this is:

Dr Cost of sales (P/L) $5k, and Cr Inventory (SoFP) $5k

The parent bears all of the unrealised profit adjustment as the parent made the sales to the subsidiary.

Tutorial note

Ensure that you can identify whether sales have been based on 'cost-plus' or a sales margin as this will affect the calculation of the provision for unrealised profit.

(W2) **Non-controlling interest share of consolidated profit**

	$000
NCI% of S's profit × 8/12 = 30% × $54 × 8/12	10.8

Note that the non-controlling interest does not bear any part of the unrealised profit on inventory adjustment as the parent made the sale.

Task 2

State whether each of the following statements is true or false. **(3 marks)**

		True/False
(i)	Accounting for the acquisition of a subsidiary always includes recognition and accounting for a non-controlling interest	False
(ii)	Accounting for the acquisition of a subsidiary can be achieved by using equity accounting	False
(iii)	The share capital and share premium account balances of a subsidiary are not included in the consolidated statement of financial position	True

The first statement is false as control could be obtained by acquisition of all of the shares in a subsidiary – there would be no non-controlling interest to account for in this situation. The second statement is false as equity accounting is used to account for an interest in an associate.

Task 3

(a)   Using the individual entity financial statements, calculate the following ratios for Patty and Selma for the year ended 31 December 20X1.   **(2 marks)**

Marks

Gross profit margin

Patty: (423/987 × 100) = 42.9%   *0.5*

Selma: (231/567 × 100) = 40.7%   *0.5*

Operating profit margin:

Patty: 200/987 × 100 = 20.3%   *0.5*

Selma: 108/567 × 100 = 19.0%   *0.5*

(b)   What conclusion could you arrive at regarding the relative financial performance of the two entities?   **(2 marks)**

		Selected answer
(i)	Patty is relatively better at minimising selling and administrative expenses than Quartz	Correct
(ii)	Quartz is relatively better at minimising selling and administrative expenses than Patty	
(iii)	It is not possible to arrive at a conclusion regarding which entity is relatively better at minimising selling and administrative expenses	

(Total: 15 marks)

Marking scheme	
	Marks
Task 1 – Consolidated statement of profit or loss per answer	8
Task 2 – 1 mark for each correct answer	3
Task 3a – 0.5 mark per ratio calculated correctly	2
Task 3b – 2 marks for correct answer	2
	——
Total	**15**
	——

11   PENTAGON AND SQUARE

Key answer tips

Task 1 of this question tests your knowledge of how to calculate goodwill on acquisition. Task 2 deals with preparation of a consolidated statement of financial position.

To answer this question fully, you also need to understand how to account for intra-group transactions and unrealised profit, together with calculation of the non-controlling interest share of the result for the year.

Task 1

(a) **Calculate the fair value of consideration paid to acquire the shares in Square.**

(1 mark)

	$	
Fair value of consideration paid:	N/A	
Cash paid	150,000	
FV of shares issued (75% × 40,000 × 4/3 × $2.50)	100,000	Add
	250,000	

(b) **State the accounting entries required by Pentagon to record the issue of shares used as part of the consideration to acquire control of Square.** **(2 marks)**

	$	Credit/Debit	Marks
Investment in Square	100,000	Debit	0.5
Issued share capital 75% × 40,000 × 4/3 × $1	40,000	Credit	0.5
Retained earnings			
Revaluation surplus			
Share premium 75% × 40,000 × 4/3 × $1.50	60,000	Credit	1

(c) **Select the correct formula to calculate goodwill arising on the acquisition of Square.**

(1 mark)

		Selected answer
(i)	Fair value of consideration paid Plus: Fair value of non-controlling interest at acquisition Plus: Fair value of net assets at acquisition date	
(ii)	Fair value of consideration paid Less: Fair value of non-controlling interest at acquisition Plus: Fair value of net assets at acquisition date	
(iii)	Fair value of consideration paid Plus: Fair value of non-controlling interest at acquisition Less: Fair value of net assets at acquisition date	Correct

Task 2

Calculate the amounts that each of the following items should be included in the consolidated statement of financial position as at 31 December 20X4. **(6 marks)**

	$	$000	
Property, plant and equipment	454,000	205 + 179 + 70 (W2)	2 marks
Inventories	127,000	80 + 50 – 3 (W1)	2 marks
Trade and other receivables	159,000	60 + 99	1 mark
Cash and cash equivalents	51,000	0 + 51	1 mark

Workings:

(W1) Provision for unrealised profit

Profit on intra-group sales = $30,000 × 30% = $9,000

The proportion of this profit remaining in inventory must be eliminated:

1/3 × $9,000 = $3,000. The double entry to adjust for this is:

Dr Cost of sales (P/L)$3,000, and Cr Inventory (SOFP) $3,000

(W2) Fair value adjustment

FV of land = $170,000 less carrying amount $100,000 = $70,000

Task 3

Select the formula which correctly calculates the non-controlling interest to be included in the consolidated statement of financial position as at 31 December 20X4.   **(2 marks)**

	All figures are in $	Selected answer
(i)	(25% × $75,000) + (25% × ($279,000 – $120,000))	
(ii)	$75,000 + (25% × ($279,000 + $120,000))	
(iii)	$75,000 + (25% × ($279,000 – $120,000))	Correct

Task 4

(a) Using the individual financial statements, calculate the quick (acid test) ratio for Pentagon and Square as at 31 December 20X4.   **(2 marks)**

Pentagon	1.0 :1	(60/(12+48))	1 mark
Square	3.0 :1	(99 + 51)/50	1 mark

(b) Complete the following statement relating to the quick (acid test) ratio.   **(1 mark)**

The quick (acid test) ratio is a measure of **liquidity**. A quick (acid test) ratio of 0.75:1 indicates that an entity has a **lower** value of current assets than current liabilities. For the purposes of this ratio, inventories are **excluded** within the definition of current assets.   **(Total: 15 marks)**

Marking scheme	
	Marks
Task 1 – Goodwill calculation	4
Task 2 – Consolidated statement of financial position assets	6
Task 3 – Calculate NCI to include in SOFP	2
Task 4a – Ratio calculations	2
Task 4b – Interpretation of financial statements	1
Total	15

12   PIKE AND SALMON

Key answer tips

This question tests your knowledge of how to deal with a mid-year acquisition – you need to pro-rate the retained earnings for the year into pre- and post-acquisition elements. Ensure that you know how to account for intra-group (IG) transactions and balances; in particular, (a) unrealised profits when the subsidiary sells to the parent, (b) cancellation of intra-group balances for receivables and payables and (c) cancellation of intra-group loans from parent to subsidiary.

Task 1

(a)   Select the formula which correctly calculates Salmon's retained earnings at the date of acquisition.   **(2 marks)**

	All figures are in $000	Selected answer
(i)	$6,090 + $240 + (3/12 × $240)	
(ii)	$1,290 – $240 + (9/12 × $240)	Correct
(iii)	$1,290 – $240 + (3/12 × $240)	

(b)   Select the formula which correctly calculates the fair value of net assets of Salmon at the date of acquisition.   **(2 marks)**

	All figures are in $000	Selected answer
(i)	$4,800 + $1,290 + $1,000	
(ii)	$4,800 – $1,230 + (3/12 × $240) + $1,000	
(iii)	$4,800 + $1,290 – (3/12 × $240) + $1,000	Correct

(c)   Select the formula which correctly calculates goodwill at acquisition.   **(2 marks)**

	All figures are in $000	Selected answer
(i)	$9,720 + $2,400 – $7,030	
(ii)	$8,720 + $2,400 – $7,030	Correct
(iii)	$8,720 + $2,400 – $6,030	

Task 2

(a)   What amount should be included in the consolidated statement of financial position for the 5% Loan notes as at 31 March 20X6?   **(2 marks)**

| $26,620,000 | $16,440 + $11,180 – $1,000 (IG)

(b)   What amount should be included in the consolidated statement of financial position for retained earnings at 31 March 20X6?   **(2 marks)**

| $12,495,000 | $12,480 + (75% × $60) – (75% × $40) PURP

Task 3

Complete the following table to state at what amount each of the following items should be included in the consolidated statement of financial position at 31 March 20X6.

(5 marks)

		$000		
(i)	Non-current assets	40,950	$26,280 + 13,670 + $1,000 (FVA)	1 mark
(ii)	Current assets	9,480	$4,760 + $5,010 − $250 (IG) − $40 (PURP)	1.5 marks
(iii)	Current liabilities	3,800	$2,640 + $1,410 − $250 (IG)	1 mark
(iv)	Non-controlling interest	2,405	$2,400 + (25% × $60) − (25% × $40 (PURP))	1.5 marks

Tutorial note

For non-current assets, remember to include the increase in the fair value of land as at the date of acquisition (i.e. $170,000 − $100,000).

For current assets, remember remove the unrealised profit of $40,000 (80% × $50,000) within closing inventory.

Also, remember to eliminate the intra-group receivable and payable. Half of the invoice value of intra-group sales is still outstanding i.e. $250,000.

Tutorial note

For non-controlling interest remember to deduct their share of the unrealised profit on inventory of $10,000 ($50,000 × 80% × 25%). This must be done as the subsidiary sold goods to the parent at a profit and not all of it has been realised by the reporting date.

(Total 15 marks)

Marking scheme	
	Marks
Task 1 – Goodwill calculation	6
Task 2 – Consolidated statement of financial position items	4
Task 3 – Consolidated statement of financial position items	5
	——
Total	**15**
	——

13   PLATE AND SAUCER

Key answer tips

This question requires you to deal with preparation of a consolidated statement of profit or loss. Ensure that you know how to deal with elimination of intra-group sales and purchases, along with unrealised profit arising on those transactions. There is also an additional aspect of intra-group trading as the parent has made a loan to the subsidiary – there is loan interest income and expense to eliminate from the consolidated statement of profit or loss. Note that the loan was made part-way through the accounting year. You therefore need to time-apportion the interest calculation. Finally, you need to cancel this intra-group item of income and expense as part of the consolidated process.

Task 1

Complete the following consolidated statement of profit or loss for the year ended 31 December 20X4.   **(9 marks)**

Consolidated statement of profit or loss for the year ended 31 December 20X4.

	$000	*Marks*
Revenue ($1,500 + $700 – $150 (IG))	2,050	2.0
Less: Cost of sales ((775 + $370 – $150 (IG) + $5 (W1)) (Item 1)	1,000	2.0
Gross profit	1,050	
Less: Administrative expenses ($317 + $135)	452	1.0
Operating profit	598	
Add: Interest income ($15 + $0 – ($1,000 × 6% × 3/12) (IG))	Nil	1.0
Profit before financing and income tax	598	
Less: Interest expense ($60 + $20 – ($1,000 × 6% × 3/12)) (item 2)	65	1.0
Profit before income taxes	533	
Less: Income tax expense ($96 + $45)	141	0.5
Profit for the year	392	
Profit attributable to:		
Owners of Plate (β)	N/A	
Non-controlling interest (W2) (Item 3)	37.5	1.5
	N/A	**9.0**

Tutorial note

Note that the loan from the parent to the subsidiary was made part-way through the accounting year. Therefore, you need to calculate the interest receivable by the parent from the subsidiary. This then needs to be eliminated on consolidation from interest income and interest expense, just like any other transaction between the parent and subsidiary during the accounting period.

Item 1: Select the formula which correctly calculates cost of sales

	All figures are in $000	Selected answer
(i)	$775 + $370 + 150 − $5	
(ii)	$775 + $370 − $150 + $5	Correct
(iii)	$775 + $370 − $150 − $5	

Item 2: Select the formula which correctly calculates interest expense

	All figures are in $000	Selected answer
(i)	$60 − $20 + ($1,000 × 6% × 9/12)	
(ii)	$60 + $20 − ($1,000 × 6%)	
(iii)	$60 + $20 − ($1,000 × 6% × 3/12)	Correct

Item 3: Select the formula which correctly calculates the non-controlling interest share of the consolidated profit for the year

		Selected answer
(i)	(NCI% × Subsidiary's profit) − (NCI share of unrealised profit on inventory)	Correct
(ii)	(NCI% × Subsidiary's profit) + NCI share of unrealised profit on inventory	
(iii)	(NCI% × Subsidiary's profit before income taxes) − NCI share of unrealised profit on inventory	

Task 2

Select which one of the following is the correct accounting treatment for an associate in the consolidated statement of financial position. **(2 marks)**

		Selected answer
(i)	All assets and liabilities of the associate are summed on a line-by-line basis with all other assets and liabilities of the group	
(ii)	The group share of the net assets of the associate are summed on a line-by-line basis with all other assets and liabilities of the group	
(iii)	The investment in the associate is presented as a separate line item in non-current assets	Correct

Task 3

(a) **Using the individual entity financial statements of Plate and Saucer, calculate the operating profit margin for each entity for the year ended 31 December 20X4.**

(2 marks)

Plate	27.2%	408/1,500	1 mark

Saucer	27.9%	195/700	1 mark

(b) **State whether each of the following statements is true or false** **(2 marks)**

		True/False	
(i)	The operating profit margin will be affected by a change in the value of closing inventory, if all other factors remain unchanged	True	1 mark
(ii)	The operating profit margin is not affected by interest expenses incurred during the accounting period	True	1 mark

(Total: 15 marks)

Workings:

(W1) PURP

$150,000/120 × 20 = $25,000

The proportion of this profit remaining in inventory must be eliminated:

$25,000 × 1/5 = $5,000

The double entry to adjust for this is:

Dr Cost of sales (P/L) $5,000, Cr Inventory (SOFP) $5,000

(W2) Non-controlling interest

	$000
NCI % of S's PAT (30% × $130,000)	39,000
NCI % of PURP (30% × $5,000 (W1))	(1,500)
	────
	37,500
	────

Marking scheme	
	Marks
Task 1 – Consolidated statement of profit or loss	9
Task 2 – Accounting for an associate	2
Task 3 – Ratio calculations and interpretation of financial statements	4
	──
Total	**15**
	──

14   PORT AND STARBOARD

Key answer tips

This question comprises five tasks. Task 1 requires the calculation and accounting classification of goodwill. Tasks 2 and 3 require you to calculate individual items for inclusion in the consolidated statement of financial position. Task 4 deals with accounting for an associate and Task 5 tests your understanding of the current ratio of a business.

Task 1:

(a)   **Select the formula which correctly calculates goodwill on acquisition of Starboard.**

(2 marks)

		Selected answer
(i)	$300,000 + $80,000 − ($60,000 + $150,000 + $30,000)	
(ii)	$300,000 + $80,000 − ($70,000 + $150,000 + $30,000)	Correct
(iii)	$300,000 + $80,000 − ($70,000 + $150,000 − $30,000)	

(b)   **Identify which one of the following wold be the correct classification for goodwill in the consolidated statement of financial position.**   **(1 mark)**

		Selected answer
(i)	A tangible non-current asset	
(ii)	A current asset	
(iii)	An intangible non-current asset	Correct

Task 2

Complete the following table to state at what amount each of the following items should be included in the consolidated statement of financial position at 31 December 20X6.

(5 marks)

		$000	$000	
(i)	Property, plant and equipment	645	$350 + $265 + $30 (FVA)	1 mark
(ii)	Inventories	184	$109 + $80 − $5 (PURP)	1 mark
(iii)	Trade receivables	144	$79 + $95 − $30 (IG)	1 mark
(iv)	Trade and other payables	185	$155 + 60 − $30 (IG)	1 mark
(v)	7% Bank loan 20X9	385	$300 + $85	1 mark

Tutorial note

When totalling the net assets at the reporting date, don't forget to include any fair value adjustments for land and buildings within non-current assets. In addition, remember to eliminate any unrealised profit on closing inventory and any receivables/payables balances outstanding between parent and subsidiary at the reporting date.

Task 3

(a) What amount should be included in the consolidated statement of financial position for the non-controlling interest as at 31 December 20X6? **(2 marks)**

$100,000   See (W1)

(b) What amount should be included in the consolidated statement of financial position for retained earnings at 31 December 20X6? **(2 marks)**

$370,000   See (W2)

Workings:

(W1) Non-controlling interest

	$000
FV of NCI at acquisition	80
20% × (250 – 150)	20
	–––––
	100
	–––––

(W2) Retained earnings

	$000
Port	295
Starboard 80% × (250 – 150)	80
Less: PURP ($50 × 25% × 40%)	(5)
	–––––
	370
	–––––

Note that the calculation of the provision for unrealised profit is based on 40% of the intra-group sales still held in inventory. The question provides the proportion of those goods that had been sold, rather than unsold, by the reporting date.

Task 4

Which TWO of the following factors would be relevant when accounting for an associate? **(1 mark)**

		Selected answer	Marks
(i)	Control of Astern		
(ii)	Exercising significant influence over Astern	Correct	0.5
(iii)	Owning the majority of the equity shares of Astern		
(iv)	Owning between 20% and 50% of the equity shares of Astern	Correct	0.5
(v)	Accounting for goodwill		
(vi)	Accounting for the non-controlling interest in Astern		

Task 5

State whether each of the following statements is true or false.   **(2 marks)**

		True/False	Marks
(i)	If the gross profit margin of a business improves, the current ratio will also improve	False	*1*
(ii)	If a bonus issue of shares is made, this will have no effect on the current ratio	True	*1*

(Total 15 marks)

Marking scheme	
	Marks
Task 1 – Accounting for goodwill	3
Task 2 – Items to include in consolidated SOFP	5
Task 3 – Items to include in consolidated SOFP	4
Task 4 – Accounting for an associate	1
Task 5 – Interpretation of financial statements	2
	——
Total	**15**
	——

15   HIDE AND SEEK

Key answer tips

This question requires you to calculate goodwill on acquisition (an item included in the consolidated statement of financial position) and also to complete the consolidated statement of profit or loss. Note that this was a mid-year acquisition, and the results of the subsidiary will need to be pro-rated accordingly. There is also intra-group trading (by definition, this will be post-acquisition) along with accounting for unrealised profit on inventory.

Task 1

Calculate goodwill arising on acquisition of Seek by Hide. **(3 marks)**

	$000	$000	Marks
Fair value of consideration paid:			
Cash paid	24,000	3,000 × $8	1
	———		
Fair value of the NCI at acquisition	4,000	1,000 × $4	1
	———		
Fair value of net assets at acquisition:			
Share capital	4,000		
Retained earnings (Item 1)	20,000	$9,500 + (9/12 × $14,000)	1
Fair value adjustment	2,000		
	———		
	26,000		
	———		
Goodwill on acquisition (Item 2)	2,000		
	———		

Item 1: Select the formula which correctly calculates retained earnings of Seek at the date of acquisition

	All figures are in $000	Selected answer
(i)	$9,500 + (3/12 × $14,000)	
(ii)	$9,500 + $14,000	
(iii)	$9,500 + (9/12 × $14,000)	Correct

Item 2: Select which of the following correctly calculates goodwill

		Selected answer
(i)	Fair value of consideration paid plus fair value of non-controlling interest at acquisition date plus fair value of net assets at acquisition	
(ii)	Fair value of consideration paid plus fair value of non-controlling interest at acquisition date minus fair value of net assets at acquisition	Correct
(iii)	Fair value of consideration paid minus fair value of non-controlling interest at acquisition date + fair value of net assets at acquisition	

Task 2

Consolidated statement of profit or loss for the year ended 30 June 20X6

	$000	Marks
Revenue ($200,000 + (3/12 × $100,000) − $12,500 (W1))	212,500	2.0
Less: Cost of sales ($110,000 + (3/12 × $50,000) − $12,500 + $1,000 (W1)) (Item 1)	111,000	2.5
	————	
Gross profit	101,500	
Less: Selling expenses ($20,000 + (3/12 × $10,000))	22,500	1.0
Less: General and administrative expenses ($40,000 + (3/12 × $20,000))	45,000	1.0
	————	
Operating profit/Profit before financing and income taxes	34,000	
Income tax expense ($10,500 + (3/12 × $6,000))	12,000	1.5
	————	
Profit for the year	22,000	
	————	
Profit attributable to:		
Owners of Hide (β)	21,375	
Non-controlling interest (W2) (item 2)	625	2.0
	————	————
	22,000	**10.0**
	————	————

Tutorial note

As this was a mid-year acquisition, remember to time-apportion each item of revenue and expense in the subsidiary's SOPL between pre-acquisition (9/12) and post-acquisition (3/12). Only the post-acquisition element is included in the consolidated SOPL on a line-by-line basis.

Item 1: Select the formula which correctly calculates cost of sales

	All figures are in $000	**Selected answer**
(i)	$110,000 + (3/12 × $50,000) − $12,500 − $1,500	
(ii)	$110,000 + (3/12 × $50,000) − $12,500 + $1,000	Correct
(iii)	$110,000 + (3/12 × $50,000) + $12,500 + $1,500	

Item 2: Select which of the following correctly calculates the non-controlling interest share of group profit.

		Selected answer
(i)	Non-controlling interest share of Seek's profit for the year, minus provision for unrealised profit on inventory	
(ii)	Non-controlling interest share of Seek's post-acquisition profit for the year, plus non-controlling interest share of provision for unrealised profit on inventory	
(iii)	Non-controlling interest share of Seek's post-acquisition profit for the year, minus non-controlling interest share of provision for unrealised profit on inventory	Correct

Workings:

(W1) Intra-group sales and PURP

	$000
Cost of goods sold by Seek to Hide	10,000
Add: 25% mark up	2,500
Selling price of goods	12,500
PURP = $2,500 × 40% in inventory	1000

(W2) Non-controlling interest

	$000
NCI share of PAT: 25% × ($14,000 × 3/12)	875
NCI share of PURP: 25% × $1,000	(250)
	625

Task 3

Based on the individual financial statements of Hide and Seek, Hide has a lower gross profit margin than Seek.

Which one of the following statements could be a plausible explanation for this situation?

(2 marks)

		Selected answer
(i)	Seek has lower levels of inventory than Hide at the start and end of the reporting period	
(ii)	Seek is able to purchase cheaper materials and has a lower wastage rate of material than Hide	Correct
(iii)	Seek has lower selling expenses and general and administrative expenses than Hide	

(Total: 15 marks)

Marking scheme	
	Marks
Task 1 – Accounting for goodwill	3
Task 2 – Items to include in consolidated SOPL	10
Task 3 – Interpretation of financial statements	2
Total	**15**

16   PUSH AND SHOVE

Key answer tips

This question is a challenge as it requires you to prepare selected figures for both the statement of financial position and statement of profit or loss. Consequently, it is not time-efficient to adopt the standard approach of working through the normal consolidation workings. You should therefore try to prepare specific workings for each individual figure required in the question.

Task 1

(a)   **State the accounting entries required to account for the issue of shares by Push on the acquisition of Shove.**   **(2 marks)**

	$000	Credit/Debit
Revaluation surplus		
Issued share capital (60% × 4,000 × 5/6 × $1)	2,000	Credit
Investment in Shove (60% × 4,000 × 5/6 × $6)	12,000	Debit
Retained earnings		
Share premium (60% × 4,000 × 5/6 × $5)	10,000	Credit

(b)   **Calculate goodwill on acquisition of Shove**   **(3 marks)**

	$000	Marks
Fair value of consideration paid (Item 1) (60% × 4,000 × 5/6 × $6)	12,000	1
	———	
Fair value of the NCI at acquisition (40% × 4,000 × $3.50)	5,600	0.5
	———	
Fair value of net assets at acquisition:		
Share capital	4,000	0.5
Retained earnings (Item 2)	12,400	1
	———	
	16,400	
	———	
Goodwill on acquisition (Item 3)	1,200	
	———	

Item 1: Select the formula which correctly calculates the fair value of consideration paid

	All figures are in $000	Selected answer
(i)	4,000 × 60% × $6	
(ii)	4,000 × 60% × 5/6 × $1	
(iii)	4,000 × 60% × 5/6 × $6	Correct

Item 2: Select the formula which correctly calculates retained earnings of Shove at the date of acquisition.

	All figures are in $000	Selected answer
(i)	$16,500	
(ii)	$16,500 – $4,100	Correct
(iii)	$35,400 – $4,100	

Item 3: Select which of the following correctly calculates goodwill

		Selected answer
(i)	Fair value of consideration paid plus fair value of non-controlling interest at acquisition date plus fair value of net assets at acquisition	
(ii)	Fair value of consideration paid minus fair value of non-controlling interest at acquisition date + fair value of net assets at acquisition	
(iii)	Fair value of consideration paid plus fair value of non-controlling interest at acquisition date minus fair value of net assets at acquisition	Correct

Tutorial note

As the parent gained control of the subsidiary on the first day of the accounting period, the subsidiary's profit must all be post-acquisition. Any retained earnings prior to that date must have been earned up to the date of acquisition.

	$000
Subsidiary retained earnings at reporting date	*16,500*
Less: Profit for the year (from P/L)	*4,100*
Retained earnings up to date of acquisition	*12,400*

Task 2

Calculate the following figures for inclusion in the consolidated statement of financial position: (3 marks)

		$000	$000
(i)	Non-current assets	63,200	40,600 + $22,600
(ii)	Current assets	21,350	$16,000 + $6,600 – $1,000 (W1) – $250 (W1)
(iii)	Current liabilities	11,900	$8,200 + $4,700 – $1,000 (W1)

(W1) Intra-group sales and PURP

	$000
Cost of goods sold by Shove to Push (100%)5,000	
Add: 20% mark-up	1,000
Selling price of goods by Shove to Push (120%)	6,000
PURP = $1,000 × 25% in inventory	250

Note – as Shove was the seller, the PURP is allocated between the controlling group and NCI based on their respective shareholdings.

Group share = 60% × $250 = $150 and NCI share = 40% × $250 = $100.

This information will be relevant for the calculation of retained earnings and non-controlling interest at the reporting date.

Task 3

Select which of the following correctly calculates each of the following items for inclusion in the consolidated statement of financial position: (4 marks)

(a) Non-controlling interest at the reporting date

	All figures are in $000	Selected answer
(i)	(4,000 × 40% × $1) + (40% × (4,100 + 250))	
(ii)	(4,000 × 40% × $3.50) + (40% × (4,100 – 250))	Correct
(iii)	(4,000 × 40% × $6) + (40% × (4,100 + 250))	

(b) Retained earnings at the reporting date

	All figures are in $000	Selected answer
(i)	$35,400 – (60% × (4,100 + 250))	
(ii)	$45,400 – (60% × (4,100 – 250))	
(iii)	$35,400 + (60% × (4,100 – 250))	Correct

Task 4

Select which of the following correctly calculates each of the following items for inclusion in the consolidated statement of financial position: **(3 marks)**

(a) **Revenue**

	All figures are in $000	Selected answer
(i)	$85,000 + $42,000 – $6,000	Correct
(ii)	$85,000 + (40% × ($42,000 – $6,000)	
(iii)	$85,000 + $42,000 + $6,000	

(b) **Cost of sales**

	All figures are in $000	Selected answer
(i)	$63,000 + $32,000 – $6,000 – $250	
(ii)	$63,000 + $32,000 – $6,000 + $250	Correct
(iii)	$63,000 + (40% × ($32,000 – $6,000 + $250))	

(Total 15 marks)

Marking scheme	
	Marks
Task 1 – Accounting for goodwill	5
Task 2 – Items to include in consolidated SOFP	3
Task 3 – Retained earnings and NCI for SOFP	4
Task 4 – Revenue and cost of sales for SOPL	3
	——
Total	**15**
	——

Section 5

SPECIMEN EXAM QUESTIONS

SECTION A

ALL 35 questions are compulsory and MUST be attempted

Each question is worth 2 marks.

1   **Which of the following calculates a sole trader's profit for a period?**

   A   Closing net assets + drawings - capital introduced – opening net assets

   B   Closing net assets - drawings + capital introduced – opening net assets

   C   Closing net assets – drawings – capital introduced – opening net assets

   D   Closing net assets + drawings + capital introduced – opening net assets

2   **Which of the following statements best explains the imprest system of operating petty cash?**

   A   All expenditure out of the petty cash must be properly authorised

   B   Regular equal amounts of cash are transferred into petty cash at intervals

   C   The exact amount of expenditure is reimbursed at intervals to maintain a fixed float

   D   Weekly expenditure cannot exceed a set amount

3   **Which of the following statements are TRUE about limited liability companies?**

   1   The company exposure to debt and liability is limited

   2   Financial statements must be produced

   3   A company continues to exist regardless of the identity of its owners

   A   2 and 3 only

   B   1, 2 and 3

   C   1 and 3 only

   D   1 and 2 only

4   Annie is a sole trader who does not keep full accounting records. The following details relate to her transactions with credit customers and suppliers for the year ended 30 June 20X6:

	$
Receivables, 1 July 20X5	130,000
Payables, 1 July 20X5	60,000
Cash received from customers	686,400
Cash paid to suppliers	302,800
Discounts received	2,960
Contra between payables and receivables	2,000
Receivables, 30 June 20X6	181,000
Payables, 30 June 20X6	84,000

What figure should appear in Annie's statement of profit or loss for the year ended 30 June 20X6 for purchases?

$ [   ]

5   Kirk's opening balance on the payables account was $32,978. During the year, Kirk made credit purchases of $178,509, returned goods back to a supplier totalling $4,945 and made payments to suppliers of $163,948.

What amount should be recognised in the payables general ledger account at the year end?

A $14,561

B $47,539

C $42,594

D $13,472

6   At 31 December 20X5 the following require inclusion in a company's financial statements:

1   On 1 January 20X5 the entity made a loan of $12,000 to an employee, repayable on 1 January 20X6, charging interest at 2% per year. On the due date the employee repaid the loan and paid the whole of the interest due on the loan to that date.

2   The entity paid an annual insurance premium of $9,000 in 20X5, covering the year ending 31 August 20X6.

3   In January 20X6 the entity received rent from a tenant of $4,000 covering the six months to 31 December 20X5.

For these items, what total figures should be included in the entity's statement of financial position as at 31 December 20X5?

A   Current assets $10,240   Current liabilities $nil

B   Current assets $16,240   Current liabilities $6,000

C   Current assets $22,240   Current liabilities $nil

D   Current assets $10,000   Current liabilities $12,240

7 A company's statement of profit or loss for the year ended 31 December 20X5 showed a profit of $83,600. It was later found that $18,000 paid for the purchase of a motor van had been debited to the motor expenses account. It is the company's policy to depreciate motor vans at 25% per year on the straight-line basis, with a full year's charge in the year of acquisition.

What would the profit be after adjusting for this error?

$ [   ]

8 Xena has the following working capital ratios:

	20X9	**20X8**
Current ratio	1·2:1	1·5:1
Receivables collection period	75 days	50 days
Payables payment period	30 days	45 days
Inventory holding period	42 days	35 days

Which of the following statements about Xena is CORRECT?

A Xena's liquidity and working capital has improved in 20X9

B Xena is taking longer to pay suppliers in 20X9

C Xena is suffering from a worsening liquidity position in 20X9

D Xena is receiving cash from customers more quickly in 20X9 than in 20X8

9 **Are the following statements true or false?**

	True	**False**
A statement of cash flows prepared using the direct method produces a different figure for net cash from operating activities compared to that produced if the indirect method is used		
Rights issues of shares do not feature in a statement of cash flows		
A surplus on revaluation of a non-current asset will not appear as an item in a statement of cash flows		
A profit on the sale of a non-current asset will appear as an item under cash flows from investing activities in the statement of cash flows		

10 A company receives rent from a significant number of properties. The total received in the year ended 30 April 20X6 was $481,200.

The following were the amounts of rent in advance and in arrears at 30 April 20X5 and 20X6:

	30 April 20X5	30 April 20X6
	$	$
Rent received in advance	28,700	31,200
Rent in arrears (all subsequently received)	21,200	18,400

What amount of rental income should appear in the company's statement of profit or loss for the year ended 30 April 20X6?

A $460,900

B $486,500

C $501,500

D $475,900

11 **Which TWO of the following are differences between sole traders and limited liability companies?**

	Selected answer
A sole trader's financial statements are private; a company's financial statements are sent to shareholders and may be publicly filed	
Only companies have capital invested into the business	
A sole trader is fully and personally liable for any losses that the business might make	
Revaluations can be carried out in the financial statements of a company, but not in the financial statements of a sole trader	

12 **Which of the following statements is TRUE?**

	Selected answer
Ratios based on historical data can predict the future performance of an entity	
An entity's management will not assess an entity's performance using financial ratios	
The interpretation of an entity's financial statements using ratios is only useful for potential investors	
The analysis of financial statements using ratios provides useful information when compared with previous performance or industry averages	

13 A company's motor vehicles (at cost) account at 30 June 20X6 is as follows:

Motor vehicles – cost

	$		$
Balance b/f	35,800	Disposal	12,000
Additions	12,950	Balance c/f	36,750
	———		———
	48,750		48,750
	———		———

What opening balance should be included in the following period's general ledger for Motor vehicles (at cost) at 1 July 20X6?

A $48,750 Dr

B $48,750 Cr

C $36,750 Cr

D $36,750 Dr

14 **Which TWO of the following items must be disclosed in the note to the financial statements for intangible assets?**

	Selected answer
A list of all intangible assets purchased or developed in the period	
A description of the development projects that have been undertaken during the period	
The useful lives of intangible assets capitalised in the financial statements	
Impairment losses written off intangible assets during the period	

15 **Which of the following statements are correct?**

1   Capitalised development expenditure must be amortised over a period not exceeding five years.

2   Capitalised development costs are shown in the statement of financial position under the heading of non-current assets.

3   All research expenditure must be recognised as an intangible asset.

A   1 and 3

B   2 and 3

C   1 only

D   2 only

16 The following transactions relate to Rashid's other operating expenses general ledger account for the year ended 30 June 20X9:

	$
Prepayment brought forward	550
Cash paid	5,400
Accrual carried forward	650

What amount should be charged to the statement of profit or loss in the year ended 30 June 20X9 for other operating expenses?

A $5,500

B $5,400

C $6,600

D $5,300

17 At 30 June 20X5 a company's allowance for receivables was $39,000. At 30 June 20X6 receivables totalled $517,000. It was decided to write off debts totalling $37,000 and to adjust the allowance for receivables to the equivalent of 5% of the receivables based on past events.

What figure should appear in the statement of profit or loss for the year ended 30 June 20X6 for these items?

$ [   ]

18 Nancy purchased a building on 1 January 20X1 for $200,000. The building had a useful life of 20 years at the date of acquisition and is depreciated on a straight-line basis. On 1 January 20X5, Nancy had the building professionally valued and its fair value was deemed to be $340,000.

What is the revaluation gain that will be recorded for the building on 1 January 20X5?

$ [   ]

19 According to IAS 2 *Inventories*, which TWO of the following costs should be included in valuing the inventories of a manufacturing company?

	Selected answer
Carriage outwards	
Depreciation of factory plant	
Carriage inwards	
General administrative overheads	

20 Prisha has not kept accurate accounting records during the financial year. She had opening inventory of $6,700 and purchased goods costing $84,000 during the year. At the year-end she had $5,400 left in inventory. All sales were made at a mark-up on cost of 20%.

What is Prisha's gross profit for the year?

$ [   ]

21   At 31 December 20X4 a company's capital structure was as follows:

	$
Equity share capital	125,000
(500,000 shares of 25c each)	
Share premium account	100,000

In the year ended 31 December 20X5 the company made a rights issue of 1 share for every 2 held at $1 per share and this was taken up in full. Later in the year the company made a bonus issue of 1 share for every 5 held, using the share premium account for the purpose.

What was the company's capital structure at 31 December 20X5?

A   Equity share capital $225,000   Share premium account $325,000

B   Equity share capital $225,000   Share premium account $250,000

C   Equity share capital $212,500   Share premium account $262,500

D   Equity share capital $450,000   Share premium account $25,000

22   **Which of the following should be presented in a company's statement of changes in equity?**

1   Total comprehensive income for the year

2   Amortisation of capitalised development costs

3   Surplus on revaluation of non-current assets

A   1 and 3 only

B   2 and 3 only

C   1 and 2 only

D   1, 2 and 3

23   The general ledger account for the historical cost of plant and machinery of a business for the year ended 31 December 20X5 was as follows:

Plant and machinery (at cost)

20X5	$	20X5	$
1 Jan Balance b/f	240,000	31 Mar Transfer to disposal account	60,000
30 Jun Cash purchase of plant	160,000	31 Dec Balance c/f	340,000
	400,000		400,000

The company's policy is to charge depreciation at 20% per year on the straight-line basis, with proportionate depreciation in the years of purchase and disposal. No item of plant and machinery is fully depreciated.

What should be the depreciation charge for the year ended 31 December 20X5?

A $64,000

B $55,000

C $68,000

D $61,000

24 **The following extracts are from Hassan Co's financial statements:**

	$
Operating profit	10,200
Interest expenses on borrowings	(1,600)
Profit before income taxes	8,600
Income tax expense	(3,300)
Profit	5,300

	$
Share capital	20,000
Other components of equity	15,600
	35,600
Loan liability (repayable 20X9)	6,900
	42,500

What is Hassan Co's return on capital employed?

| | %

25 **Is each of the following statements about sales tax true or false?**

	True	False
Sales tax is recorded as income in the accounts of the entity selling the goods		
Sales tax is an expense to the ultimate consumer of the goods purchased when the ultimate consumer is not registered for sales tax		

26 **Using the table below, identify whether the following ledger accounts will appear on the debit side or credit side of the trial balance.**

	Debit	Credit
Sales		
Sales returns		
Purchases		
Purchase returns		

27   Prior to the financial year end of 31 July 20X9, Cannon Co received a claim of $100,000 from a customer for providing poor quality goods which damaged the customer's plant and equipment. Cannon Co's lawyers have stated that there is a 20% chance that Cannon will successfully defend the claim.

Which of the following is the correct accounting treatment for the claim in the financial statements for the year ended 31 July 20X9?

A   Cannon Co should provide for an expected cost of $20,000

B   Cannon Co should disclose a contingent liability of $100,000

C   Cannon Co should provide for the expected cost of the claim of $100,000

D   Cannon Co should neither provide for nor disclose the claim

28   Gareth, who is registered for sales tax, purchased a computer for use in his business. The invoice for the computer showed the following costs related to the purchase:

	$
Hardware	890
Operating system	95
Delivery	10
Installation	20
Maintenance (1 year)	25
	1,040
Sales tax (17.5%)	182
Total	1,222

How much should Gareth capitalise as a non-current asset in relation to the purchase?

$ [   ]

29   Aim Co has an overdraft per the bank account of $3,860. The following bank reconciliation statement has been prepared by a trainee accountant:

	$
Overdraft per bank statement	3,860
Less: Unpresented cheques	9,160
	5,300
Add: Outstanding lodgements	16,690
Cash at bank	21,990

What should be the correct balance per the cash at bank ledger?

A $3,670 overdrawn

B $21,990 cash at bank as stated

C $11,390 cash at bank

D $3,670 cash at bank

30 Which TWO of the following are characteristics that are required to ensure faithful representation?

	Selected answer
Accruals	
Completeness	
Going concern	
Neutrality	

31 The following general ledger account contains errors:

Receivables account

	$		$
Balance brought forward	308,600	Cash received from credit customers	147,200
Credit sales	152,800	Irrecoverable debts written off	4,900
Cash sales	88,100	Interest charges on overdue debts	2,400
Contras against payables	4,600	Allowance for receivables	2,800
		Balance carried forward	396,800
	554,100		544,100

What should the closing balance be when all the errors in the receivables' general ledger account have been corrected?

A $395,200

B $309,500

C $307,100

D $304,300

32 Are the following material events, that have occurred after the reporting date and before the financial statements are approved, adjusting events?

	Yes	No
A valuation of property providing evidence of impairment in value at the reporting date		
Sale of inventory held at the reporting date for less than cost		
Discovery of fraud or error affecting the financial statements		
The insolvency of a customer with a debt owing at the reporting date which is still outstanding		

33 A company values its inventory using the FIFO (first in, first out) method. At 1 May 20X5 the company had 700 engines in inventory, valued at $190 each. During the year ended 30 April 20X6 the following transactions took place:

20X5

1 July	Purchased	500 engines at $220 each
1 November	Sold	400 engines for $160,000

20X6

1 February	Purchased	300 engines at $230 each
15 April	Sold	250 engines for $125,000

What is the value of the company's closing inventory of engines at 30 April 20X6?

A $188,500

B $195,500

C $166,000

D $176,800

34 Amy is a sole trader and had assets of $569,400 and liabilities of $412,840 on 1 January 20X8. During the year ended 31 December 20X8 she paid $65,000 capital into the business and withdrew $800 per month.

At 31 December 20X8, Amy had assets of $614,130 and liabilities of $369,770.

What is Amy's profit for the year ended 31 December 20X8?

$

35 Nigel has produced his trial balance for the year ended 30 June 20X5. A suspense account was included at the amount of $4,139 (credit).

Which of the following errors could have resulted in the suspense account being required?

A The omission of a customer (sales) invoice of $4,139

B A manual journal entry for accrued motor expenses of $4,139 was correctly recognised in expenses but the corresponding entry created the suspense account

C A manual journal entry for prepaid rent expenses of $4,139 was correctly recognised against expenses but the corresponding entry created the suspense account

D A payment of $4,139 for wages being recorded as $1,439 in the wages account

(Total 70 marks)

SECTION B

BOTH questions are compulsory and MUST be attempted

36   Background

Keswick Co acquired 80% of the share capital of Derwent Co on 1 June 20X5. The draft statements of profit or loss for the year ended 31 May 20X6 are shown below:

	Keswick Co	Derwent Co
	$000	$000
Revenue	8,400	3,200
Less: Cost of sales	4,600	1,700
Gross profit	3,800	1,500
Operating expenses:		
Less: Selling expenses	1,500	510
General and administrative expenses	700	450
Profit before income taxes	1,600	540
Less: Income tax expense	600	140
Profit (for the year)	1,000	400

During the year, Keswick Co sold goods costing $1,000,000 to Derwent Co for $1,500,000. At 31 May 20X6, 30% of these goods remained in Derwent Co's inventory.

Task 1   **(11 marks)**

Use the information to complete the following financial statement:

∇ Drop down list for the title of the financial statement	Selection
Consolidated statement of profit or loss as at 31 May 20X6	
Statement of profit or loss for the year ended 31 May 20X6	
Consolidated statement of profit or loss for the year ended 31 May 20X6	
Statement of profit or loss as at 31 May 20X6	

∇ Drop down list for Revenue calculation	Selection
8,400 + 3,200 – 1,500	
8,400 + (80% × 3,200) – 1,500	
8,400 + 3,200	
8,400 + 3,200 + 1,500	
8,400 + 3,200 – 1,000	

∇ Drop down list for Cost of sales calculation	Selection
4,600 + 1,700 – 1,000	
4,600 + (80% × 1,700) – 1,500	
4,600 + 1,700 – 1,500 – (30% × 500)	
4,600 + (80% × 1,700)	
4,600 + 1,700 – 1,500 + (30% × 500)	
4,600 + 1,700	

Gross profit

Less: Selling expenses

General and administrative expenses

Profit before income taxes

Less: Income tax expense

Profit

Attributable to:

∇ Drop down list for Owners of Keswick Co

	Selection
Keswick Co profit for the year	
Group profit for the year– Non-controlling interest	
Group profit for the year + Non-controlling interest	
Group profit for the year	

Non-controlling interest

Task 2   **(4 marks)**

Does the existence of each of the following factors illustrate the existence of a parent-subsidiary relationship?

	Yes	**No**
50% of all debt being held by an investor		
Greater than 50% of the preference shares and debt being held by an investor		
Non-controlling interest of 10%		
Greater than 50% of preference shares and debt being held by an investor		
Greater than 50% of the equity shares held by an investor		
Significant influence		
100% of the equity shares being held by an investor		
Control		

(Total 15 marks)

37 Background

Malright Co has an accounting year end of 31 October. The accountant is preparing the financial statements as at 31 October 20X7. A trial balance has been prepared but no year-end adjustments have been made.

Task 1 (4 marks)

Should each of the following amounts be used to determine the figures to be reported in the statement of financial position (SOFP) as at 31 October 20X7 before any year-end adjustments?

	Dr	Cr	Yes/No
	$000	$000	
Buildings at cost	740		
Buildings accumulated depreciation at 1 November 20X6		60	
Plant at cost	220		
Plant accumulated depreciation at 1 November 20X6		110	
Bank balance		70	
Revenue		1,800	
Net purchases	1,140		
Inventory at 1 November 20X6	160		
Cash	20		
Payables		250	
Receivables	320		
General and administrative expenses	325		
Allowance for receivables at 1 November 20X6		10	
Retained earnings at 1 November 20X6		130	
Equity shares, $1		415	
Share premium account		80	
	2,925	2,925	

Task 2 (3 marks)

The allowance for receivables is to be increased to 5% of receivables. The allowance for receivables is treated as an administrative expense.

The year-end journal for allowance for receivables is given below. Prepare the double entry by selecting the correct option for each row.

	Debit	Credit	No debit or credit
Receivables			
Administrative expenses			
Allowance for irrecoverable debts			
Revenue			

Complete the following:

The amount included in the statement of profit or loss after the allowance is increased to 5% of receivables is:

$\boxed{\$\qquad}$ '000

Task 3 (5 marks)

Plant is depreciated at 20% per annum using the reducing balance method and buildings are depreciated at 5% per annum on their original cost. Depreciation is treated as a cost of sales expense.

The year-end journal for buildings and plant depreciation is given blow. Using the information above, prepare the double entry by selecting the correct option for each row.

	Debit	Credit	No debit or credit
General and administrative expenses			
Cost of sales			
Buildings cost			
Plant cost			
Buildings accumulated depreciation			
Plant accumulated depreciation			

Calculate the depreciation charge calculated for the year ended 31 October 20X7. Use the information above to help you.

Buildings	$	'000
Plant	$	'000

Task 4 (1.5 marks)

Closing inventory has been counted and is valued at $75,000.

Ignoring the depreciation charge calculated earlier, what is the cost of sales for the year?

$\boxed{\$\qquad}$ '000

Task 5 (1.5 marks)

An invoice of $15,000 for energy costs relating to the quarter ended 30 November 20X7 was received on 2 December 20X7. Energy costs are included in administrative expenses.

Complete the following statements:

The double entry to post the year end adjustment for energy costs is:

	Debit	Credit
Accrual		
General and administrative expenses		

The amount to be posted within the year end adjustment double entry above is:

$\boxed{\$\qquad}$ '000

(Total 15 marks)

Section 6

ANSWERS TO SPECIMEN EXAM QUESTIONS

SECTION A

1   A

Opening net assets + profit − drawings + capital introduced = Closing net assets

Therefore: profit = Closing net assets + drawings − capital introduced − opening net assets

2   C

The exact amount pf expenditure, as supported by vouchers, is reimbursed at intervals to maintain a fixed float.

3   A

Items (2) and (3) only are true. Only the liability of members of a company (i.e. its shareholders) is limited; the liability of the company is not limited.

4 $331,760

Payables			
	$		$
Cash paid to suppliers	302,800	Balance b/fwd	60,000
Discount received	2,960	**Purchases (β)**	**331,760**
Contra	2,000		
Balance c/fwd	84,000		
	———		———
	391,760		391,760
	———		———

5   C $42,594

Opening 32,978 + Credit purchases 178,509 − Returns 4,945 − Payments 163,948 = 42,594

6   C

	$
Loan asset	12,000
Interest (12,000 × 12%) 240	240
Prepayment (8/12 × 9,000)	6,000
Accrued rent	4,000
	———————
Current assets	22,240 and current liabilities $0
	———————

7 $97,100

	$
Profit	83,600
Reduce motor expenses for cost of car	18,000
Depreciation charge ($18,000 × 25%)	(4,500)
	———————
Adjusted profit	97,100
	———————

8   C

Xena is suffering from a worsening liquidity position in 20X9.

9

	True	False
A statement of cash flows prepared using the direct method produces a different figure for net cash from operating activities compared to that produced if the indirect method is used.		✓
Rights issues of shares do not feature in a statement of cash flows		✓
A surplus on revaluation of a non-current asset will not appear as an item in a statement of cash flows	✓	
A profit on the sale of a non-current asset will appear as an item under cash flows from investing activities in the statement of cash flows		✓

10   D

	$
Balance b/f (advance)	28,700
Balance b/f (arrears)	(21,200)
Cash received	481,200
Balance c/f (advance)	(31,200)
Balance c/f (arrears)	18,400
	———————
Rental income receivable	475,900
	———————

11

	Selected answer
A sole trader's financial statements are private; a company's financial statements are sent to shareholders and may be publicly filed	✓
Only companies have capital invested into the business	
A sole trader is fully and personally liable for any losses that the business might make	✓
Revaluations can be carried out in the financial statements of a company, but not in the financial statements of a sole trader	

Regarding the incorrect statements:

- All sole traders, partnerships and companies have 'capital' – an irremovable element of the accounting equation.

- Revaluations may be carried out by sole traders, partnerships and companies – only companies must apply IFRS Accounting Standards in doing so.

12

	Selected answer
Ratios based on historical data can predict the future performance of an entity	
An entity's management will not assess an entity's performance using financial ratios	
The interpretation of an entity's financial statements using ratios is only useful for potential investors	
The analysis of financial statements using ratios provides useful information when compared with previous performance or industry averages	✓

Regarding the incorrect statements:

- Ratio analysis is used by a wide range of stakeholders.

- Although financial information has a predictive value (a qualitative characteristic), this does not mean a ratio can determine future results without exception.

- Management are one of the stakeholder groups which uses ratio analysis.

13   D

The c/f amount on the credit side of the cost account at the end of the current period is the b/f debit balance at the beginning of the following period.

14

	Selected answer
A list of all intangible assets purchased or developed in the period	
A description of the development projects that have been undertaken during the period	
The useful lives of intangible assets capitalised in the financial statements	✓
Impairment losses written off intangible assets during the period	✓

15   D

Capitalised development costs are shown in the statement of financial position under the heading of non-current assets.

16   C

	$
Balance b/f	550
Expense incurred (cash)	5,400
Accrual c/f	650
	———
	6,600
	———

17 $22,000

	$	$
Debts written off		37,000
Closing allowance: (517 − 37) × 5%	24,000	
Less: opening allowance	39,000	
	———	(15,000)
		———
Expense to profit of loss		22,000
		———

18 $180,000

	$
Cost at 1 January 20X1	200,000
Accumulated depreciation (4/20 years x $200,000)	(40,00)
Carrying amount at 31 December 20X4	160,000
Fair value at 1 January 20X5	340,000
	———
Revaluation increase	180,000
	———

19

	Selected answer
Carriage outwards	
Depreciation of factory plant	✓
Carriage inwards	✓
General administrative overheads	

20 $17,060

(6,700 + 84,000 − 5,400) × 20% = $17,060

21   B

	Equity share capital	Share premium account
	$	$
Balance b/f	125,000	100,000
Rights issue	62,500	187,500
Bonus issue	37,500	(37,500)
Balance c/f	225,000	250,000

22   A

Amortisation of development costs is charged to profit or loss as an expense.

23   B

Depreciation	$	
Jan – Mar	12,000	(240,000 × 20%) × 3/12
Apr – Jun	9,000	(240,000 – 60,000) × 20% × 3/12
Jul – Dec	34,000	(180,000 + 160,000) × 20% × 6/12
	55,000	

24   24%

ROCE = Operating profit /(Equity + Non-current liabilities)
= (10,200/42,500) × 100 = 24%

25

	True	False
Sales tax is recorded as income in the accounts of the entity selling the goods		✓
Sales tax is an expense to the ultimate consumer of the goods purchased when the ultimate consumer is not registered for sales tax	✓	

26

	Debit	Credit
Sales		✓
Sales returns	✓	
Purchases	✓	
Purchase returns		✓

27   C

It is probable (80% chance) that Cannon Co will lose the case. As it is probable and results from a past transaction or event and can be reliably measured provision for the full amount should be made.

28 $1,015

$1,040 – $25 maintenance = $1,015.

Note that, as the business is registered to account for sales tax, the amount of sales tax charged by the supplier cannot be capitalised as part of the cost of the computer. The maintenance cost cannot be capitalised – that is written off to profit or loss over the period of the maintenance contract.

29   D

	$
Overdraft per bank statement	(3,860)
Less: unpresented cheques	(9,160)
Add: outstanding lodgements	16,690
	———
Cash at bank	3,670
	———

30

	Selected answer
Accruals	
Completeness	✔
Going concern	
Neutrality	✔

31   C

Receivables' ledger account

	$		$
Opening balance	308,600	Cash from credit customers	147,200
Credit sales	152,800	Contras	4,600
Interest charged on overdue accounts	2,400	Irrecoverable debts	4,900
		Closing balance	307,100
	———		———
	463,800		463,800
	———		———

32

	Yes	No
A valuation of property providing evidence of impairment in value at the reporting date	✓	
Sale of inventory held at the reporting date for less than cost	✓	
Discovery of fraud or error affecting the financial statements	✓	
The insolvency of a customer with a debt owing at the reporting date which is still outstanding	✓	

33   A

Closing inventory	**$**
50 × $190	9,500
500 × $220	110,000
300 × $230	69,000
	188,500

34 $32,400

	$
Opening net assets ($569,400 − $412,840)	156,560
Capital introduced	65,000
Drawings ($800 × 12)	(9,600)
Profit for the year (β)	**32,400**
Closing net assets ($614,130 − $369,770)	244,360

35   B

SECTION B

36 Task 1 (11 marks)

Use the information to complete the following financial statement:

▽ Drop down list for the title of the financial statement	Selection
Consolidated statement of profit or loss as at 31 May 20X6	
Statement of profit or loss for the year ended 31 May 20X6	
Consolidated statement of profit or loss for the year ended 31 May 20X6	✓
Statement of profit or loss as at 31 May 20X6	

▽ Drop down list for Revenue calculation	Selection
8,400 + 3,200 - 1,500	✓
8,400 + (80% × 3,200) – 1,500	
8,400 + 3,200	
8,400 + 3,200 + 1,500	
8,400 + 3,200 – 1,000	

▽ Drop down list for Cost of sales calculation	Selection
4,600 + 1,700 – 1,000	
4,600 + (80% × 1,700) – 1,500	
4,600 + 1,700 – 1,500 – (30% × 500)	
4,600 + (80% × 1,700)	
4,600 + 1,700 – 1,500 + (30% × 500)	✓
4,600 + 1.700	

Gross profit	5,150
Less: Selling expenses (1,500 + 510)	2,010
General and administrative expenses (700 + 450)	1,150
Operating profit/Profit before financing and income taxes	1,990
Less: Income tax expense (600 + 140)	740
Profit (for the year)	1,250

Attributable to:

▽ Drop down list for Equity owners of Keswick Co	Selection
Keswick Co profit for the year	
Group profit for the year – Non-controlling interest	✓
Group profit for the year + Non-controlling interest	
Group profit for the year	

Non-controlling interest (20% × 400)	80

Task 2 (4 marks)

Does the existence of each of the following factors illustrate the existence of a parent-subsidiary relationship?

	Yes	No
50% of all debt being held by an investor		✓
Greater than 50% of the preference shares and debt being held by an investor		✓
Non-controlling interest of 10%	✓	
Greater than 50% of preference shares and debt being held by an investor		✓
Greater than 50% of the equity shares held by an investor	✓	
Significant influence		✓
100% of the equity shares being held by an investor	✓	
Control	✓	

(Total 15 marks)

37 Task 1 (4 marks)

Should each of the following amounts be used to determine the figures to be reported in the statement of financial position (SOFP) as at 31 October 20X7 before any year-end adjustments?

	Dr $000	Cr $000	Yes/No
Buildings at cost	740		✓
Buildings accumulated depreciation at 1 November 20X6		60	No
Plant at cost	220		✓
Plant accumulated depreciation at 1 November 20X6		110	No
Bank balance		70	✓
Revenue		1,800	No
Net purchases	1,140		No
Inventory at 1 November 20X6	160		No
Cash	20		✓
Payables		250	✓
Receivables	320		✓
General and administrative expenses	325		No
Allowance for receivables at 1 November 20X6		10	No
Retained earnings at 1 November 20X6		130	No
Equity shares, $1		415	✓
Share premium account		80	✓
	2,925	2,925	

Note: the accumulated depreciation balances as at 1 November 20X6 would not appear on the statement of financial positon as at 31 October 20X7. Those balances would need to be updated for the depreciation charge for the year ended 31 October 20X7, along with any adjustment that may be required for additions and/or disposals in the year. Similarly, the allowance for receivables as at 1 November 20X6 would need to be adjusted to the circumstances existing at 31 October 20X7.

Task 2   **(3 marks)**

The year-end journal for allowance for receivables is given below. Prepare the double entry by selecting the correct option for each row.

	Debit	Credit	No debit or credit
Receivables			✓
Administrative expenses	✓		
Allowance for irrecoverable debts		✓	
Revenue			✓

Complete the following:

The amount included in the statement of profit or loss after the allowance is increased to 5% of receivables is:

| $6 | '000   (5% × 320,000) – 10,000

Task 3   **(5 marks)**

The year-end journal for buildings and plant depreciation is given blow. Using the information above, prepare the double entry by selecting the correct option for each row.

	Debit	Credit	No debit or credit
General and administrative expenses			✓
Cost of sales	✓		
Buildings cost			✓
Plant cost			✓
Buildings accumulated depreciation		✓	
Plant accumulated depreciation		✓	

Calculate the depreciation charge calculated for the year ended 31 October 20X7. Use the information above to help you.

Buildings	$37	'000	5% × 740,000
Plant	$22	'000	20% × (220,000 – 110,000)

Task 4   **(1.5 marks)**

Ignoring the depreciation charge calculated earlier, what is the cost of sales for the year?

| $1,225 | '000 | 160,000 + 1,140,000 – 75,000

Task 5 (1.5 marks)

Complete the following statements:

The double entry to post the year end adjustment for energy costs is:

	Debit	Credit
Accrual		✓
Administrative expenses	✓	

The amount to be posted within the year end adjustment double entry above is:

$10   '000   2/3 × 15,000

(Total 15 marks)

Section 7

REFERENCES

The Board (2024) *Conceptual Framework for Financial Reporting*. London: IFRS Foundation.

The Board (2024) *IAS 2 Inventories*. London: IFRS Foundation.

The Board (2024) *IAS 7 Statement of Cash Flows*. London: IFRS Foundation.

The Board (2024) *IAS 16 Property, Plant and Equipment*. London: IFRS Foundation.

The Board (2024) *IAS 27 Separate Financial Statements*. London: IFRS Foundation.

The Board (2024) *IAS 28 Investments in Associates and Joint Ventures*. London: IFRS Foundation.

The Board (2024) *IAS 37 Provisions, Contingent Liabilities and Contingent Assets*. London: IFRS Foundation.

The Board (2024) *IAS 38 Intangible Assets*. London: IFRS Foundation.

The Board (2024) *IFRS 3 Business Combinations*. London: IFRS Foundation.

The Board (2024) *IFRS 10 Consolidated Financial Statements*. London: IFRS Foundation.

The Board (2024) *IFRS 15 Revenue from Contracts with Customers*. London: IFRS Foundation.

The Board (2024) IFRS 18 *Presentation and Disclosure in Financial Statements*. London: IFRS Foundation

The Board (2024) IFRS S1 *General Requirements for Disclosure of Sustainability-related Financial Disclosures*. London: IFRS Foundation

The Board (2024) IFRS S2 *Climate-related Disclosures*. London: IFRS Foundation